CORPORATE ENVIRONMENTALISM AND PUBLIC POLICY

CORPORATE ENVIRONMENTALISM AND PUBLIC POLICY

Dr. Chandrama Singh

RANDOM PUBLICATIONS

NEW DELHI - 110 002 (INDIA)

Corporate Environmentalism and Public Policy

ISBN 978-93-51117-19-3

Published in 2015 in India by

RANDOM PUBLICATIONS

4376-A/4B, Gali Murari Lal, Ansari Road
New Delhi-110 002
Phone: +9111-43580356, 23289044
E-mail: randomexports@gmail.com; sales@randompublications.com;
info@randompublications.com

Type Setting by: Friends Media, Delhi-110089
Printed at : Mehra Printers, Delhi-110092

Preface

Globalization is here to stay and, as a result, the speed with which ideas, products and services travel around the world is changing the way companies do business. Various trends and processes associated with globalization are generating conditions and pressures conducive to corporate environmental responsibility. As trade continues to liberalize, flows of goods, services and capital render traditional geopolitical borders increasingly irrelevant and traditional approaches to managing the environment obsolete. Corporate environmentalism has taken on new meaning both in operational and philosophical terms. The factors promoting it are more diverse, the scope broader, the rigor greater. Doing a good job on the environment and crafting strategies to address sustainable development no longer represent unproductive costs but, increasingly, opportunities whose benefits may be vital and necessary for the survival of companies.

Six trends seem particularly important in terms of promoting or facilitating corporate environmental management and business responsibility for sustainable development. First, as companies seek greater uniformity in process, production and product standards, geographic location is becoming less important. On the other hand, socio-economic and environmental distinctions are becoming more important in shaping corporate image and consumer decisions. Second, the movement from product-based manufacturing into service-based commerce in some sectors has significant implications for environment and development in both developed and developing countries. Third, as investment in developing country research and development increases, and as corporate authority within transnational firms is increasingly decentralized, southern-based firms and institutions are playing a more important role in the development and production of goods and services. Fourth, international attention to corporate activities is increasing as multilateral organizations establish global rules and standards concerning evironmental management, and as communications technology and civil society networks facilitate surveillance. Fifth, globalization means that the range of any particular company's stakeholders is broad. Many companies are recognizing that their ability to operate effectively depends on their accountability and standing among stakeholders. At the same time, they also recognize that doing a good job on the environment cannot be separated from social and community responsibility issues. Finally, legal systems and frameworks, at both national and international levels, continue to expand and, as business and government recognize the limits of command and control approaches to environmental protection, more collaborative approaches to resolving environmental problems are emerging. Considerable progress has been made by firms over the past few years in coming to grips with their environmental responsibilities. Companies are being pushed to consider environmental concerns in the full range of their decisions, and they are challenging themselves constantly to respond to new market opportunities and reconceptualize their core businesses. It is also apparent that as leading companies strive to make sustainable development operational, the issues of environment, economics and social responsibility are increasingly indistinguishable. While companies are undergoing transformations, governments are simultaneously seeking ways to increase the effectiveness of their policies. Approaches that reflect corporate self-interest may result in significant improvements to the environment at relatively modest societal costs. As part of this approach, however, policy makers will have to develop a more complete understanding than they now have of the forces driving corporate environmental responsibility. Company response to environment issues is a topic that has received insufficient attention from policy makers, academicians and non-governmental organizations. Understanding the forces driving corporate responsibility in the environmental field creates the possibility of crafting policies that are more effective and less contentious than those currently in place. While it would be naive and inaccurate to suggest that all companies are taking seriously their responsibility towards the environment, there are an increasing number of ways through which company practice is revealed to the public and subjected to scrutiny.

This is one of the few books that provide a hard-headed economic view of the voluntary approaches to environmental issues, especially toxic chemicals, waste disposal and global warming, that have become prominent in recent years.

I thank all members of my team who have helped in the preparation of the book. My special thanks go to "Random Publications" who have published the book.

— Dr. Chandrama Singh

Contents

1. **Corporate Environmentalism ... 1**
   - Environmental Corporate Responsibility ... 2
   - Sustainable Business ... 6
   - Corporate Sustainability ... 15
   - Cleaner Production ... 17
   - Clean Energy Trends ... 18
   - Low-Carbon Economy ... 20
   - Business Action on Climate Change ... 29
   - Corporations and the Environment ... 37
   - Green Brands ... 41
   - Triple Bottom Line ... 43
   - Sustainable Procurement ... 51
2. **Markets, Politics and Models ... 57**
   - How to Write an Environmental Policy ... 57
   - The Benefits of an Environmental Policy ... 58
   - Creating Content for an Environmental Policy ... 59
   - Environmental Governance ... 63
   - Environmental Issues ... 66
   - Policies ... 95
   - Ecotax ... 106
   - Environmental Tariff ... 111
   - Ecolabel ... 113
3. **Preempting Future Regulation ... 119**
   - Toxic Waste ... 119
   - Hazardous Waste ... 123
   - Chemical Waste ... 127
   - Construction Waste ... 128

Industrial Waste 129
Radioactive Waste 130
Wastewater 151
Industrial Wastewater Treatment 157
Mining Processing Chemicals 158
4. Industrial Ecology 166
History of Industrial Ecology 166
Environmental Impact Assessment 177
Canadian Environmental Assessment Act 183
Environmental Impact Design 197
Life-Cycle Assessment 198
Design for the Environment 210
Design Impact Measures 216
Cradle-to-Cradle Design 218
Eco-Industrial Park 225
Eco-Industrial Development 227
Industrial Symbiosis 230
Extended Producer Responsibility 232
Eco-Efficiency 237
Eco-Costs Value Ratio 241
Sustainable Value 248
Source Reduction 251
Eco-Innovation 252
5. Concepts in Corporate Ecology 254
Circular Economy 254
Founding Principles 256
Ecological Modernisation 259
Efficient Energy Use 262
Rebound Effect (Conservation) 271
Polluter Pays Principle 278
Precautionary Principle 279
Waste Hierarchy 290
Bibliography 293
Index 295

Chapter

Corporate Environmentalism

Edgar S. Woolard, CEO, Dupont Corporation, defines corporate environmentalism as "an attitude and a performance commitment that place corporate environmental stewardship fully in line with public desires and expectations."

In 1993, Baker and Miner defined corporate environmentalism as that which "superficially promises easy and risk-free solutions to complex, pressing environmental issues such as: the destruction of the ozone layer; the gradual warming of the earth's atmosphere; the solid waste disposal dilemma; and the continued pollution of the soil, water and air." But concerns for the environment on issues that have been affecting the earth and its people have been on since the 1960s. Questions concerning issues of resources are raised by more and people who are becoming "green consumers."

In the 1980s, the rich corporate were seen as evil, constantly raping Mother Earth of her natural resources for corporate riches, but fortunately they were restrained from this by law. They were forced to recycle goods and reduce emissions. A decade later, these corporate kings actually began caring for their environment. They got into deals with environmental activists across the US and began to show concern in planet saving. In the earlier decade, since corporate environmentalism was imposed, companies fulfilled the letter of the law but did not innovate, leading to a situation called "greenwashing." So companies thought it better to ward off excessive government regulation, improve their bottom line, and get some acclaim too by teaming up with environmental groups.

By the end of the century, Greenpeace, Environmental Defence, et al. saw that the government wasn't a reliable ally in their mission anymore and looked to partner with corporations to go far beyond regulations. Certain companies decided to strike a balance between the demands of shareholders and those of Greenpeace. One such company who decided to go environmental in the full glare of the public was British Petroleum or BP. It began by describing itself as going "Beyond Petroleum" and declaring that now it had begun "thinking outside the barrel."

It positioned itself to convince the world that it was a company that sucked dead dinosaurs out of the earth, turned it into gas that runs SUVs and is environmentally friendly too. On the face of it, this company supports stricter pollution rules and calls for reducing greenhouse gas emissions, but it really spends less than half of one percent of its revenue.

The money BP spends in partnership with environmental groups might look like a bribe to some people but corporations are learning to react to what Tom Murray of Environmental Defence said are "carrots in a system which is, in many ways, all sticks."

Home Depot does its own bit of corporate environmentalism and in 1999 Ron Jarvis' bosses asked him to quit his job and go over as the environmental global product manager at their Atlanta headquarters. Since then, Jarvis has become the vice president of merchandising for lumber products. So much of corporate environmentalism has happened at Home Depot that in 2005 the company's website boasted that "typical Team Depot activities include conservation projects, beautification efforts, and cleanups." At $400 million, today the Home Depot is the world's largest lumber buyer. And Jarvis has the power to cancel contracts with suppliers who bring harm to endangered forests or harm the environment in any way.

Today, more and more companies see merit in being corporate environmentalists.

Environmental Corporate Responsibility

Environmental corporate responsibility, in which a company seeks to reduce its operating impacts on the land, is often considered a portion of total corporate social responsibility. In addition to government pressure that regulates many business practices, corporations today often take voluntary measures to account for and mitigate environmental influences. Green practices, for example, may include selling non-toxic products, reducing air emissions and minimizing water pollutants. Environmental responsibility may also be evidenced in charity work, staff training, volunteer efforts and eco-labels. The surge in such practices is likely driven by both economic and political factors.

A business operating in today's competitive marketplace often wants to be perceived as ethical and responsible. Not only do customers often expect such behaviour, but government regulations may demand it as well. Corporate social responsibility (CSR), often defined as a form of self-regulation integrated into a business model, is one axis of this practice. CSR policy, therefore, often monitors a business to ensure it meets legal and ethical standards relative to its practices and the community. Such policy may also promote public interest with community development and voluntary elimination of harmful practices.

In addition to monitoring its community influences, an ethical corporation often measures and reduces its environmental impacts as well. Government pressure usually improves business practices with public initiatives and laws, such as the increased road tax for higher-emission vehicles in the United Kingdom. Even without such regulations, however, mounting environmental corporate responsibility is visible in many industry sectors. Toyota and Bank of America, for example, have buildings that are Gold-certified by the United States Building Council, Dell Computers allows customers to buy carbon offsets when they purchase new computers and British retailer Marks and Spencer plans to make all of its British and Irish operations carbon neutral by 2012.

The basic principle of environmental corporate responsibility is to hold a company accountable for its impact on the world around it. Such accountability may mean that companies incorporate into their own operations solutions for environmental problems. An automobile manufacturer, for example, often releases toxins into the air that are largely borne by surrounding citizens and businesses. To reflect its corporate conscience, the manufacturer may begin using more earth-friendly production materials or identify new processes that emit fewer pollutants. Such practices have evolved into what is known as green corporate responsibility, in which some companies produce and sell non-toxic products, reduce industry-related air emissions and implement processes to minimize water pollutants.

A commitment to mitigate the ways in which operations affect the planet is often a measure of a company's social performance. In some instances, that commitment manifests itself in the form of charity work within a community. To illustrate, Coco-Cola partners with Ocean Conservancy to sponsor the annual one-day event of International Coastal Cleanup. This increases awareness of marine litter and helps remove trash from worldwide beaches and waterways. Such a display of environmental corporate responsibility often provides a company with a positive social image. To this end, many companies also teach staff members about the issues of environmental responsibility. Hazardous waste management, for example, is often a component of training in many manufacturing and engineering facilities. In some countries, proper waste handling and disposal is strictly regulated, and industrial companies must routinely follow local and national guidelines.

Some companies further promote the idea of environmental corporate responsibility by encouraging employees to recycle paper and aluminum products. Still other firms sponsor community clean-up days, whereby employees actively remove litter from roadsides, parks and downtown areas. Eco-labels provide another way in which corporations voluntarily attempt to communicate sustainability efforts with the public. These labels generally indicate a product's overall environmental impacts or identify it as having passed local or national environmental standards. Such industries as those of home appliances, forestry products and organic foods often use eco-labelling.

Numerous applications for and explanations of environmental corporate responsibility can be provided. Some economists regard pollution as symptomatic of broader production inefficiencies. Thus, pollution reduction and cost savings may go hand-in-hand to generate greater profits. Other forces, including market responses by consumers seeking green products and services as well as such political steps as regulatory threats, may also be the drivers behind increasing CSR.

Essential Matter: Corporate Environmentalism: From Rhetoric to Results

Globalization is here to stay and, as a result, the speed with which ideas, products and services travel around the world is changing the way companies do business. How will the environment fare under globalization, and how will firms use environmental management strategies to maintain or improve their competitiveness?

Various trends and processes associated with globalization are generating conditions and pressures conducive to corporate environmental responsibility. As trade continues to liberalize, flows of goods, services and capital render traditional geopolitical borders increasingly irrelevant and traditional approaches to managing the environment obsolete. Corporate environmentalism has taken on new meaning both in operational and philosophical terms. The factors promoting it are more diverse, the scope broader, the rigor greater. Doing a good job on the environment and crafting strategies to address sustainable development no longer represent unproductive costs but, increasingly, opportunities whose benefits may be vital and necessary for the survival of companies.

Six trends seem particularly important in terms of promoting or facilitating corporate environmental management and business responsibility for sustainable development. First, as companies seek greater uniformity in process, production and product standards, geographic location is becoming less important. On the other hand, socio-economic and environmental distinctions are becoming more important in shaping corporate image and consumer decisions. Second, the movement from product-based manufacturing into service-based commerce in some sectors has significant implications for environment and development in both developed and developing countries. Third, as investment in developing country research and development increases, and as corporate authority within transnational firms is increasingly decentralized, southern-based firms and institutions are playing a more important role in the development and production of goods and services. Fourth, international attention to corporate activities is increasing as multilateral organisations establish global rules and standards concerning environmental management, and as communications technology and civil society networks facilitate surveillance. Fifth, globalization means that the range of any particular company's stakeholders is broad. Many companies are recognising that their ability to operate effectively depends on their accountability and standing among stakeholders. At the same time, they also recognise that doing a good job on the environment cannot be separated from social and community responsibility issues. Finally, legal systems and frameworks, at both national and international levels, continue to expand and, as business and government recognise the limits of command and control approaches to environmental protection, more collaborative approaches to resolving environmental problems are emerging.

Considerable progress has been made by firms over the past few years in coming to grips with their environmental responsibilities. Companies are being pushed to consider environmental concerns in the full range of their decisions, and they are challenging themselves constantly to respond to new market opportunities and reconceptualize their core businesses. It is also apparent that as leading companies strive to make sustainable development operational, the issues of environment, economics and social responsibility are increasingly indistinguishable.

While companies are undergoing transformations, governments are simultaneously seeking ways to increase the effectiveness of their policies. Approaches that reflect corporate self-interest may result in significant improvements to the environment at relatively modest societal costs. As part of this approach, however, policy makers will have to develop a more complete understanding than they now have of the forces driving corporate environmental responsibility.

Company response to environment issues is a topic that has received insufficient attention from policy makers, academicians and non-governmental organisations. Understanding the forces driving corporate responsibility in the environmental field creates the possibility of crafting policies that are more effective and less contentious than those currently in place. While it would be naive and inaccurate to suggest that all companies are taking seriously their responsibility toward the environment, there are an increasing number of ways through which company practice is revealed to the public and subjected to scrutiny. This increasing transparency represents an enormous opportunity for developing countries to shape company decisions in directions that favour sustainable development.

Sustainable Business

Sustainable business, or green business, is an enterprise that has minimal negative impact on the global or local environment, community, society, or economy—a business that strives to meet the triple bottom line. Often, sustainable businesses have progressive environmental and human rights policies. In general, business is described as green if it matches the following four criteria:

1. It incorporates principles of sustainability into each of its business decisions.
2. It supplies environmentally friendly products or services that replaces demand for nongreen products and/or services.
3. It is greener than traditional competition.
4. It has made an enduring commitment to environmental principles in its business operations.

A sustainable business is any organisation that participates in environmentally friendly or green activities to ensure that all processes, products, and manufacturing activities adequately address current environmental concerns while maintaining a profit. In other words, it is a business that "meets the needs of the present world without compromising the ability of the future generations to meet their own needs." It is the process of assessing how to design products that will take advantage of the current environmental situation and how well a company's products perform with renewable resources.

The Brundtland Report emphasized that sustainability is a three-legged stool of people, planet, and profit. Sustainable businesses with the supply chain try to balance all three through the triple-bottom-line concept—using sustainable development and sustainable distribution to affect the environment, business growth, and the society.

Everyone affects the sustainability of the marketplace and the planet in some way. Sustainable development within a business can create value for customers, investors, and the environment. A sustainable business must meet customer needs while, at the same time, treating the environment well.

Sustainability is often confused with corporate social responsibility (CSR), though the two are not the same. Bansal and DesJardine (2014) state that the notion of 'time' discriminates sustainability from CSR and other similar concepts. Whereas ethics, morality, and norms permeate CSR, sustainability only obliges businesses to make intertemporal trade-offs to safeguard intergenerational equity. Short-termism is the bane of sustainability.

Green business has been seen as a possible mediator of economic-environmental relations, and if proliferated, would serve to diversify our economy, even if it has a negligible effect at lowering atmospheric CO_2 levels. The definition of "green jobs" is ambiguous, but it is generally agreed that these jobs, the result of green business, should be linked to clean energy, and contribute to the reduction of greenhouse gases. These corporations can be seen as generators of not only "green energy", but as producers of new "materialities" that are the product of the technologies these firms developed and deployed.

Sustainable business, or green business, is an enterprise that has minimal negative impact on the global or local environment, community, society, or economy—a business that strives to meet the triple bottom line. Often, sustainable businesses have progressive environmental and human rights policies. In general, business is described as green if it matches the following four criteria:

1. It incorporates principles of sustainability into each of its business decisions.
2. It supplies environmentally friendly products or services that replaces demand for nongreen products and/or services.
3. It is greener than traditional competition.
4. It has made an enduring commitment to environmental principles in its business operations.

A sustainable business is any organisation that participates in environmentally friendly or green activities to ensure that all processes, products, and manufacturing activities adequately address current environmental concerns while maintaining a profit. In other words, it is a business that "meets the needs of the present world without compromising the ability of the future generations to meet their own needs." It is the process of assessing how to design products that will take advantage of the current environmental situation and how well a company's products perform with renewable resources.

The Brundtland Report emphasized that sustainability is a three-legged stool of people, planet, and profit. Sustainable businesses with the supply chain try to balance all three through the triple-bottom-line concept—using sustainable development and sustainable distribution to affect the environment, business growth, and the society.

Everyone affects the sustainability of the marketplace and the planet in some way. Sustainable development within a business can create value for customers, investors, and the environment. A sustainable business must meet customer needs while, at the same time, treating the environment well.

Sustainability is often confused with corporate social responsibility (CSR), though the two are not the same. Bansal and DesJardine (2014) state that the notion of 'time' discriminates sustainability from CSR and other similar concepts. Whereas ethics, morality, and norms permeate CSR, sustainability only obliges businesses to make intertemporal trade-offs to safeguard intergenerational equity. Short-termism is the bane of sustainability.

Green business has been seen as a possible mediator of economic-environmental relations, and if proliferated, would serve to diversify our economy, even if it has a negligible effect at lowering atmospheric CO2 levels. The definition of "green jobs" is ambiguous, but it is generally agreed that these jobs, the result of green business, should be linked to clean energy, and contribute to the reduction of greenhouse gases. These corporations can be seen as generators of not only "green energy", but as producers of new "materialities" that are the product of the technologies these firms developed and deployed.

Environmental Sphere

A major initiative of sustainable businesses is to eliminate or decrease the environmental harm caused by the production and consumption of their goods. The impact of such human activities in terms of the amount of greenhouse gases produced can be measured in units of carbon dioxide and is referred to as the *carbon footprint*. The carbon footprint concept is derived from ecological footprint analysis, which examines the ecological capacity required to support the consumption of products.

Businesses take a wide range of green initiatives. One of the most common examples is the act of "going paperless" or sending electronic correspondence in lieu of paper when possible. On a higher level, examples of sustainable business practices include: *refurbishing used products* (e.g., tuning up lightly used commercial fitness equipment for resale); *revising production processes* in order to eliminate waste (such as using a more accurate template to cut out designs); and choosing nontoxic raw materials and processes. For example, Canadian farmers have found that hemp is a sustainable alternative to rapeseed in their traditional crop rotation; hemp grown for fibre or seed requires no pesticides or herbicides. Sustainable business leaders also take into account the *life cycle costs* for the items they produce. Input costs must be considered in regards to regulations, energy use, storage, and disposal. *Designing for the environment* (DFE) is also an element of sustainable business. This process enables users to consider the potential environmental impacts of a product and the process used to make that product.

Among large corporations, Ford Motor Company occupies an odd role in the story of sustainability. Ironically, founder Henry Ford was a pioneer in the sustainable business realm, experimenting with plant-based fuels during the days of the Model T. Ford Motor Company also shipped the Model A truck in crates that then became the vehicle floorboards at the factory destination. This was a form of *upcycling*, retaining high quality in a closed-loop industrial cycle. Furthermore, the original auto body was made of a stronger-than-steel hemp composite. Today, of course, Fords aren't made of hemp or running on the most sensible fuel. Currently, Ford's claim to eco-friendly fame is the use of seat fabric made from 100% post-industrial materials and renewable soy foam seat bases. Ford executives recently appointed the company's first senior vice president of sustainability, environment, and safety engineering. This position is responsible for establishing a long-range sustainability strategy and environmental policy. The person in this position will also help develop the products and processes necessary to satisfy both customers and society as a whole while working toward energy independence. It remains to be seen whether Ford will return to its founder's vision of a petroleum-free automobile, a vehicle powered by the remains of plant matter.

Smaller companies such as Nature's Path, an organic cereal and snack making business, have also made significant sustainability gains in the 21st century. CEO Arran Stephens and his associates have ensured that the quickly growing company's products are produced without toxic farm chemicals. Furthermore, employees are constantly encouraged to find ways to reduce consumption. Sustainability is an essential part of corporate discussions. Another example comes from Salt Spring Coffee, a company created in 1996 as a certified organic, fair trade, coffee producer. In recent years they have become carbon neutral, lowering emissions by reducing long-range trucking and using bio-diesel in delivery trucks, upgrading to energy efficient equipment and purchasing carbon offsets. The company claims to offer the first carbon neutral coffee sold in Canada. Salt Spring Coffee was recognised by the David Suzuki Foundation in the 2010 report *Doing Business in a New Climate*. A third example comes from Korea, where rice husks are used as a nontoxic packaging for stereo components and other electronics. The same material is later recycled to make bricks.

The many possibilities for adopting green practices have led to considerable pressure being put upon companies from consumers, employees, government regulators and other stakeholders. Some companies have resorted to greenwashing instead of making meaningful changes, merely marketing their products in ways that suggest green practices. For example, various producers in the bamboo fibre industry have been taken to court for advertising their products as more "green" than they are. Still, countless other companies have taken the sustainability trend seriously and are enjoying profits. The *Gort Cloud* written by Richard Seireeni, (2009), documents the experiences of sustainable businesses in America and their reliance on the vast but invisible green community, referred to as the gort cloud, for support and a market.

Green investment firms are consequently attracting unprecedented interest. In the UK, for instance, the Green Investment Bank is devoted exclusively to supporting renewable domestic energy. However, the UK and Europe as a whole are falling behind the impressive pace set by developing nations in terms of green development. Thus, green investment firms are creating more and more opportunities to support sustainable development practices in emerging economies. By providing micro-loans and larger investments, these firms assist small business owners in developing nations who seek business education, affordable loans, and new distribution networks for their "green" products.

Social Sphere

Organisations that give back to the community, whether through employees volunteering their time or through charitable donations are often considered to be socially sustainable. Organisations also can encourage education in their communities by training their employees and offering internships to younger members of the community. Practices such as these increase the education level and quality of life in the community.

In order for a business to be truly sustainable, it must sustain not only the necessary environmental resources, but also its social resources, including employees, customers (the community), and its reputation.

Organisations

The European community's Restriction of Hazardous Substances Directive restricts the use of certain hazardous materials in the production of various electronic and electrical products. Waste Electrical and Electronic Equipment (WEEE) directives provide collection, recycling, and recovery practices for electrical goods. The World Business Council for Sustainable Development and the World Resources Institute are two organisations working together to set a standard for reporting on corporate carbon footprints. From October 2013, all quoted companies in the UK are legally required to report their annual greenhouse gas emissions in their directors' report, under the Companies Act 2006 (Strategic and Directors' Reports) Regulations 2013.

Lester Brown's Plan B 2.0 and Hunter Lovins's Natural Capitalism provide information on sustainability initiatives.

Corporate Sustainability Strategies

Corporate sustainability strategies can aim to take advantage of sustainable revenue opportunities, while protecting the value of business against increasing energy costs, the costs of meeting regulatory requirements, changes in the way customers perceive brands and products, and the volatile price of resources.

Not all eco-strategies can be incorporated into a company's Eco-portfolio immediately. The widely practiced strategies include: Innovation, Collaboration, Process Improvement and Sustainability reporting.

Innovation & Technology: This introverted method of sustainable corporate practices focuses on a company's ability to change its products and services towards less waste production and sustainable best practices.

Collaboration: The formation of networks with similar or partner companies facilitates knowledge sharing and propels innovation.

Process Improvement: Continuous process surveying and improvement is essential to reduction in waste. Employee awareness of company-wide sustainability plan further aids the integration of new and improved processes.

Sustainability Reporting: Periodic reporting of company performance in relation to goals. These goals are often incorporated in to the corporate mission (as in the case of Ford Motor Co.).

Additionally, companies might consider implementing a sound monitoring system with readjustment procedures, as well as a regular forum for all stakeholders to discuss sustainability issues.

Standards

Enormous economic and population growth worldwide in the second half of the twentieth century aggravated the factors that threaten health and the world — ozone depletion, climate change, depletion, fouling of natural resources, and extensive loss of biodiversity and habitat. In the past, the standard approaches to environmental problems generated by business and industry have been regulatory-driven "end-of-the-pipe" remediation efforts. In the 1990s, efforts by governments, NGOs, corporations, and investors began to grow substantially to develop awareness and plans for investment in business sustainability.

One critical milestone was the establishment of the ISO 14000 standards whose development came as a result of the Rio Summit on the Environment held in 1992. ISO 14001 is the cornerstone standard of the ISO 14000 series. It specifies a framework of control for an Environmental Management System against which an organisation can be certified by a third party. Other ISO 14000 Series Standards are actually guidelines, many to help you achieve registration to ISO 14001. They include the following:

- ISO 14004 provides guidance on the development and implementation of environmental management systems
- ISO 14010 provides general principles of environmental auditing (now superseded by ISO 19011)
- ISO 14011 provides specific guidance on audit an environmental management system (now superseded by ISO 19011)
- ISO 14012 provides guidance on qualification criteria for environmental auditors and lead auditors (now superseded by ISO 19011)

- ISO 14013/5 provides audit program review and assessment material.
- ISO 14020+ labelling issues
- ISO 14030+ provides guidance on performance targets and monitoring within an Environmental Management System
- ISO 14040+ covers life cycle issues

LEED Certification

The Leadership in Energy and Environmental Design standards were developed by the US Green Building Council in an effort to propel green building design in the United States. LEED certification is very prestigious title and can be attained through "compliance with all environmental laws and regulations, occupancy scenarios, building permanence and pre-rating completion, site boundaries and area-to-site ratios, and obligatory five-year sharing of whole building energy and water use data from the start of occupancy (for new construction) or date of certification (for existing buildings)".[15].

Six Essential Characteristics

Matthew Tueth, Ph.D. reiterates the ideas put forward by authors such as Paul Hawken (*The Ecology of Commerce* and *Natural Capitalism*), Bill McDonough and Michael Braungart (*Cradle to Cradle*), and Janine Benyus (*Biomimicry*) when he proposes that a mature and authentic sustainable business contains six essential characteristics.

Triple Top-Line Value Production

"The TTL Establishes three *simultaneous requirements* of sustainable business activities - financial benefits for the company, natural world betterment, and social advantages for employees and members of the local community—with each of these three components recognised as equal in status." Whereas many businesses use the triple bottom line, "triple top line" stresses the importance of initial design and is a term attributable to McDonough and Braungart in their book *Cradle to Cradle.*

Nature-based Knowledge and Technology

"This biomimicry-based principal [sic] involves the conscious emulation of natural-world genius in terms of growing our food, harnessing our energy, constructing things, conducting business healing ourselves, processing information and designing our communities"

Products of Service to Products of Consumption

"*Products of service* are durable goods routinely leased by the customer that are made of technical materials and are returned to the manufacturer and re-processed into a new generation of products when they are worn out.(These products are mostly non-toxic to human and environmental health but toxic materials that are used will be kept within a closed loop type system and not be able to escape into the environment). *Products of consumption* are shorter lived items made only of biodegradable materials. They are broken down by the detritus organisms after the products lose their usefulness.(These are also non-hazardous to human or environmental health). This principal requires that we manufacture only these two types of products and necessitates the gradual but continual reductions of products of service and their replacement with products of consumption as technological advancements allow."

Solar, Wind, Geothermal and Ocean Energy

"This principal[sic] advocates employing only sustainable energy technology—solar, wind, ocean and geothermal—that can meet our energy needs indefinitely without negative effects for life on earth." Other authors, such as Paul Hawken, have referred to this as utilising current solar income.

Local-based Organisations and Economies

"This ingredient includes durable, beautiful and healthy communities with locally owned and operated businesses and locally managed non-profit organisations, along with regional corporations and shareholders working together in a dense web of partnerships and collaborations."

Continuous Improvement Process

"Operational processes inside successful organisations include provisions for constant advancements and upgrade as the company does its business. The continuous process of monitoring, analyzing, redesigning and implementing is used to intensify TTL value production as conditions change and new opportunities emerge."

Challenges and Opportunities

Implementing sustainable business practices may have an effect on profits and a firm's financial 'bottom line'. At first blush, this challenge might make many corporate executives cringe. However, during a time where environmental awareness is popular, green strategies are likely to be embraced by employees, consumers, and other stakeholders. In fact, according to many studies, a positive correlation exists between environmental performance and economic performance.

Companies leading the way in sustainable business practices can be said to be taking advantage of sustainable revenue opportunities: according to the Department for Business, Innovation and Skills the UK market for low-carbon goods and services is set to grow by £5 billion a year to £140 billion by 2015, and the average internal rate of return on energy efficiency investments for large businesses is 48%. A 2013 survey suggests that demand for green products appears to be increasing: 27% of respondents said they are more likely to buy a sustainable product and/or service than 5 years ago. Furthermore, sustainable business practices may attract talent and generate tax breaks.

Corporate Sustainability

Corporate sustainability is a business approach that creates long-term consumer and employee value by creating a "green" strategy aimed toward the natural environment and taking into consideration every dimension of how a business operates in the social, cultural, and economic environment. It also formulates strategies to build a company that fosters longevity through transparency and proper employee development.

Corporate sustainability is an evolution on more traditional phrases describing ethical corporate practice. Phrases such as corporate social responsibility (CSR) or corporate citizenship continue to be used but are increasingly superseded by the broader term *corporate sustainability*. Unlike phrases that focus on "added-on" policies, *corporate sustainability* describes business practices built around social and environmental considerations.

The phrase is derived from two keys sources. The Brundtland Commission's Report, *Our Common Future*, described sustainable development as, "development that meets the needs of the present without compromising the ability of future generations to meet their own needs". This desire to grow without damaging future generations' prospects is becoming more and more central to business philosophies. Within more academic management circles, Elkington (1999) developed the concept of the Triple Bottom Line which proposed that business goals were inseparable from the societies and environments within which they operate. Whilst short-term economic gain could be chased, a failure to account for social and environmental impacts would make those business practices unsustainable.

Strategy for Corporate Sustainability

Business Case for Sustainability: The challenge for many businesses in this new field is to quantify the positive impacts of sustainability. Sustainability can increase revenue, reduce energy expenses, reduce waste expenses, reduce materials and water expenses, increase employee productivity, reduce hiring and attrition expenses, and reduce strategic and operational risks. Furthermore, sustainable business practices may attract talent and generate tax breaks.

Transparency: Transparency deals with the idea that by having an engaging and open environment in the company as well as the community will improve performance and increase profits. It is an open culture that promotes employee involvement in the innovation and creative processes. Reaching out to the community creates a much bigger team is extremely cheap and provides evaluation from all angles. Companies are looking inward and realising changes must be made to fulfill environment needs such as energy efficiency, limiting product waste and toxicity, and designing innovative products. One way for companies to accomplish this is through open communications with stakeholders characterized by high levels of information disclosure, clarity, and accuracy.

Stakeholder Engagement: Sustainability requires a company to look internally and externally to understand their environmental and social impacts. This requires the engagement of stakeholders to understand impacts and concerns. A business can address sustainability internally by educating employees and seeking to reduce impacts through waste reduction, energy efficiency, etc. Employee engagement can be a powerful motivator by having a philanthropy committee or a green team. As a company looks externally, stakeholders include customers, suppliers, community, and non-government organisations.

Thinking Ahead: Companies have adapted by implementing new creative ideas related to sustainability, such as preparing upgraded technology that can transform the product rather than throwing away old materials. New solutions that improve recycling and waste redirecting can ultimately reduce costs and increase profits. For example, Wal-Mart has redirected more than 64 percent of the waste generated by stores and Sam's Club facilities. In 2009 alone, they recycled more than 1.3 million pounds of aluminum, 120 million pounds of plastics, 11.6 million pounds of mixed paper and 4.6 billion pounds of cardboard. Annually, they expect to save around $20 million and prevent 38 million pounds of waste being sent to landfills.

Professionals

Companies focused on sustainability are appointing chief sustainability officers leading a department with a mandate to proactively develop and implement a corporate sustainability strategy.

Cleaner Production

Cleaner production is a preventive, company-specific environmental protection initiative. It is intended to minimize waste and emissions and maximize product output. By analysing the flow of materials and energy in a company, one tries to identify options to minimize waste and emissions out of industrial processes through source reduction strategies. Improvements of organisation and technology help to reduce or suggest better choices in use of materials and energy, and to avoid waste, waste water generation, and gaseous emissions, and also waste heat and noise.

The concept was developed during the preparation of the Rio Summit as a programme of UNEP (United Nations Environmental Programme) and UNIDO (United Nations Industrial Development Organisation) under the leadership of Jacqueline Aloisi de Larderel, the former Assistant Executive Director of UNEP. The programme was meant to reduce the environmental impact of industry. It built on ideas used by 3M in its 3P programme (pollution prevention pays). It has found more international support than all other comparable programmes. The programme idea was described "...to assist developing nations in leapfrogging from pollution to less pollution, using available technologies". Starting from the simple idea to produce with less waste Cleaner Production was developed into a concept to increase the resource efficiency of production in general. UNIDO has been operating a National Cleaner Production Centre Programme with centres in Latin America, Africa, Asia and Europe.

In the US, the term pollution prevention is more commonly used for cleaner production.

Examples for cleaner production options are:

- Documentation of consumption (as a basic analysis of material and energy flows, e. g. with a Sankey diagram)
- Use of indicators and controlling (to identify losses from poor planning, poor education and training, mistakes)
- Substitution of raw materials and auxiliary materials (especially renewable materials and energy)

- Increase of useful life of auxiliary materials and process liquids (by avoiding drag in, drag out, contamination)
- Improved control and automatisation
- Reuse of waste (internal or external)
- New, low waste processes and technologies

One of the first European initiatives in cleaner production was started in Austria in 1992 by the BMVIT (Bundesministerium für Verkehr, Innovation und Technologie). This resulted in two initiatives: "Prepare" and EcoProfit.

The "PIUS" initiative was founded in Germany in 1999. Since 1994, the United Nations Industrial Development Organisation operates the National Cleaner Production Centre Programme with centres in Central America, South America, Africa, Asia, and Europe.

Clean Energy Trends

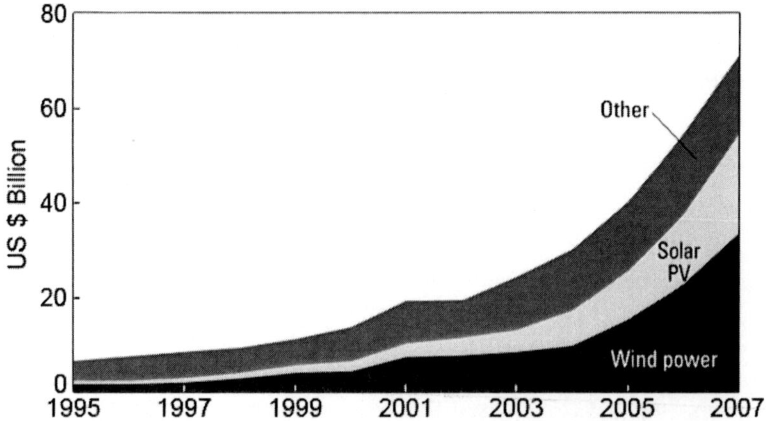

Figure: *Global renewable energy investment growth (1995-2007)*

Clean Energy Trends is a series of reports by Clean Edge which examine markets for solar, wind, geothermal, fuel cells, biofuels, and other clean energy technologies. Since the publication of the first *Clean Energy Trends* report in 2002, Clean Edge has provided an annual snapshot of both the global and U.S. clean energy sector markets.

2006 Trends

In 2006 most climate change skeptics began to change their views. Scientists, investors, business leaders, and politicians moved the agenda from whether climate change was occurring to what should be done about it. The acceptance of climate change as "real" helped to unlock latent interest in clean energy technologies on the part of corporate and political leaders. In Washington and other capitals, clean energy became a bipartisan issue. In corporate boardrooms, it is said to be fast becoming an imperative and clean energy markets are growing:

> *"We have reached the point where the steady and rapid growth of clean energy has become an old story. Each year, it seems, brings an ever-higher plateau of success. This appears to be the future of clean energy: a rolling series of technology breakthroughs, landmark corporate investments, industry consolidation, and the not-infrequent emergence of new and sometimes surprising players entering the field."*

2007 Trends

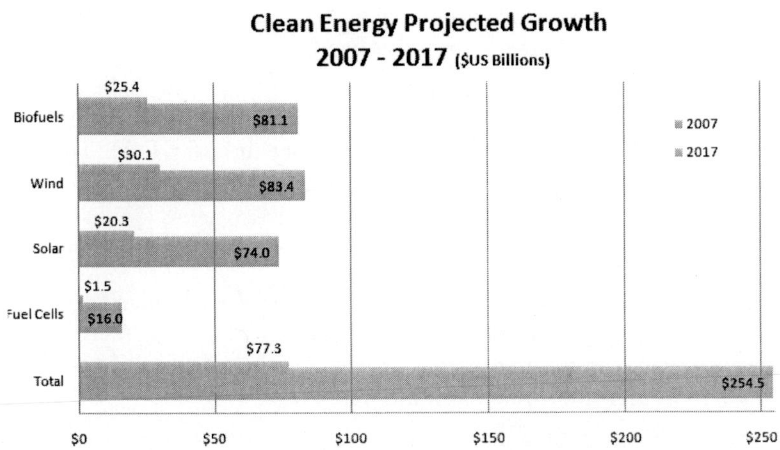

Figure: *Projected renewable energy investment growth globally (2007-2017)*

Clean Energy Trends 2007 shows markets for four benchmark technologies — solar photovoltaics, wind power, biofuels, and fuel cells — continuing their steady climb. Annual revenue for these four technologies increased nearly 39% in one year — to $55 billion in 2006 up from $40 billion in 2005. Clean Edge forecasts that this trajectory will continue to become a $226 billion market by 2016.

Several developments have helped to strengthen clean energy markets in 2007:

- "a near tripling in venture investments in energy technologies in the U.S. to more than $2.4 billion"
- "a new level of commitment by U.S. politicians at the regional, state, and federal levels"

- "significant corporate investments in clean energy acquisitions and expansion initiatives"

Low-Carbon Economy

A low-carbon economy (LCE), low-fossil-fuel economy (LFFE), or decarbonised economy is an economy based on low carbon power sources that therefore has a minimal output of greenhouse gas (GHG) emissions into the environment biosphere, but specifically refers to the greenhouse gas carbon dioxide. GHG emissions due to anthropogenic (human) activity are increasingly either causing climate change (global warming) or making climate change worse. Scientists are concerned about the negative impacts of climate change on humanity in the near future.

Globally implemented LCEs are therefore proposed by those having drawn this conclusion, as a means to avoid catastrophic climate change, and as a precursor to the more advanced, zero-carbon economy.

In terms of large industrialized nations, mainland France, due primarily to 75% of its electricity being produced by nuclear power, has the lowest carbon dioxide production per unit of GDP in the world and it is the largest exporter of electricity in the world, earning it approximately €3 billion annually in sales.

Rationale and Aims

Nations may seek to become low-carbon or decarbonised economies as a part of a national climate change mitigation strategy. A comprehensive strategy to mitigate, if that is possible, climate change is carbon neutrality and geoengineering.

The aim of a LCE is to integrate all aspects of itself from its manufacturing, agriculture, transportation, and power-generation, etc. around technologies that produce energy and materials with little GHG emission, and, thus, around populations, buildings, machines, and devices that use those energies and materials efficiently, and, dispose of or recycle its wastes so as to have a minimal output of GHGs. Furthermore, it has been proposed that to make the transition to an LCE economically viable we would have to attribute a cost (per unit output) to GHGs through means such as emissions trading and/or a carbon tax.

Some nations are presently low carbon: societies that are not heavily industrialised or populated. In order to avoid climate change on a global level, all nations considered carbon intensive societies, and societies that are heavily populated might have to become zero-carbon societies and economies. Several of these countries have pledged to cut their emissions by 100% via offsetting emissions rather than ceasing all emissions (carbon neutrality); in other words, emitting will not cease but will continue and will be *offset* to a different geographical area. EU emission trading system allows companies to buy international carbon credits, thus the companies can channel clean technologies to promote other countries to adopt low-carbon developments.

Energy Policy

Renewable Energy and Energy Efficiency: Recent advances in technology and policy will allow renewable energy and energy efficiency to play major roles in displacing fossil fuels, meeting global energy demand while reducing carbon dioxide emissions. Renewable energy technologies are being rapidly commercialized and, in conjunction with efficiency gains, can achieve far greater emissions reductions than either could independently.

Renewable energy is energy that comes from natural resources such as sunlight, wind, rain, tides, and geothermal heat, which are renewable (naturally replenished). In 2008, about 19% of global final energy consumption came from renewables. During the five years from the end of 2004 through 2009, worldwide renewable energy capacity grew at rates of 10–60 percent annually for many technologies. For wind power and many other renewable technologies, growth accelerated in 2009 relative to the previous four years. More wind power capacity was added during 2009 than any other renewable technology. However, grid-connected photovoltaics increased the fastest of all renewables technologies, with a 60 percent annual average growth rate for the five-year period.

Energy efficiency gains in recent decades have been significant, but there is still much more that can be achieved. With a concerted effort and strong policies in place, future energy efficiency improvements are likely to be very large. Heat is one of many forms of "energy wastage" that could be captured to significantly increase useful energy without burning more fossil fuels.

Smart Grid

One proposal from Karlsruhe University developed as a virtual power station is the use of solar and wind energy for base load with hydro and biogas for make up or peak load. Hydro and biogas are used as energy storage. This requires the development of a smart intelligent grid hopefully including local power networks than use energy near the site of production, thereby minimising electrical grid losses.

Methane Cycle

A further development of this at Kassel University, Fraunhofer Institute, Negawatt Institute, etc. is the use of the carbon capture, hydrogen and its conversion into methane (SNG synthetic natural gas) to act as a storage for intermittent renewables.

$$CO_2 + 4H_2 \rightarrow CH_4 + 2H_2O \text{ Sabatier reaction}$$

This involves the use of the existing natural gas (methane) grid as the store. In this case, the carbon dioxide is given economic value as a component of energy carrier. This "solar fuel" cycle uses the excess electrical renewable energy that cannot be used instantaneously in the grid, which otherwise would be wasted to create hydrogen via electrolysis of water. The hydrogen is then combined with CO_2 to create synthetic or substitute natural gas SNG and stored in the natural gas network.

The natural gas is used to create electrical energy (and the heat used as well in CHP) on demand when there is not enough sun (photovoltaic, CSP...) or wind (turbines) or water (hydro, ocean current, waves,...). The German natural gas grid, for example, has two months of storage, more than enough to outlast renewable energy low production points.

Nuclear Power and CCS

Nuclear power and/or the proposed strategies of carbon capture and storage (CCS) have been offered as the primary means to achieve a LCE while continuing to exploit non-renewable resources; there is concern, however, with the matter of spent-nuclear-fuel storage, security, and the uncertainty of costs and time needed to successfully implement CCS worldwide and with guarantees that the stored emissions will not leak into the biosphere. The liquid fluoride thorium reactor (LFTR) has been suggested as a solution to the concerns posed by conventional nuclear.

Combined Heat and Power

Combined Heat and Power (CHP) is a technology which by allowing the more efficient use of fuel will at least reduce carbon emissions; should the fuel be biomass or biogas or hydrogen used as an energy store then in principle it can be a zero carbon option. CHP can also be used with a nuclear reactor as the energy source, there are examples of such installations in the far North of the Russian Federation.

Primary Sector

Agriculture: Most of the agricultural facilities in the developed world are mechanized due to rural electrification. Rural electrification has produced significant productivity gains, but it also uses a lot of energy. For this and other reasons (such as transport costs) in a low-carbon society, rural areas would need available supplies of renewably produced electricity. Irrigation can be one of the main components of an agricultural facility's energy consumption. In parts of California, it can be up to 90%. In the low carbon economy, irrigation equipment will be maintained and continuously updated and farms will use less irrigation water.

Crops

Different crops require different amounts of energy input. For example, glasshouse crops, irrigated crops, and orchards require a lot of energy to maintain, while row crops and field crops do not need as much maintenance. Those glasshouse and irrigated crops that do exist will incorporate the following improvements:

Glasshouse Crops:

- environmental control systems
- heat recovery using condensers
- heat storage using buffer tanks
- heat retention using thermal screens
- alternative fuels (e.g., waste wood)
- cogeneration (heat and power)

Irrigated Arable Crops:

- soil moisture measurement to regulate irrigation
- variable-speed drives on pumps

Livestock

Livestock operations can also use a lot of energy depending on how they are run. Feed lots use animal feed made from corn, soybeans, and other crops. Energy must be expended to produce these crops, process, and transport them. Free-range animals find their own vegetation to feed on. The farmer may expend energy to take care of that vegetation, but not nearly as much as the farmer growing cereal and oil-seed crops.

Many livestock operations currently use a lot of energy to water their livestock. In the low-carbon economy, such operations will use more water conservation methods such as rainwater collection, water cisterns, etc., and they will also pump/distribute that water with on-site renewable energy sources (most likely wind and solar).

Due to rural electrification, most agricultural facilities in the developed world use a lot of electricity. In a low-carbon economy, farms will be run and equipped to allow for greater energy efficiency. The dairy industry, for example, will incorporate the following changes:

Irrigated Dairy:

- heat recovery on milk vats
- variable speed drives on motors/pumps
- heat recovery from hot water wash
- soil moisture measurement to regulate irrigation
- biodigester with cogen (heat & power)
- vat wrap
- solar water heating
- ripple control
- ice bank
- chemical substitute for hot-water wash

Hunting and Fishing

Fishing is quite energy intensive. Improvements such as heat recovery on refrigeration and trawl net technology will be common in the low-carbon economy.

Forestry

In the low-carbon economy, forestry operations will be focused on low-impact practices and regrowth. Forest managers will make sure that they do not disturb soil-based carbon reserves too much. Specialised tree farms will be the main source of material for many products. Quick maturing tree varieties will be grown on short rotations in order to maximize output.

Mining

Flaring and venting of natural gas in oil wells is a significant source of greenhouse gas emissions. Its contribution to greenhouse gases has declined by three-quarters in absolute terms since a peak in the 1970s of approximately 110 million metric tons/year, and in 2004 accounted for about 1/2 of one percent of all anthropogenic carbon dioxide emissions.

The World Bank estimates that 134 billion cubic metres of natural gas are flared or vented annually (2010 datum), an amount equivalent to the combined annual gas consumption of Germany and France or enough to supply the entire world with gas for 16 days. This flaring is highly concentrated: 10 countries account for 70% of emissions, and twenty for 85%.

The top-ten leading contributors to world gas flaring in 2010, were (in declining order): Russia (26%), Nigeria (11%), Iran (8%), Iraq (7%), Algeria (4%), Angola (3%), Kazakhstan (3%), Libya (3%), Saudi Arabia (3%), and Venezuela (2%).

Secondary Sector

Basic Metals Processing:

- high efficiency electric motors
- induction furnaces
- heat recovery

Nonmetallic Product Processing:

- variable speed drives
- injection molding - replace hydraulic with electric servo motors

Wood Processing:

- high efficiency motors
- high efficiency fans
- dehumidifier driers

Paper and Pulp Making:

- variable speed drives
- high efficiency motors

Food Processing:

- high efficiency boilers
- heat recovery e.g. refrigeration
- solar hot water for pre-heating
- bio fuels e.g. tallow, wood

Tertiary Sector

Retail: Retail operations in the low-carbon economy will have several new features. One will be high-efficiency lighting such as compact fluorescent, halogen, and eventually LED light sources. Many retail stores will also feature roof-top solar panel arrays. These make sense because solar panels produce the most energy during the daytime and during the summer. These are the same times that electricity is the most expensive and also the same times that stores use the most electricity.

Transportation Services

Decarbonisation of (urban) mobility by means of:

- More energy efficiency and alternative propulsion:
    - o Increased focus on fuel efficient vehicle shapes and configurations, with more vehicle electrification, particularly through plug-in hybrids.
    - o More alternative and flex-fuel vehicles (based on local conditions and availability)
    - o Driver training for more fuel efficiency.
    - o Low-carbon biofuels cellulosic (biodiesel, bioethanol, biobutanol)
    - o Petroleum fuel surcharges will be a more significant part of consumer costs.
- Less international trade of physical objects, despite more overall trade (as measure by value of goods)
- Greater use of marine and electric rail transport, less use of air and truck transport.
- Increased non-motorised transport (i.e. walking and cycling) and public transport usage, less reliance on private motor vehicles.
- More pipeline capacity for common fluid commodities such as water, ethanol, butanol, natural gas, petroleum, and hydrogen (in addition to gasoline and diesel).

Health Services

There have been some moves to investigate the ways and extent to which health systems contribute to greenhouse gas emissions and how they may need to change to become part of a low-carbon world. The Sustainable Development Unit of the NHS in the UK is one of the first official bodies to have been set up in this area, whilst organisations such as the Campaign for Greener Healthcare are also producing influential changes at a clinical level. This work includes

- Quantification of where the health services emissions stem from.
- Information on the environmental impacts of alternative models of treatment and service provision

Some of the Suggested Changes Needed are

- Greater efficiency and lower ecological impact of energy, buildings, and procurement choices (e.g., in-patient meals, pharmaceuticals, and medical equipment).

- A shift from focusing solely on cure to prevention, through the promotion of healthier, lower-carbon lifestyles, e.g. diets lower in red meat and dairy products, walking or cycling wherever possible, better town planning to encourage more outdoor lifestyles.
- Improving public transport and liftsharing options for transport to and from hospitals and clinics.

Initial Steps

A good overview of the history of international efforts towards a low-carbon economy, from its initial seed at the inaugural UN Conference on the Human Environment in Stockholm in 1972, has been given by David Runnals. On the international scene, the most prominent early step in the direction of a low-carbon economy was the signing of the Kyoto Protocol, which came into force on February 16, 2005, under which most industrialized countries committed to reduce their carbon emissions. Importantly, all member nations of the Organisation for Economic Co-operation and Development except the United States have ratified the protocol. Europe is the leading geopolitical continent in defining and mobilising decarbonisation policies. For instance, the UITP - an organisation advocating sustainable mobility and public transport - has an EU office, but less well developed contacts with, for example, the US. The European Union Committee of the UITP wants to promote decarbonisation of urban mobility in Europe. Although Europe is nowadays the leading geopolitical continent with regard to lowering emissions, Europe is quickly losing ground to Asia, with countries such as China and South Korea. However, the 2014 *Global Green Economy Index™ (GGEI)* ranks 60 nations on their green economic performance, finding that the Nordic countries and Switzerland have the best combined performance around climate change and green economy.

Countries

Costa Rica: Costa Rica sources much of its energy needs from renewables and is undertaking reforestation projects. In 2007, the Costa Rican government announced the commitment for Costa Rica to become the first carbon neutral country by 2021.

Iceland: Iceland began utilising renewable energy early in the 20th century and so since has been a low-carbon economy. However, since dramatic economic growth, Iceland's emissions have increased significantly per capita. As of 2009, Iceland energy is sourced from mostly geothermal energy and hydropower, renewable energy in Iceland

and, since 1999, has provided over 70% of the nation's primary energy and 99.9% of Iceland's electricity. As a result of this, Iceland's carbon emissions per capita are 62% lower than those of the United States despite using more primary energy per capita, due to the fact that it is renewable and thus limitless and costs Icelanders almost nothing. Iceland seeks carbon neutrality and expects to use 100% renewable energy by 2050 by generating hydrogen fuel from renewable energy sources.

Australia: Australia has implemented schemes to start the transition to a low-carbon economy but carbon neutrality has not been mentioned and since the introduction of such scheme emissions have increased. The Second Rudd Government pledged to lower emissions by 5-15%. In 2001, The Howard Government introduced a Mandatory Renewable Energy Target (MRET) scheme. In 2007, the Government revised the MRET - 20 percent of Australia's electricity supply to come from renewable energy sources by 2020. Renewable energy sources provide 8-10% of the nation's energy, and this figure will increase significantly in the coming years. However coal dependence and exporting conflicts with the concept of Australia as a low-carbon economy. Carbon-neutral businesses have received no incentive; they have voluntarily done so. Carbon-offset companies offer assessments based on lifecycle impacts to businesses that seek carbon neutrality. The Carbon Reduction Institute is one such offset provider, that has produced a certification procedure to promote a low-carbon economy in Australia. Though the only true certified carbon neutral scheme is the Australian governments National Carbon Offset Standard (NCOS). Businesses are now moving from unaccredited schemes such as noco2 and transitioning to NCOS as the only one that is externally audited. Most of leading carbon management companies have also aligned with NCOS such as Net Balance, Pangolin Asscociates, Energetics and the big four accounting firms.

In 2011 the Gillard Government introduced a price on carbon dioxide emissions for businesses. Although often characterised as a tax, it lacked the revenue-raising nature of a true tax. In 2013, on the election of the Abbott government, immediate legislative steps were taken to repeal the so-called carbon tax. The price on carbon was repealed on the 17th July 2014 by an act of parliament. As it stands Australia currently has no mechanism to deal with climate change.

China: In China, the city of Dongtan is to be built to produce zero net greenhouse gas emissions. The Chinese State Council announced in 2009 it aimed to cut China's carbon dioxide emissions per unit of GDP by 40%-45% in 2020 from 2005 levels. However carbon dioxide emissions were still increasing by 10% a year by 2013 and China was emitting more carbon dioxide than the next two biggest countries combined (U.S.A. and India). Total carbon dioxide emissions were projected to increase until 2030.

United Kingdom: In the United Kingdom, the Climate Change Act 2008 outlining a framework for the transition to a low-carbon economy became law on November 26, 2008. This legislation requires an 80% cut in the UK's carbon emissions by 2050 (compared to 1990 levels), with an intermediate target of between 26% and 32% by 2020. Thus, the UK became the first country to set such a long-range and significant carbon reduction target into law.

A meeting at the Royal Society on 17–18 November 2008 concluded that an integrated approach, making best use of all available technologies, is required to move toward a low-carbon future. It was suggested by participants that it would be possible to move to a low-carbon economy within a few decades, but that 'urgent and sustained action is needed on several fronts'.

In June 2012, the UK coalition government announced the introduction of mandatory carbon reporting, requiring around 1,100 of the UK's largest listed companies to report their greenhouse gas emissions every year. Deputy Prime Minister Nick Clegg confirmed that emission reporting rules would come into effect from April 2013 in his piece for The Guardian.

In July 2014, the UK Energy Savings Opportunity Scheme (ESOS) came into force. This requires all large businesses in the UK to undertake mandatory assessments looking at energy use and energy efficiency opportunities at least once every four years.

The low carbon economy has been described as a "UK success story", accounting for more than £120 billion in annual sales and employing almost 1 million people. A 2013 report suggests that over a third of the UK's economic growth in 2011/12 was likely to have come from green business.

Cities: Companies are planning large scale developments without using fossil fuels. Development plans such as those by World Wide Assets LLC for entire cities using only geothermal energy for electricity, geothermal desalination, and employing full recycling systems for water and waste are under development (2006) in Mexico and Australia.

Business Action on Climate Change

Business action on climate change includes a range of activities relating to global warming, and to influencing political decisions on global-warming-related regulation, such as the Kyoto Protocol. Major multinationals have played and to some extent continue to play a significant role in the politics of global warming, especially in the United States, through lobbying of government and funding of global warming skeptics. Business also plays a key role in the mitigation of global warming, through decisions to invest in researching and implementing new energy technologies and energy efficiency measures.

Overview

In 1989 in the US, the petroleum and automotive industries and the National Association of Manufacturers created the Global Climate Coalition (GCC) to oppose mandatory actions to address global warming. In 1997, when the US Senate overwhelmingly passed a resolution against ratifying the Kyoto Protocol, the industry funded a $13 million industry advertising blitz in the run-up to the vote.

In 1998 the *New York Times* published an American Petroleum Institute (API) memo outlining a strategy aiming to make "recognition of uncertainty ... part of the 'conventional wisdom.'" The memo has been compared to a late 1960s memo by tobacco company Brown and Williamson, which observed: "Doubt is our product since it is the best means of competing with the 'body of fact' that exists in the mind of the general public. It is also the means of establishing a controversy." Those involved in the memo included Jeffrey Salmon, then executive director of the George C. Marshall Institute, Steven Milloy, a prominent skeptic commentator, and the Competitive Enterprise Institute's Myron Ebell. In June 2005 a former API lawyer, Philip Cooney, resigned his White House post after accusations of politically motivated tampering with scientific reports.

In 2002 the GCC considered its work in the US against regulation on global warming to have been so successful that it "deactivated" itself, although the loss of some leading members may also have been a factor.

At the same time, since 1989 many previously skeptical petroleum and automobile industry corporations have changed their position as the political and scientific consensus has grown, with the creation of the Kyoto Protocol and the publication of the International Panel on Climate Change's Second and Third Assessment Reports. These corporations include major petroleum companies like Royal Dutch Shell, Texaco, and BP, as well as automobile manufacturers like Ford, General Motors, and DaimlerChrysler. Some of these have joined with the Centre for Climate and Energy Solutions (formerly the Pew Centre on Global Climate Change), a non-profit organisation aiming to support efforts to address global climate change.

Since 2000, the Carbon Disclosure Project has been working with major corporations and investors to disclose the emissions of the largest companies. By 2007, the CDP published the emissions data for 2400 of the largest corporations in the world, and represented major institutional investors with $41 trillion combined assets under management. The pressure from these investors had some success in working with companies to reduce emissions.

The World Business Council for Sustainable Development, a CEO-led association of some 200 multinational companies, has called on governments to agree on a global targets, and suggests that it is necessary to cut emissions by 60-80 percent from current levels by 2050.

Global Climate Coalition

A central organisation in climate skepticism was the Global Climate Coalition (1989–2002), a group of mainly United States businesses opposing immediate action to reduce greenhouse gas emissions. The coalition funded skeptical scientists to be public spokespeople, provided industry a voice on climate change, and fought the Kyoto Protocol. The *New York Times* reported that "even as the coalition worked to sway opinion [towards skepticism], its own scientific and technical experts were advising that the science backing the role of greenhouse gases in global warming could not be refuted."

In the year 2000, the rate of corporate members leaving accelerated when they became the target of a national divestiture campaign run by John Passacantando and Phil Radford with the organisation Ozone Action. According to the New York Times, when Ford Motor Company was the first company to leave the coalition, it was "the latest sign of divisions within heavy industry over how to respond to global warming." After that, between December, 1999 and early March, 2000, the GCC was deserted by Daimler-Chrysler, Texaco, the Southern Company and General Motors. The organisation closed in 2002, or in their own words, 'deactivated'.

U.S. Climate Action Partnership

The U.S. Climate Action Partnership (USCAP) was formed in January 2007 with the primary goal of influencing the US government's regulation of greenhouse gas emissions. Original members included General Electric, Alcoa, Natural Resources Defence Council, etc., but they were joined in April, 2007 by ConocoPhilips and AIG.

Energy Industry

ExxonMobil: ExxonMobil has been a leading figure in the business world's position on climate change, providing substantial funding to a range of global-warming-skeptical organisations. *Mother Jones* counted some 40 ExxonMobil-funded organisation that "either have sought to undermine mainstream scientific findings on global climate change or have maintained affiliations with a small group of "skeptic" scientists who continue to do so." Between 2000 and 2003 these organisations received more than $8m in funding.

It has also had a key influence in the Bush administration's energy policy, including on the Kyoto Protocol, supported by both $55m spent on lobbying since 1999, and direct contacts between the company and leading politicians. It was a leading member of the Global Climate Coalition. It encouraged (and may have been instrumental in) the replacement in 2002 of the head of the IPCC, Robert Watson. . It has also invested $100m into the Global Climate and Energy Project, with Stanford University, and other programs at institutions such as the Massachusetts Institute of Technology, Carnegie Mellon University and the International Energy Agency Greenhouse Gas Research and Development Program.

Some of Exxon's activities on climate change produced strong criticism from environmental groups, including reactions such as a leaflet produced by the Stop Esso campaign, saying 'Don't buy E$$o', and featuring a tiger hand setting fire to the Earth. The company's carbon dioxide emissions are more than 50% higher than those of British rival BP, despite the US firm's oil and gas production being only slightly larger.

According to a 2004 study commissioned by Friends of the Earth, ExxonMobil and its predecessors caused 4.7 to 5.3 percent of the world's man-made carbon dioxide emissions between 1882 and 2002. The group suggested that such studies could form the basis for eventual legal action.

BP

BP left the Global Climate Coalition in 1997 and said that global warming was a problem that had to be dealt with, although it subsequently joined others in lobbying the Australian government not to sign the Kyoto Protocol unless the US did. In March 2002 BP's chief executive, Lord Browne, declared in a speech that global warming was real and that urgent action was needed, saying that "Companies composed of highly skilled and trained people can't live in denial of mounting evidence gathered by hundreds of the most reputable scientists in the world.". In 2005 BP was considering testing carbon sequestration in one of its North Sea oil fields, by pumping carbon dioxide into them (and thereby also increasing yields). Throughout 2006 BP, led by their CEO Lord John Browne, has continued to take a leadership stance on climate change. It has cut its own operational emissions of CO_2 by 10%. It is investing $8 billion in renewable energy over the next 10 years. And most recently it has launched a 'target zero' campaign in the UK to encourage its customers to offset their vehicle emissions when they fill up at the petrol station.

BP's American division is a member of the U.S. Climate Action Partnership (USCAP).

Koch Industries

From 2005 to 2008, Koch Industries donated $5.7 million on political campaigns and $37 million on direct lobbying to support fossil fuel industries. Between 1997 and 2008, Koch Industries donated a total of nearly $48 million to climate opposition groups. According to Greenpeace, Koch Industries is the major source of funds of what Greenpeace calls "climate denial". Koch Industries and its subsidiaries spent more than $20 million on lobbying in 2008 and $12.3 million in 2009, according to the Centre for Responsive Politics, a nonpartisan research group.

Others

American Electric Power, the world's largest private producer of carbon dioxide, said in 2005 that targets for carbon reduction "represent a common-sense approach that can begin the process of lowering emissions along a gradual, cost-effective path." The company complained that "uncertainties over the cost of carbon" made it very difficult to make decisions about capital investment.

DuPont has cut its greenhouse gas emissions by 65% since 1990, saving hundreds of millions of dollars in the process. "Give us a date, tell us how much we need to cut, give us the flexibility to meet the goals, and we'll get it done", Xcel Energy CEO Wayne Brunetti told *Business Week* in 2004.

Duke Energy, FPL Group, and PG&E Corporation are members of the U.S. Climate Action Partnership (USCAP).

Transportation

A large proportion of carbon dioxide emissions occur because of transportation. Several companies have formed or invested in electric substitutes for standard automobiles. The Tesla Roadster is an all-electric sports car, available now (production ended). Tesla produces a sedan, Tesla Model S now. Vectrix produces and sells an electric scooter rated for 100 km/h (60 MPH).

There has also been greatly increased interest in personal rapid transit, which applies system engineering principles to reduce energy use, eliminate traffic jams, and produce an acceptable substitute to replace cars, all at the same time. Most systems fully meet Kyoto Treaty carbon emission goals now, 60 years ahead of schedule. Korean steel maker POSCO and its partner Vectus Ltd. have produced a working safety case, including test track and vehicles, that remains fully functional in Swedish winters. Vectus and Suncheon S. Korea signed a memorandum of understanding to install a system. Advanced Transportation Systems' ULTra passed safety certification by the UK Rail Inspectorate in 2003, and won a demonstration project at Heathrow Airport due to be in service in early 2010. ATS Ltd. estimates its ULTra PRT will consume 839 BTU per passenger mile (0.55 MJ per passenger km). By comparison, automobiles consume 3,496 BTU, and personal trucks consume 4,329 BTU per passenger mile. 2getthere Inc. sells automated electric freight handling and transit vehicles designed to share existing rights of way with normal traffic. The company recently won the personal rapid transit competition for Masdar.

Insurance Industry

In 2004 Swiss Re, the world's second largest reinsurance company, warned that the economic costs of climate-related disasters threatened to reach $150 billion a year within ten years.

In 2006 Lloyd's of London, published a report highlighting the latest science and implications for the insurance industry.

Swiss Re, has said that if the shore communities of four Gulf Coast states choose not to implement adaptation strategies, they could see annual climate-change related damages jump 65 percent a year to $23 billion by 2030. "Society needs to reduce its vulnerability to climate risks, and as long as they remain manageable, they remain insurable, which is our interest as well," said Mark D. Way, head of Swiss Re's sustainable development for the Americas.

AIG is a member of the U.S. Climate Action Partnership (USCAP).

Media

In the UK, some newspapers (*Daily Mail, Daily Telegraph*) are significantly skeptical, while most others (with varying enthusiasm, *The Independent* giving it most prominence) support action on global warming. Overall, British newspapers have given the issue three times more coverage than US newspapers. In 2006 (*British Sky Broadcasting* (Sky) became the world's first media company to go 'climate neutral' by purchasing enough carbon offsets. The CEO of the company James Murdoch (son of Rupert Murdoch and heir apparent for the News International empire) is a strong advocate of action on climate change and is thought to be influential on the issue within the wider group of companies, *The Sun* announced it was "going green" and now covers the global warming issue extensively. In June 2006, to much industry interest, Rupert Murdoch invited Al Gore to make his climate change presentation at the annual News Corp (including the Fox Network) gathering at the Pebble Beach golf resort, (USA). In August 2007, Rupert Murdoch announced plans for News Corp. to be carbon neutral by 2010.

More on Business Action

Businesses take action on climate change for several reasons. Action improves corporate image and better aligns corporate actions with the environmental interests of owners, employees, suppliers, and customers. Action also occurs to reduce costs, increase return on investments, and to reduce dependency on uncontrollable costs.

Increased Energy Efficiency

For many companies, looking at more efficient energy use can pay off in the medium to long term; unfortunately, shareholders need to be satisfied in the short term, so regulatory intervention is often required, to encourage prudent conservation measures. However, as carbon intensity starts to show up on balance books through organisations such as the Carbon Disclosure Project, voluntary action is starting to take place.

Recently there has been a spate of companies acting to improve their energy efficiency. Possibly the most prominent of these companies is Wal-Mart. Wal-Mart, the largest retailer in the US, has announced specific environmental goals to reduce energy use in its stores and pressure its 60,000 suppliers in its worldwide supply chain to follow its lead. On energy efficiency, Wal-Mart wants to increase the fuel efficiency of its truck fleet by 25% over the next three years and double it within ten years, moving from 6.5 mpg. This seems an attainable goal, and by 2020, it is expected to save the company $494 million a year. The company also wants to build a store that is at least 25% more energy efficient within four years.

Use of Renewable Energies

In August 2002, the largest gathering of ministers in the history of the world met at the World Summit on Sustainable Development WSSD in Johannesburg. The global environmental community discussed the role of renewables and energy efficiency in lowering carbon emissions, mitigating poverty reduction (energy access) and improving energy security. One result from WSSD was the formation of Partnerships for Sustainable Development to carry forward the international dialogue on sustainable energy and its role in the energy mix.

Partnerships formed include the Renewable Energy and Energy Efficiency Partnership REEEP, the Global Village Energy Partnership GVEP, the Johannesburg Renewable Energy Coalition (JREC), and the Global Network on Energy for Sustainable Development GNESD.

Renewable energies and renewable energy technologies have many advantages over their fossil fuel counterparts. These advantages include the absence of local pollution such as particulates, sulphur oxides (SOX's) and nitrous oxides (NOX's). For the business community, the economic advantages are also becoming clearer. Numerous studies have shown that the working environment has a significant effect on workforce morale. Renewable energy solutions are a part of this, wind turbines in particular being seen by many as a potent symbol of a new modernity, where environmental considerations are taken seriously. A workforce seeing a forward-looking and responsible company is more likely to feel good about working for such a company. A happier workforce is a more productive workforce.

More directly, the high petroleum (oil) and gas prices of 2005 have only added to the attraction of renewable energy sources. Although most renewable energies are more expensive at current fuel prices, the difference is narrowing, and uncertainty in oil and gas markets is a factor worth considering for highly energy-intensive businesses.

Another factor affecting the uptake of renewable energies in Europe is the EU Energy Trading Scheme (ETS or EUTS). Many large businesses are fined for increases in emissions, but can sell any "excess" reductions they make.

Companies with high-profile renewable energy portfolios include an aluminium smelter (Alcan), a cement company (Lafarge), and a microchip manufacturer (Intel). Many examples of corporate leadership in this area can be found on the website of The Climate Group, an independent organisation set up for promoting such action by business and government.

Carbon Offsets

The principle of carbon offset is fairly simple: a business decides that it doesn't want to contribute further to global warming, and it has already made efforts to reduce its carbon (dioxide) emissions, so it decides to pay someone else to further reduce its net emissions by planting trees or by taking up low-carbon technologies. Every unit of carbon that is absorbed by trees—or not emitted due to funding of renewable energy deployment—offsets the emissions from fossil fuel use. In many cases, funding of renewable energy, energy efficiency, or tree planting—particularly in developing nations—can be a relatively cheap way of making an event, project, or business "carbon neutral". Many carbon offset providers—some as inexpensive as $0.10 per ton of carbon dioxide—are referenced in the Carbon Offset article of this encyclopedia.

Many businesses are now looking to carbon offset all their work. An example of a business going carbon neutral is FIFA: their 2006 World Cup Final will be carbon neutral. FIFA estimate they are offsetting one hundred thousand tons of carbon dioxide created by the event, largely as a result of people travelling there. Other carbon neutral companies include the bank HSBC, the consumer staples manufacturer Annie's Homegrown, world leading society publisher Blackwell Publishing, and the publishing house New Society Publishers. The Guardian newspaper also offsets its carbon emissions resulting from international air travel.

Corporations and the Environment

In the developing world, many development projects have come under criticism for damaging the environment, even when they are presented as helping it. Concerns have increased in line with the rising investment in the developing world.

In the late 1990s attention was drawn to a United Nations (U.N.) project to get corporate collaboration/sponsorship in development projects, supporting human rights and the environment, and being generally more responsible and accountable. However it fell under a lot of criticism for involving corporations that are known to have contributed or caused some of the more severe human rights and environment problems, allowing these companies to attempt to repair their tarnished image, while not actually tackling the problems.

In May 2002, the United Nations Environment Program (UNEP) released an extensive report saying that, "there was a growing gap between the efforts to reduce the impact of business and industry on nature and the worsening state of the planet" and that "this gap is due to the fact that only a small number of companies in each industry are actively integrating social and environmental factors into business decisions." (The actual quote is from a U.N. News Centre article, 15 May 2002 that introduces the report.)

One sharp example of environmental problems caused by multinational corporations, is the drive to extract oil from Nigeria. As the previous link, from this site's section on Africa shows, corporations have even backed the military to harass, even kill, local people who continue to protest at the environmental and other problems the activities of the various oil companies have caused. Some local groups have become extreme themselves, kidnapping foreigners for example.

The interests of the various big polluters, such as the auto, mining, oil and chemical corporations influenced the Kyoto Global Climate Change Conference outcome. And with biotechnology and genetically engineered food production, companies are accused of following a profit motive even as they promote the technology as a means to address world hunger. Environmental concerns also feature quite strongly on this issue.

With increased consumerism, there has been a rise in the number of environmental groups campaigning on various issues such as environmentally friendly products. To varying extents then, environmental concerns are issues that sometimes make the mainstream news. However, a cover story, of *Down To Earth* magazine from Delhi-based Centre for Science and Environment as an example, warns that the latest craze in green and ethical consumerism may just be another way for corporations to exploit people and make money by misrepresenting the facts. As another example of this, EarthDay Resources' annual Don't Be Fooled Awards highlight some of what they call the corporate "greenwashing" that goes on through advertising and lobbying campaigns.

There are countless examples where corporate involvement in various issues could contribute to environmental problems as a result. Corporations are major entities in the world and thus have an enormous impact (negative and positive) on all our lives. And concerns of overly corporate-led globalization contributing to environmental problems are increasing, as reported and documented by countless environmental and social justice groups around the world.

But Corporations are also Locked into a Destructive Mode that is Hard to Break out of

It is not that managers of corporations are necessarily "evil" and *want* to degrade the environment (especially their own, where they live). One might argue that when they operate in countries or regions that they don't live, they might not care, but the other aspect which may be more fundamental is that it is perhaps a result of the nature of today's businesses and how they feel compelled to operate, compete and stay alive, which might have an enormous impact here. This is summarized well by the opening paragraphs of an on-line book:

> *I was driving through Maine one late summer day when I stopped to admire a river running through a pretty wooded area. I noticed big, slick bubbles of industrial discharge corroding the vegetation along the riverbank, and I wondered: Who wants this to happen? Not the owners of the company, the shareholders. Not the managers or employees, who want to live in a healthy environment. Not the board of directors, not the community, not the government. I could not think of anyone connected with the company emitting the effluent who wanted the result I saw. This was an unintended consequence of the corporate structure.*

In some respects, many corporations are also victims of the ideologies that are prevalent in current mainstream economics that treat the environment in certain regards. Some corporations might wish to be more environmentally friendly but are unable to do so due to fears that their competitors will get away with it (sort of seen in the fiasco of the politics behind global warming issues).

As the Simultaneous Policy highlights, "Over" competition (or the drive by larger players to reduce the threat of competition and head towards unaccountable monopolies and oligopolies) may be detrimental in this regards too. It is hard for an individual corporation or even group of corporations to effectively break out of this cycle due to fear of competitors being able to take the advantage. Hence this becomes a political as well as economic and environmental issues.

Politics and Corporate Interests often Intertwined

On the political side of things, there have been countless measures pushed and lobbied for that favours corporations directly or indirectly getting out of some of their responsibilities on environmental issues by passing on the costs to others. Various environmental groups constantly campaign on such issues, so this comes as no surprise to state this.

But political frameworks can often cause enormous problems from the onset.

Even what appeared in an *Economist* article, by a foremost pusher of Structural Adjustment, we see that politics can affect markets to help or worsen environmental issues.

Furthermore, corporations are afforded excuses to avoid refitting factories in the first world with their costly environmentally oriented measures and protections, and move elsewhere where regulations have been reduced or removed thanks to economic "agreements". As a result, we may see a relatively cleaner environment in the industrialized world, but it is not all explainable by using newer technologies (which is certainly one of the explanations).

Ideologies and Politics can Drive How Corporations Treat the Environment

Due to the centrality of corporations in many issues as important players, they can greatly influence the impact on the environment (positive or negative, directly or indirectly).

For example, in many cases corporate lobbies have pushed for policies that will benefit them and let them get away with harming the environment. Yet other political processes or even misguided development projects may in some way employ corporations to perform the actual tasks which are damaging to the environment and corporations. This may not be the corporation's fault, per se, however, though in some cases companies do push for such projects, as it is in their interest to gain those lucrative accounts.

Many corporate lobbies and think tanks that they fund push for policies which favour such actions in order to make more money. For example, see this site's sections on

- some of the causes of hunger and the dams section in particular.
- Behind consumption and consumerism that looks at many examples
- (Many issues presented throughout this site that have corporate involvement could be looked at with this perspective in mind. I leave it to the reader to explore the rest of this site, than attempt to list all those pages here!)

Corporations therefore can also be positive engines for the environment as well.

- That is, if the environment and related factors were central concerns in politics, media, and so forth, then public pressure and other factors would of course require corporations to be more accountable.
- Furthermore corporations typically have a lot of capital, knowledge, and resources to research, pursue, develop, and market environmentally friendly/sustainable products, but only if that is the political driver.
- If the current economic and political systems allow corporations to socialize such costs while they benefit, then there is no real

or effective interest in being environmentally friendly as it hurts rather than improves profits and public opinion.

Related Issues

This issue of environmental problems by actions, directly, or indirectly, of various corporations is enormous! This site can't expect to document many examples here, although some links above and throughout this site and section on trade related issues provide more information. In fact, due to the centrality of corporations in many issues, because they are no doubt important players, many parts of this web site discusses their impact, either directly or indirectly.

Green Brands

Green brands are those brands that consumers associate with environmental conservation and sustainable business practices.

Such brands appeal to consumers who are becoming more aware of the need to protect the environment. A green brand can add a unique selling point to a product and can boost corporate image. However, if a company is found or perceived to overstate its green practices its green brand may be criticised as greenwash.

Increase in Green Brands

Ethical consumerism has led to an increase in green brands. In the food and drinks industry only 5 green brand products were launched in 2002, increasing to 328 in 2007 (Mintel global database).

Packaging

In the case of consumer brands packaging can be a key element in communicating a green brand. This is because packaging communicates information to the consumer at the point-of-sale, and because of the environmental impact of the packaging itself.

Companies may claim sustainable packaging, recycled and/or recyclable material, or reduce excess packaging. Packaging is of especially high brand importance when the packaging is part of the aesthetic appeal of the product and brand, as in the case of the cosmetics and toiletries sector. Packaging material may have to not only reinforce environmental credentials, but also communicate the high-quality and luxury image of the brand.

Advertisement and Marketing Standards Concerns

In Europe concerns have been raised that consumers might be confused or mislead as a result of a recent increase in green brands.

Because green brands can add a unique selling point there is little consistency from brand to brand. In the food and drinks industry it has been observed that companies are reluctant to use existing and widely recognised green logos, such as the mobius loop, because using their own makes the brand more easily distinguishable for the consumer.

In Britain, the Advertising Standards Authority (ASA) warned consumers in mid-2007, that some "green" claims might not be authentic. The ASA stated that green claims have become noticeably more prevalent in advertisement, and has investigated and upheld several complaints regarding "unsubstantiated environmental claims". The ASA Director General has stated that "the ASA needs to see robust evidence to back up any eco-friendly claims".

The ASA in Britain has also raised concerns that as awareness about climate change increase among consumers, the cases of unsubstantiated carbon claims (e.g. carbon emissions and carbon neutral claims) rises. The ASA has upheld a number of complaints against energy companies, including Scottish and Southern Energy car manufacturers, including Toyota, Lexus and Volkswagen, and airlines, including EasyJet, for misleading claims regarding carbon emissions and carbon neutrality.

Recent cases before the British ASA involved environmental claims such as "local". In December 2006 for example the ASA upheld a complaint against Tesco, where the company advertised British products as "local", which the ASA ruled to be misleading because in this particular case the consumers were likely to interpret "local" as referring to their immediate surrounding region.

In August 2008 the British ASA ruled that Shell had misled the public in an advertisement which claimed that a $10bn oil sands project in Alberta, northern Canada, was a "sustainable energy source". The ASA upheld a complaint by the World Wide Fund for Nature about Shell's advert in the Financial Times. Explaining the ruling the ASA stated that "We considered that the Department for Environment, Food and Rural Affairs (Defra) best practice guidance on environmental claims stated that green claims should not 'be vague or ambiguous, for instance by simply trying to give a good impression about general concern for the environment. Claims should always avoid the vague use of terms such as 'sustainable', 'green', 'non-polluting' and so on." Furthermore the ASA ruling stated "Defra had made that recommendation because, although 'sustainable' was a widely used term, the lack of a universally agreed definition meant that it was likely to be ambiguous and unclear to consumers. Because we had not seen data that showed how Shell was effectively managing carbon emissions from its oil sands projects in order to limit climate change, we concluded that the ad was misleading"

In the United States the Federal Trade Commission issues the "Green Guides" (last updated 2012) - environmental marketing guidelines. The guidelines give advice on the types of substantiation needed to support environmental claims, and give examples of claims that are to be avoided. The Federal Trade Commission has recognised that these guidelines need updating, as for example they currently contain no guidance on carbon neutrality, or the terms sustainable or renewable. The Green Guides do contain guidance on the term recyclable, recycled and biodegradable.

The marketing and brand building experiences of many American green brands was documented in the book *The Gort Cloud* by Richard Seireeni, 2009. The gort cloud refers to the green community that provides support and a market to green brands.

Triple Bottom Line

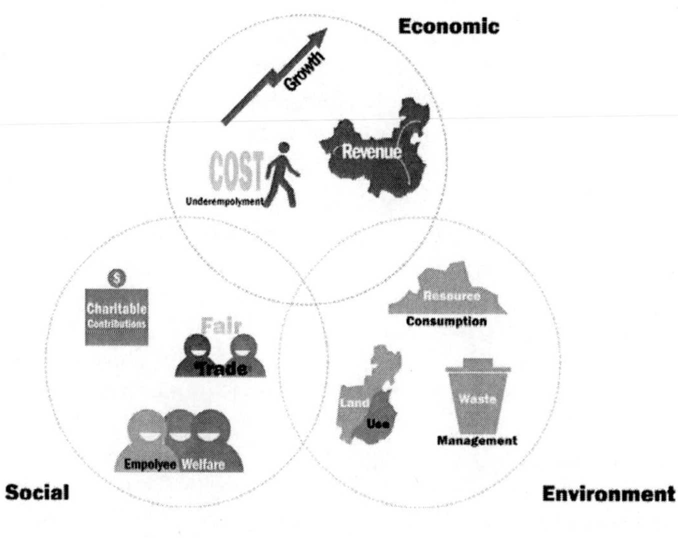

***Figure:** Graphic describing the three types of bottom lines*

Triple bottom line (abbreviated as TBL or 3BL) is an accounting framework with three parts: social, environmental (or ecological) and financial. These three divisions are also called the three Ps: people, planet and profit, or the "three pillars of sustainability". Interest in triple bottom line accounting has been growing in both for-profit, nonprofit and government sectors. Many organisations have adopted the TBL framework to evaluate their performance in a broader context. The term was coined by John Elkington in 1994.

In traditional business accounting and common usage, the "bottom line" refers to either the "profit" or "loss", which is usually recorded at the very bottom line on a statement of revenue and expenses. Over the last 50 years, environmentalists and social justice advocates have struggled to bring a broader definition of bottom line into public consciousness by introducing full cost accounting. For example, if a corporation shows a monetary profit, but their asbestos mine causes thousands of deaths from asbestosis, and their copper mine pollutes a river, and the government ends up spending taxpayer money on health care and river clean-up, how do we perform a full societal cost benefit analysis? The triple bottom line adds two more "bottom lines": social and environmental (ecological) concerns. With the ratification of the United Nations and ICLEI TBL standard for urban and community accounting in early 2007, this became the dominant approach to public sector full cost accounting. Similar UN standards apply to natural capital and human capital measurement to assist in measurements required by TBL, e.g. the EcoBudget standard for reporting ecological footprint. The TBL seems to be fairly widespread in South African media, as found in a 1990-2008 study of worldwide national newspapers.

An example of an organisation seeking a triple bottom line would be a social enterprise run as a non-profit, but earning income by offering opportunities for handicapped people who have been labelled "unemployable", to earn a living recycling. The organisation earns a profit, which is controlled by a volunteer Board, and ploughed back into the community. The social benefit is the meaningful employment of disadvantaged citizens, and the reduction in the society's welfare or disability costs. The environmental benefit comes from the recycling accomplished. In the private sector, a commitment to CSR implies a commitment to transparent reporting about the business' material impact for good on the environment and people. Triple bottom line is one framework for reporting this material impact. This is distinct from the more limited changes required to deal only with ecological issues. The triple bottom line has also been extended to encompass four pillars, known as the quadruple bottom line (QBL). The fourth pillar denotes a future-oriented approach (future generations, intergenerational equity, etc.). It is a long-term outlook that sets sustainable development and sustainability concerns apart from previous social, environmental, and economic considerations.

According to Slaper and Hall (2011) The challenges of putting the TBL into practice relate to the measurement of social and ecological categories: Finding applicable data and determining how a project or policy contributes to sustainability. Despite this, the TBL framework enables organisations to take a longer-term perspective and thus evaluate the future consequences of decisions.

Definition

Sustainable development was defined by the Brundtland Commission of the United Nations in 1987. Triple bottom line (TBL) accounting expands the traditional reporting framework to take into account social and environmental performance in addition to financial performance. In 1981, Freer Spreckley first articulated the triple bottom line in a publication called 'Social Audit - A Management Tool for Co-operative Working'. In this work, he argued that enterprises should measure and report on social, environmental and financial performance.

The phrase "triple bottom line" was coined by John Elkington in his 1997 book *Cannibals with Forks: the Triple Bottom Line of 21st Century Business*. A *Triple Bottom Line Investing* group advocating and publicizing these principles was founded in 1998 by Robert J. Rubinstein.

For reporting their efforts companies may demonstrate their commitment to Corporate social responsibility (CSR) through the following:

- Top-level involvement (CEO, Board of Directors)
- Policy Investments
- Programs
- Signatories to voluntary standards
- Principles (UN Global Compact-Ceres Principles)
- Reporting (Global Reporting Initiative)

The concept of TBL demands that a company's responsibility lies with stakeholders rather than shareholders. In this case, "stakeholders" refers to anyone who is influenced, either directly or indirectly, by the actions of the firm. According to the stakeholder theory, the business entity should be used as a vehicle for coordinating stakeholder interests, instead of maximizing shareholder (owner) profit. A growing number of financial institutions incorporate a triple bottom line approach in their work. It is at the core of the business of banks in the Global Alliance for Banking on Values, for example.

Bottom Lines

The triple bottom line consists of social equity, economic, and environmental factors. "People, planet and profit" succinctly describes the triple bottom lines and the goal of sustainability. The phrase, "people, planet, profit", was coined by John Elkington in 1994 while at SustainAbility, and was later adopted as the title of the Anglo-Dutch oil company Shell's first sustainability report in 1997. As a result, one country in which the 3P concept took deep root was The Netherlands.

"People" pertains to fair and beneficial business practices toward labour and the community and region in which a corporation conducts its business. A TBL company conceives a reciprocal social structure in which the well-being of corporate, labour and other stakeholder interests are interdependent.

An enterprise dedicated to the triple bottom line seeks to benefit many constituencies and not to exploit or endanger any group of them. The "upstreaming" of a portion of profit from the marketing of finished goods back to the original producer of raw materials, for example, a farmer in fair trade agricultural practice, is a common feature. In concrete terms, a TBL business would not use child labour and monitor all contracted companies for child labour exploitation, would pay fair salaries to its workers, would maintain a safe work environment and tolerable working hours, and would not otherwise exploit a community or its labour force. A TBL business also typically seeks to "give back" by contributing to the strength and growth of its community with such things as health care and education. Quantifying this bottom line is relatively new, problematic and often subjective. The Global Reporting Initiative (GRI) has developed guidelines to enable corporations and NGOs alike to comparably report on the social impact of a business.

"Planet" (natural capital) refers to sustainable environmental practices. A TBL company endeavours to benefit the natural order as much as possible or at the least do no harm and minimise environmental impact. A TBL endeavour reduces its ecological footprint by, among other things, carefully managing its consumption of energy and non-renewables and reducing manufacturing waste as well as rendering waste less toxic before disposing of it in a safe and legal manner. "Cradle to grave" is uppermost in the thoughts of TBL manufacturing businesses, which typically conduct a life cycle assessment of products to determine what the true environmental cost is from the growth and harvesting of raw materials to manufacture to distribution to eventual disposal by the end user. A triple bottom line company does not produce harmful or destructive products such as weapons, toxic chemicals or batteries containing dangerous heavy metals, for example.

Currently, the cost of disposing of non-degradable or toxic products is borne financially by governments and environmentally by the residents near the disposal site and elsewhere. In TBL thinking, an enterprise which produces and markets a product which will create a waste problem should not be given a free ride by society. It would be more equitable for the business which manufactures and sells a problematic product to bear part of the cost of its ultimate disposal.

Ecologically destructive practices, such as overfishing or other endangering depletions of resources are avoided by TBL companies. Often environmental sustainability is the more profitable course for a business in the long run. Arguments that it costs more to be environmentally sound are often specious when the course of the business is analyzed over a period of time. Generally, sustainability reporting metrics are better quantified and standardized for environmental issues than for social ones. A number of respected reporting institutes and registries exist including the Global Reporting Initiative, CERES, Institute 4 Sustainability and others.

The eco bottom line is akin to the concept of Eco-capitalism. "Profit" is the economic value created by the organisation after deducting the cost of all inputs, including the cost of the capital tied up. It therefore differs from traditional accounting definitions of profit. In the original concept, within a sustainability framework, the "profit" aspect needs to be seen as the real economic benefit enjoyed by the host society. It is the real economic impact the organisation has on its economic environment. This is often confused to be limited to the internal profit made by a company or organisation (which nevertheless remains an essential starting point for the computation). Therefore, an original TBL approach cannot be interpreted as simply traditional corporate accounting profit *plus* social and environmental impacts unless the "profits" of other entities are included as a social benefit.

Subsequent Development

Following the initial publication of the Triple Bottom Line concept, students and practitioners have sought greater detail in how pillars can be evaluated.

The People concept for example can be viewed in three dimensions - The organisation needs, the personal needs and the community issues associated with supplying future people into the business.

Equally, Profit is a function of both a healthy sales stream, which needs a high focus on customer service, coupled with the adoption of a strategy to develop new customers to replace those that die away.

And Plant can be divided into a multitude of subdivisions, although Reduce Reuse and Recycle is a succinct way of steering though.

Supporting Arguments

The following business-based arguments support the concept of TBL:

- Reaching untapped market potential: TBL companies can find financially profitable niches which were missed when money alone was the driving factor. Examples include:
  1. Adding ecotourism or geotourism to an already rich tourism market such as the Dominican Republic
  2. Developing profitable methods to assist existing NGOs with their missions such as fundraising, reaching clients, or creating networking opportunities with multiple NGOs
  3. Providing products or services which benefit underserved populations and/or the environment which are also financially profitable.
- Adapting to new business sectors: Since many business opportunities are developing in the realm of social enterpreneurialism, businesses hoping to reach this expanding market must design themselves to be financially profitable, socially beneficial and ecologically sustainable or fail to compete with those companies who do design themselves as such. For example, Fair Trade and Ethical Trade companies require ethical and sustainable practices from all of their suppliers and service providers. A business which is planning to work with Fair Trade or Ethical Trade companies must design their business model to be TBL.

Fiscal policy of governments usually claims to be concerned with identifying social and natural deficits on a less formal basis. However, such choices may be guided more by ideology than by economics. The primary benefit of embedding one approach to measurement of these deficits would be first to direct monetary policy to reduce them, and eventually achieve a global monetary reform by which they could be systematically and globally reduced in some uniform way.

The argument is that the Earth's carrying capacity is at risk, and that in order to avoid catastrophic breakdown of climate or ecosystems, there is need for comprehensive reform of global financial institutions similar in scale to what was undertaken at Bretton Woods in 1944. Marilyn Waring has been a major proponent of this reform.

With the emergence of an externally consistent green economics and agreement on definitions of potentially contentious terms such as full-cost accounting, natural capital and social capital, the prospect of formal metrics for ecological and social loss or risk has grown less remote through the 1990s.

In the United Kingdom in particular, the London Health Observatory has undertaken a formal programme to address social deficits via a fuller understanding of what "social capital" is, how it functions in a real community (that being the City of London), and how losses of it tend to require both financial capital and significant political and social attention from volunteers and professionals to help resolve. The data they rely on is extensive, building on decades of statistics of the Greater London Council since World War II. Similar studies have been undertaken in North America.

Studies of the value of Earth have tried to determine what might constitute an ecological or natural life deficit. The Kyoto Protocol relies on some measures of this sort, and actually relies on some value of life calculations that, among other things, are explicit about the ratio of the price of a human life between developed and developing nations (about 15 to 1). While the motive of this number was to simply assign responsibility for a cleanup, such stark honesty opens not just an economic but political door to some kind of negotiation — presumably to reduce that ratio in time to something seen as more equitable. As it is, people in developed nations can be said to benefit 15 times more from ecological devastation than in developing nations, in pure financial terms. According to the IPCC, they are thus obliged to pay 15 times more per life to avoid a loss of each such life to climate change — the Kyoto Protocol seeks to implement exactly this formula, and is therefore sometimes cited as a first step towards getting nations to accept formal liability for damage inflicted on ecosystems shared globally.

Advocacy for triple bottom line reforms is common in Green Parties. Some of the measures undertaken in the European Union towards the Euro currency integration standardize the reporting of ecological and social losses in such a way as to seem to endorse in principle the notion of unified accounts, or unit of account, for these deficits.

Criticism

While many people agree with the importance of good social conditions and preservation of the environment, there are also many who disagree with the triple bottom line as the way to enhance these conditions. The main arguments against it are summarised below.

- *Reductive method*: In the triple bottom line, because it is a corporate-oriented approach, the social—that is, the way in which humans live and relate to each other and the environment—is treated as secondary. The economic as a domain is given an independent status which is ideologically assumed rather than analytically argued. In the most problematic versions, the economic is elevated to the master category and defined in terms that assume the dominance of a singular, historically specific, economic configuration—modern globalizing capitalism. Concurrently the environment comes to be treated as an externality or background feature, an externality that tends not to have the human dimension build into its definition. Thus, in many writings, even in those critical of the triple-bottom-line approach, the social becomes a congeries of miscellaneous considerations left over from the other two prime categories. Alternative approaches, such as Circles of Sustainability, that treat the economic as a social domain, alongside and in relation to the ecological, the political and the cultural are now being considered as more appropriate for understanding institutions, cities and regions.
- *Inertia*: The difficulty of achieving global agreement on simultaneous policy may render such measures at best advisory, and thus unenforceable. For example, people may be unwilling to undergo a depression or even sustained recession to replenish lost ecosystems.
- *Application*: According to Fred Robins' *The Challenge of TBL: A Responsibility to Whom?* one of the major weaknesses of the TBL framework is its ability to be applied in a monetary-based economic system. Because there is no single way in monetary terms to measure the benefits to the society and environment as there is with profit, it does not allow for businesses to sum across all three bottom lines. In this regard, it makes it difficult for businesses to recognise the benefits of using TBL for the company, itself.
- *Equating ecology with environment*: TBL is seen to be undermining ecological sustainability by equating ecological with environmental priorities, where in reality both economic and social viability is dependent on environmental well being. The left sees the root of the issue of environmental degradation

to be in the logic of consumerism inherent within the capitalist mode of production. Therefore, adopting 'ethical' business strategy to address the issue will fail as it is still subject to the overarching exploitative logic of capitalism. Further, TBL is viewed as an attempt by otherwise exploitative corporations to avoid legislation and taxation and generate a fictitious people-friendly & eco-friendly image for PR purposes (greenwashing).

- *Fragmenting the social*: The concept of a triple bottom line, while initially attractive, seems to ignore the reality that if one is not adding value to society it is subtracting value. So creating a third bottom line for the environment often can lead organisations to fragment the societal (or "Mega") bottom line.
- *Time dimension*: While the triple bottom line incorporates the social, economical and environmental (People, Planet, Profit) dimensions of sustainable development, it does not explicitly address the fourth dimension: time. The time dimension focuses on preserving current value in all three other dimensions for later. This means assessment of short term, longer term and long term consequences of any action.

Legislation

Legislation permitting corporations to adopt a triple bottom line is under consideration in some jurisdictions, including Minnesota and Oregon.

Some businesses have voluntarily adopted a triple bottom line as part of their articles of incorporation or bylaws, and some have advocated for state laws creating a "Sustainable Corporation" that would grant triple bottom line businesses benefits such as tax breaks.

The triple bottom line was adopted as a part of the State Sustainability Strategy, and accepted by the Government of Western Australia but its status was increasingly marginalised by subsequent premiers Alan Carpenter and Colin Barnett and is in doubt.

Sustainable Procurement

Sustainable procurement (or Green procurement) is a spending and investment process typically associated with public policy, although it is equally applicable to the private sector.

Organisations practicing sustainable procurement meet their needs for goods, services, utilities and works not on a private cost-benefit analysis, but with a view to maximising net benefits for themselves and the wider world.

In doing so they must incorporate extrinsic cost considerations into decisions alongside the conventional procurement criteria of price and quality, although in practice the sustainable impacts of a potential supplier's approach are often assessed as a form of quality consideration. These considerations are typically divided thus: environmental, economic and social (also known as the "triple bottom line").

There is no single definition of sustainable procurement– and applications vary across organisational hierarchy and sector. However, there is a general acceptance that it involves a higher degree of collaboration and engagement between all parties in a supply chain. Many businesses have adopted a broad interpretation of sustainable procurement and have developed tools and techniques to support this engagement and collaboration.

A research by INSEAD Business School has demonstrated that Sustainable Procurement could yield positive economical benefits for private companies in terms of "Risk Management", "Cost Reduction" and "Revenue Growth".

Exogenous Considerations: the "Triple Bottom Line"

Procurement - the letting of contracts for goods, works and services on the best possible terms - has historically been based on two criteria, price and quality, with a view to maximising benefits for the procuring organisation. Sustainable procurement broadens this framework to take account of third-party consequences of procurement decisions, forming a "triple baseline" of external concerns which the procuring organisation must fulfil.

Environmental

Environmental concerns are the dominant macro-level justification for sustainable procurement, born out of the growing 21st century consensus that humanity is placing excessive demands on available resources through unsustainable but well-established consumption patterns.

This is a sufficiently influential issue that environment-centric procurement (green procurement) is sometimes seen to stand alone from sustainable procurement. The most straightforward justification for green procurement is as a tool with which to address climate change, but it offers the broader capacity to mitigate over-exploitation of any and all scarce resources.

Examples of green procurement range from the purchase of energy-saving light-bulbs to the commissioning of a new building from renewably sourced timber via organic food being served in a workplace canteen. The ultimate green procurement is the avoidance of the purchase altogether.

In support of Sustainable Development the organisation should develop and publish a 'Sustainable Development Procurement Guidelines and Procedures'. When it comes to purchasing products or services, referral to these guidelines would help make the organisation become a leader in environmentally responsible purchasing.

Social

Sustainable procurement is also used to address issues of social policy, such as inclusiveness, equality, international labour standards and diversity targets, regeneration and integration.

Examples include addressing the needs – whether employment, care, welfare or other – of groups including ethnic minorities, children, the elderly, those with disabilities, adults lacking basic skills, and immigrant populations.

Economic

On a macroeconomic level, it can be argued that there are economic benefits in the form of efficiency gains from incorporating whole-life costing into decision-making. [Note: in contrast to most arguments from sustainable procurement proponents, these can be purely private benefits accrued by the procuring organisation.]

In addition, the creation of sustainable markets is essential for long-term growth while sustainable development requirements foster innovation. There are also potential global applications: sustainable procurement can favour fair trade or ethical practice, and allow extra investment to channelled towards developing countries.

On a microeconomic level, sustainable procurement offers the chance for economic redistribution. Targets might include creation of jobs and wealth in regeneration areas, or assistance for small and/or ethnic minority-owned businesses.

Applications

Central Government: In central government, sustainable procurement is typically viewed as the application of sustainable development criteria to spending and investment decisions. Given high-profile socio-economic and environmental concerns such as globalisation and climate change, governments are increasingly concerned that our actions meet the needs of the present without compromising the needs of the future. The UK in 2005 pledged to be a performance-leader in sustainable procurement by 2009 and commissioned the business-led Sustainable Procurement Task Force to formulate appropriate strategy. Broad-based procurement strategies are prominent across the EU while it is an increasingly influential concern elsewhere, most notably Canada.

Devolved and Local Government

At market-level, sustainable procurement is typically instrumental: authorities seek to address policy *through procurement*. Government departments and local bodies can use procurement to address certain chosen agendas in buying solutions that will contribute to community or environmental goals, or to diversity or equality targets.

To help local governments improve sustainability and reduce environmental impacts the California Sustainability Alliance, has developed a Green Procurement Toolkit. Green procurement can help local governments save money, create local green jobs and improve their environmental sustainability.

Under sustainable procurement criteria any procuring organisation must therefore take a broad approach to sustainability, reflecting localised economic, environmental and social needs as well as cross-cutting sustainable development targets such as whole-life costing.

ICLEI is a membership organisation of local governments who recognise the power of Public Sustainable Procurement to achieve environmental, social and economic benefits. It encourages Public Procurement of Innovation as a means for achieving sustainability. Among its various activities, it offers a Sustainable Procurement Resource Centre and a Procurement of Innovation Platform which can be used by procurers or by anyone interested in these topics.

Private Sector

Sustainable procurement is as applicable to the private sector as the public sector, and certainly its proponents aspire to seeing its application across all areas of the economy. Influencing procurement practice within a private-sector firm is not straightforward for governments, meaning that the companies themselves often have to be self-motivated to embrace sustainability.

The UK's Sustainable Procurement National Action Plan argues that it is "something the best of the private sector is already doing - whether through enlightened leadership or shareholder pressure". It also argues that government purchasing power (circa £150bn in the UK alone) can apply sustainable procurement principles to present a persuasive case to those in the private sector resisting sustainable procurement practice.

Policy Development

On December 8, 2006 the Greater London Authority became the first public-sector body to publish a sustainable procurement policy, promising to award a "distinct competitive advantage" to those companies which demonstrated a commitment to sustainable procurement concerns. The policy reflected the Mayor's enthusiasm for public procurement as a tool for fostering social inclusion, equality and environmental objectives.

The GLA also stated that their policy was "very much as a model for broader government procurement" but this expectation was not fulfilled in the UK Government's Sustainable Procurement Action Plan, published on March 5, 2007. The Action Plan, which incorporated answers to the Sustainable Procurement Task Force, was explicitly environment-oriented in approach (Ch 4.3) with wider social issues scarcely addressed.

This was perhaps surprising, as was press disinterest in the publication. Despite its acknowledged importance among senior politicians and business leaders, publication of the Action Plan received only one national newspaper report, and that was markedly flippant in tone.

Approaches

While there is no strict definition on how organisations implement sustainable procurement, there are two approaches that can be combined:

Product-Based

This is where an organisation examines a products movement along the supply chain and assesses the environmental credentials of themselves and of their suppliers. This path is commonly used when an organisation wishes to understand the impact of a product or product range for strategic and marketing purposes. This approach can also provide a vivid picture of supplier processes.

Supplier-Based

An organisation may analyse the CSR management systems of a supplier and whether its practices conform with law and with the CSR standards of "buying" organisation. Thus, the organisation measures the environmental and social risk a supplier may impose upon them.

Implemented effectively, this method will show whether a supplier meets the environmental standards of the organisation, along with whether suppliers are meeting the requirements of law. In order to assess the CSR Management systems companies can use a variety of tools :

- self-assessment questionnaires
- on site audits programs managed internally or through 3rd parties.
- specialised CSR suppliers database such as the ones operated by EICC, FLA or EcoVadis.

Chapter 2

Markets, Politics and Models

How to Write an Environmental Policy

An environmental policy is a written statement, usually signed by senior management, which outlines a business' aims and principles in relation to managing the environmental effects and aspects of its operations. Although putting one in place is voluntary, an increasing number of businesses are choosing to do so.

Having an environmental policy is essential if you want to implement an environmental management standard such as ISO 14001. It's also vital if you currently work or intend to work with large organisations, or if you need to demonstrate to customers and other stakeholders that you are committed to managing your environmental impacts in a responsible way.

This guide sets out the benefits of having an environmental policy. It makes suggestions for selecting the right format and content. It also gives useful tips on how to keep the policy up to date and how to extend its scope to include corporate social responsibility and sustainable development.

- The benefits of an environmental policy
- Selecting the right format for your environmental policy
- Creating content for an environmental policy
- Checklist: good practice for drafting an environmental policy
- Keep your environmental policy up to date
- Extend the scope of your policy

The Benefits of an Environmental Policy

An environmental policy forms the foundation of environmental improvements made for your business, as defined by senior management. It sets out key aims and principles.

Having an environmental policy can provide significant benefits to your business. These include:

- helping you to stay within the law
- improving information for employees about their environmental roles and responsibilities
- improving cost control
- reducing incidents that result in liability
- conserving raw materials and energy
- improving your monitoring of environmental impacts
- improving the efficiency of your processes

However, the benefits are not restricted simply to internal operations. By demonstrating commitment to environmental management, you can develop positive relations with external stakeholders, such as investors, insurers, customers, suppliers, regulators and the local community. This in turn can lead to an improved corporate image and financial benefits, such as increased investment, customer sales and market share.

It's important to bear in mind that these benefits are unlikely to be achieved if you just have an environmental policy in place. If you set up an environmental management system (EMS) this requires you to implement a program to systematically deliver your policy in a strategic way.

External certification of your EMS will help you demonstrate to customers, investors, regulators and other stakeholders that the environmental claims you make in your policy are credible, reliable and have been independently checked.

If you don't choose to set up a formal EMS, it's a good idea to at least apply some of the steps to ensure your policy is effective. This can include assessing the environmental impact of your business, developing appropriate key performance indicators, setting objectives and targets and reviewing these regularly.

Selecting the Right Format for Your Environmental Policy

There is no standard format for writing an environmental policy, but to give it the best chance of success, it's important you plan it carefully. For your policy to be successful you need to get buy-in from management, by emphasising the key benefits such as cost reduction, improved risk management and marketing.

Once you have secured this commitment, it's a good idea to assess where your business currently stands in terms of environmental management. This could include drawing up an environmental history of your business, its impact and the risks faced by it.

You could also carry out a benchmarking exercise to establish how you compare against similar businesses.

It's important to tailor your environmental policy to reflect your business and its culture. A good starting point is to collect and review examples of policies written by other businesses and select the format and style most appropriate to your own business. However, avoid copying someone else's policy.

There are a Few Basic Rules to Follow:

- keep the statement short - if it's longer than a sheet of 8 ½ X 11, then it's probably too long
- the statement is meant for everyone to see, so make sure it's easy to read and understand
- the statement must be realistic, achievable and relevant to your company's activities and practices
- demonstrate commitment to making the policy work and get the statement signed, dated and endorsed by the owner, managing director or other senior manager
- make the policy available on your website
- ask new employees and suppliers to read a copy of the policy

Creating Content for an Environmental Policy

There is no standard content for an environmental policy, although policies normally contain the same themes. Bear in mind that your policy should be personal to your business, and as such reflect the activities, priorities and concerns most relevant to it.

Before you write your policy you should assess which aspects of your business affect the environment and what the potential impacts are. There are a number of techniques that you could use when carrying out the assessment.

The content of your policy should be based on the results of your assessment, which should have identified the key issues that apply to your business.

Your policy should contain brief statements on the following criteria:

- The business mission and information about its operations. Bear in mind that if your business activities or operations change significantly, the policy may need to be amended.
- A commitment to continually improve your environmental performance.
- A commitment to effectively manage your significant environmental impacts.
- The expectations that your business has in relation to external parties such as suppliers and contractors.
- Recognition that you will comply with relevant environmental legislation as a minimum level of performance.
- Education and training of employees in environmental issues and the environmental effects of their activities.
- Monitoring progress and reviewing environmental performance against targets and objectives on a regular basis (usually annually or in the first six months initially).
- A commitment to communicate your business' environmental aims and objectives to all staff, as well as to customers, investors and other external stakeholders.

Additional issues relevant to your business, and which you may wish to address in your environmental policy, could include:

- transport
- recycling of packaging materials
- minimising waste
- efficient use of water and energy
- use of biodegradable chemicals
- minimising use of solvents and lead-based paints
- use of timber or wood products from sustainable (managed) forests
- procedures to minimise noise disturbance to neighbours
- phasing out of chlorofluorocarbons (CFCs) and other ozone-depleting substances

If your business is linked closely to key customers through the supply chain, obtain a copy of their environmental policy, so that your statements can reflect their requirements and needs.

Your policy should demonstrate commitment by senior management and is usually signed by the chairman or chief executive.

You may want to integrate your environmental policy with other policies on health and safety, quality management, corporate social responsibility or sustainability.

Checklist: Good Practice for Drafting an Environmental Policy

The checklist below may help you to draft a policy appropriate to your business. Choose examples of the statements that would apply to your business and make the statements as specific as possible for your operations:

- comply with environmental legislation and other requirements, such as approved codes of practice
- importance of environmental issues to your business
- assess the environmental impact of all historic, current and likely future operations
- continually seek to improve environmental performance, e.g. by doing a regular walk-around survey of your business to see if you are using energy and water efficiently and whether measures to reduce waste and pollution are effective
- reduce pollution, emissions and waste, e.g. emissions from transport, oil leaks and spills, excessive noise, heat or vibration generated by the activities of your business
- reduce the use of all raw materials, energy and supplies
- raise awareness, encourage participation and train employees in environmental matters
- expect similar environmental standards from all suppliers and contractors
- assist customers to use products and services in an environmentally sensitive way
- liaise with the local community
- participate in discussions about environmental issues
- communicate environmental aims and objectives to employees and external stakeholders
- agree to commit to environmental principles and continual improvement at the highest level in your business

Keep Your Environmental Policy up to Date

To check that your company's current activities still comply with your environmental policy, it's a good idea to carry out a regular review

- usually on an annual basis, or in the first six months initially. These are key to ensuring that there is continual improvement in environmental performance and that more specific environmental targets are set on a yearly basis. Bear in mind that if your business activities or operations change significantly, the policy may need to be amended.

If your policy is not kept up to date, and it is not backed up with some form of environmental improvement (such as a formal environmental management system or less formal program of improvements), other organisations may think that you're not taking your environmental responsibilities seriously. Consequently, they may decide to take their business elsewhere.

Similarly, if your policy says that you are taking your environmental responsibilities seriously but you fail to back this up, you may face questions over the quality of operations in other parts of your business. This could tarnish your reputation with customers and suppliers.

It's a good idea to involve employees in the reviewing process. If employees are expected to deliver on environmental policy commitments, they may be a good source of ideas for improvements. The environmental policy should be available for all new employees to read and to all existing employees if it changes significantly.

Extend the Scope of Your Policy

Your environmental policy doesn't have to exist in isolation. In fact, it can be useful to extend the scope of your policy to cover corporate social responsibility and sustainable development. You could choose to develop this either within a single policy or create separate, linked policies. An extended policy acknowledges the fact that different groups of people rely on your business and outlines how you go about minimising your impact on the environment.

By developing a corporate social responsibility (CSR) policy, you are showing that you are:

- Dealing with suppliers and employees in a responsible way - for example by being open and honest about your products and services and avoiding pressure selling. It also means going beyond the legal minimum when dealing with employees and promoting best practice.
- Building up a good relationship with the local community - for example by supporting a local charity or sponsoring a local event.

- Minimising your impact on the environment and cutting pollution and waste – by using energy efficiency measures, e.g. switching off lights, reducing the use of water. You could also consider minimising waste and reducing the environmental impact of your business generally, e.g. buying locally to cut fuel costs.

Equally, you can show that you take sustainable development seriously by:

- considering the life cycle of your products and services and designing them to be as sustainable as possible
- buying materials and resources that come from renewable sources
- reusing or recycling your waste, or passing it on to other businesses to use as a resource
- going beyond your legal obligations and anticipating changes so that you can make adjustments before legislation comes into force
- involving employees and other stakeholders in sustainable development -by involving them in training and incentives to encourage buy-in to your strategy

Environmental Governance

Environmental governance is a concept in political ecology and environmental policy that advocates sustainability (sustainable development) as the supreme consideration for managing all human activities—political, social and economic. Governance includes government, business and civil society, and emphasizes whole system management. To capture this diverse range of elements, environmental governance often employs alternative systems of governance, for example watershed-based management.

It views natural resources and the environment as global public goods, belonging to the category of goods that are not diminished when they are shared. This means that everyone benefits from for example, a breathable atmosphere, stable climate and stable biodiversity.

Public goods are non-rivalrous—a natural resource enjoyed by one person can still be enjoyed by others—and non-excludable—it is impossible to prevent someone consuming the good (breathing). Nevertheless, public goods are recognised as beneficial and therefore have value. The notion of a global public good thus emerges, with a slight distinction: it covers necessities that must not be destroyed by one person or state. The non-rivalrous character of such goods calls for a management approach that restricts public and private actors from damaging them. One approach is to attribute an economic value to the resource. Water is possibly the best example of this type of good.

As of 2013 environmental governance is far from meeting these imperatives. "Despite a great awareness of environmental questions from developed and developing countries, there is environmental degradation and the appearance of new environmental problems. This situation is caused by the parlous state of global environmental governance, wherein current global environmental governance is unable to address environmental issues due to many factors. These include fragmented governance within the United Nations, lack of involvement from financial institutions, proliferation of environmental agreements often in conflict with trade measures; all these various problems disturb the proper functioning of global environmental governance. Moreover, divisions among northern countries and the persistent gap between developed and developing countries also have to be taken into account to comprehend the institutional failures of the current global environmental governance."

Definitions

What is Environmental Governance?: Environmental governance refers to the processes of decision-making involved in the control and management of the environment and natural resources. International Union for Conservation of Nature (IUCN), define Environmental Governance as the 'Multi-level interactions (i.e., local, national, international/global) among, but not limited to, three main actors, i.e., state, market, and civil society, which interact with one another, whether in formal and informal ways; in formulating and implementing policies in response to environment-related demands and inputs from the society; bound by rules, procedures, processes, and widely accepted behaviour; possessing characteristics of "good governance"; for the purpose of attaining environmentally-sustainable development' (ICUN 2014)

Key Principles of Environmental Governance include

- Embedding the environment in all levels of decision-making and action
- Conceptualizing cities and communities, economic and political life as a subset of the environment
- Emphasizing the connection of people to the ecosystems in which they live

- Promoting the transition from open-loop/cradle-to-grave systems (like garbage disposal with no recycling) to closed-loop/ cradle-to-cradle systems (like permaculture and zero waste strategies).

Neoliberal Environmental Governance – is an approach to the theory of environmental governance framed by a perspective on neoliberalism as an ideology, policy and practice in relation to the biophysical world. There are many definitions and applications of neoliberalism e.g. in economic, international relations, etc. However, the traditional understanding of neoliberalism is often simplified to the notion of the primacy of market-led economics through the rolling back of the state, deregulation and privatisation. Neoliberalism has evolved particularly over the last 40 years with many scholars leaving their ideological footprint on the neoliberal map. Hayek and Friedman believed in the superiority of the free market over state intervention. As long as the market was allowed to act freely, the supply/demand law would ensure the 'optimal' price and reward. In Karl Polanyi's opposing view this would also create a state of tension in which self-regulating free markets disrupt and alter social interactions and "displace other valued means of living and working". However, in contrast to the notion of an unregulated market economy there has also been a "paradoxical increase in [state] intervention" in the choice of economic, legislative and social policy reforms, which are pursued by the state to preserve the neoliberal order. This contradictory process is described by Peck and Tickell as roll back/roll out neoliberalism in which on one hand the state willingly gives up the control over resources and responsibility for social provision while on the other, it engages in "purposeful construction and consolidation of neoliberalised state forms, modes of governance, and regulatory relations".

There has been a growing interest in the effects of neoliberalism on the politics of the non-human world of environmental governance. Neoliberalism is seen to be more than a homogenous and monolithic 'thing' with a clear end point. It is a series of path-dependent, spatially and temporally "connected neoliberalisation" processes which affect and are affected by nature and environment that "cover a remarkable array of places, regions and countries". Co-opting neoliberal ideas of the importance of private property and the protection of individual (investor) rights, into environmental governance can be seen in the example of recent multilateral trade agreements. Such neoliberal structures further reinforce a process of nature enclosure and primitive accumulation or "accumulation by dispossession" that serves to privatise increasing areas of nature. The ownership-transfer of resources traditionally not privately owned to free market mechanisms is believed to deliver greater efficiency and optimal return on investment. Other similar examples of neo-liberal inspired projects include the enclosure of minerals, the fisheries quota system in the North Pacific and the privatisation of water supply and sewage treatment in England and Wales. All three examples share neoliberal characteristics to "deploy markets as the solution to environmental problems" in which scarce natural resources are commercialized and turned into commodities. The approach to frame the ecosystem in the context of a price-able commodity is also present in the work of neoliberal geographers who subject nature to price and supply/demand mechanisms where the earth is considered to be a quantifiable resource (Costanza, for example, estimates the earth ecosystem's service value to be between 16 and 54 trillion dollars per year).

Environmental Issues

Main Drivers of Environmental Degradation

Economic growth – The development-centric vision that prevails in most countries and international institutions advocates a headlong rush towards more economic growth. Environmental economists on the other hand, point to a close correlation between economic growth and environmental degradation, arguing for qualitative development as an alternative to growth. As a result, the past couple of decades has seen a big shift towards sustainable development as an alternative to neo-liberal economics. There are those, particularly within the alternative globalization movement, who maintain that it is feasible to change to a degrowth phase without losing social efficiency or lowering the quality of life.

Consumption – The growth of consumption and the cult of consumption, or consumerist ideology, is the major cause of economic growth. Overdevelopment, seen as the only alternative to poverty, has become an end in itself. The means for curbing this growth are not equal to the task, since the phenomenon is not confined to a growing middle class in developing countries, but also concerns the development of irresponsible lifestyles, particularly in northern countries, such as the increase in the size and number of homes and cars per person.

Destruction of Biodiversity – The complexity of the planet's ecosystems means that the loss of any species has unexpected consequences. The stronger the impact on biodiversity, the stronger the likelihood of a chain reaction with unpredictable negative effects. Another important factor of environmental degradation that falls under this destruction of biodiversity, and must not be ignored is deforestation. Despite all the damage inflicted, a number of ecosystems have proved to be hugely resilient. Environmentalists are endorsing a precautionary principle whereby all potentially damaging activities would have to be analyzed for their environmental impact.

Population Growth – Forecasts predict 8.9 billion people on the planet in 2050. This is a subject which primarily affects developing countries, but also concerns northern countries; although their demographic growth is lower, the environmental impact per person is far higher in these countries. Demographic growth needs to be countered by developing education and family planning programs and generally improving women's status.

"Pollution" - Pollution caused by the use of fossil fuels is another driver of environmental destruction. The burning of carbon based fossil fuels such as coal and oil, releases carbon dioxide into the atmosphere. One of the major impacts of this is the climate change that is currently taking place on the planet, where the earth's temperature is gradually rising. Given that fuels such as coal and oil are the most heavily used fuels, this a great concern to many environmentalists.

"Agricultural Practices" - Destructive agricultural practices such as overuse of fertilizers and overgrazing lead to land degradation. The soil gets eroded, and leads to silting in rivers and reservoirs. Soil erosion is a continuous cycle and ultimately results in desertification of the land. Apart from land degradation, water pollution is also a possibility; chemicals used in farming can run-off into rivers and contaminate the water.

Challenges

The crisis caused by the impact of human activities on nature calls for governance. Which includes responses by international institutions, governments and citizens, who should meet this crisis by pooling the experience and knowledge of each of the agents and institutions concerned.

The environmental protection measures taken remain insufficient. The necessary reforms require time, energy, money and diplomatic negotiations. The situation has not generated a unanimous response. Persistent divisions slow progress towards global environmental governance.

The global nature of the crisis limits the effects of national or sectoral measures. Cooperation is necessary between actors and institutions in international trade, sustainable development and peace.

Global, continental, national and local governments have employed a variety of approaches to environmental governance. Substantial positive and negative spillovers limit the ability of any single jurisdiction to resolve issues.

Challenges Facing Environmental Governance include

- Inadequate continental and global agreements
- Unresolved tensions between maximum development, sustainable development and maximum protection, limiting funding, damaging links with the economy and limiting application of Multilateral Environment Agreements (MEAs).
- Environmental funding is not self-sustaining, diverting resources from problem-solving into funding battles.
- Lack of integration of sector policies
- Inadequate institutional capacities
- Ill-defined priorities
- Unclear objectives
- Lack of coordination within the UN, governments, the private sector and civil society
- Lack of shared vision
- Interdependencies among development/sustainable economic growth, trade, agriculture, health, peace and security.
- International imbalance between environmental governance and trade and finance programs, e.g., World Trade Organisation (WTO).
- Limited credit for organisations running projects within the Global Environment Facility (GEF)
- Linking UNEP, United Nations Development Programme (UNDP) and the World Bank with MEAs
- Lack of government capacity to satisfy MEA obligations
- Absence of the gender perspective and equity in environmental governance
- Inability to influence public opinion
- Time lag between human action and environmental effect, sometimes as long as a generation
- Environmental problems being embedded in very complex systems, of which our understanding is still quite weak

All of these challenges have implications on governance, however international environmental governance is necessary. The IDDRI claims that rejection of multilateralism in the name of efficiency and protection of national interests conflicts with the promotion of international law and the concept of global public goods. Others cite the complex nature of environmental problems.

On the other hand, The Agenda 21 program has been implemented in over 7,000 communities. Environmental problems, including global-scale problems, may not always require global solutions. For example, marine pollution can be tackled regionally, and ecosystem deterioration can be addressed locally. Other global problems such as climate change benefit from local and regional action.

Bäckstrand and Saward wrote, "sustainability and environmental protection is an arena in which innovative experiments with new hybrid, plurilateral forms of governance, along with the incorporation of a transnational civil society spanning the public-private divide, are taking place."

Local Governance

A 1997 report observed a global consensus that sustainable development implementation should be based on local level solutions and initiatives designed with and by the local communities. Community participation and partnership along with the decentralisation of government power to local communities are important aspects of environmental governance at the local level. Initiatives such as these are integral divergence from earlier environmental governance approaches which was "driven by state agendas and resource control" and followed a top-down or trickle down approach rather than the bottom up approach that local level governance encompasses. Local level governance shifts decision making power away from the state and/or governments to the grassroots. Local level governance is extremely important even on a global scale. Environmental governance at the global level is defined as international and as such has resulted in the marginalisation of local voices. Local level governance is important to bring back power to local communities in the global fight against environmental degradation. Pulgar Vidal observed a "new institutional framework, [wherein] decision-making regarding access to and use of natural resources has become increasingly decentralized." He noted four techniques that can be used to develop these processes:

- formal and informal regulations, procedures and processes, such as consultations and participative democracy;
- social interaction that can arise from participation in development programs or from the reaction to perceived injustice;

- regulating social behaviours to reclassify an individual question as a public matter;
- within-group participation in decision-making and relations with external actors.

He found that the key conditions for developing decentralized environmental governance are:

- access to social capital, including local knowledge, leaders and local shared vision;
- democratic access to information and decision-making;
- local government activity in environmental governance: as facilitator of access to natural resources, or as policy maker;
- an institutional framework that favours decentralized environmental governance and creates forums for social interaction and making widely accepted agreements acceptable.

The legitimacy of decisions depends on the local population's participation rate and on how well participants represent that population. With regard to public authorities, questions linked to biodiversity can be faced by adopting appropriate policies and strategies, through exchange of knowledge and experience, the forming of partnerships, correct management of land use, monitoring of biodiversity and optimal use of resources, or reducing consumption, and promoting environmental certifications, such as EMAS and/or ISO 14001. Local authorities undoubtedly have a central role to play in the protection of biodiversity and this strategy is successful above all when the authorities show strength by involving stakeholders in a credible environmental improvement project and activating a transparent and effective communication policy (Ioppolo et al., 2013).

State Governance

States play a crucial role in environmental governance, because "however far and fast international economic integration proceeds, political authority remains vested in national governments". It is for this reason that governments should respect and support the commitment to implementation of international agreements.

At the state level, environmental management has been found to be conducive to the creation of roundtables and committees. In France, the *Grenelle de l'environnement* process:

- included a variety of actors (e.g. the state, political leaders, unions, businesses, not-for-profit organisations and environmental protection foundations);

- allowed stakeholders to interact with the legislative and executive powers in office as indispensable advisors;
- worked to integrate other institutions, particularly the Economic and Social Council, to form a pressure group that participated in the process for creating an environmental governance model;
- attempted to link with environmental management at regional and local levels.

If environmental issues are excluded from e.g., the economic agenda, this may delegitimize those institutions.

"In southern countries, the main obstacle to the integration of intermediate levels in the process of territorial environmental governance development is often the dominance of developmentalist inertia in states' political mindset. The question of the environment has not been effectively integrated in national development planning and programs. Instead, the most common idea is that environmental protection curbs economic and social development, an idea encouraged by the frenzy for exporting raw materials extracted using destructive methods that consume resources and fail to generate any added value." Of course they are justified in this thinking, as their main concerns are social injustices such as poverty alleviation. Citizens in some of these states have responded by developing empowerment strategies to ease poverty through sustainable development. In addition to this, policymakers must be more aware of these concerns of the global south, and must make sure to integrate a strong focus on social justice in their policies.

Global Governance

At the global level there are numerous important actors involved in environmental governance and "a range of institutions contribute to and help define the practice of global environmental governance. The idea of global environmental governance is to govern the environment at a global level through a range of nation states and non state actors such as national governments, NGOs and other international organisations such as UNEP (United Nations Environment Programme). Global environmental governance is the answer to calls for new forms of governance because of the increasing complexity of the international agenda. It is perceived to be an effective form of multilateral management and essential to the international community in meeting goals of mitigation and the possible reversal of the impacts on the global environment. However, a precise definition of global environmental governance is still vague and there are many issues surrounding global governance. Elliot argues that "the congested institutional terrain still provides more of an appearance than a reality of comprehensive global governance." This meant that there are too many institutions within the global governance of the environment for it to be completely inclusive and coherent leaving it merely portraying the image of this to the global public. Global environmental governance is about more than simply expanding networks of institutions and decision makers. "It is a political practice which simultaneously reflects, constitutes and masks global relations of power and powerlessness." State agendas exploit the use of global environmental governance to enhance their oven agendas or wishes even if this is at the detriment of the vital element behind global environmental governance which is the environment. Elliot states that global environmental governance "is neither normatively neutral nor materially benign." As explored by Newell, report notes by The Global Environmental Outlook noted that the systems of global environmental governance are becoming increasingly irrelevant or impotent due to patterns of globalisation such as; imbalances in productivity and the distribution of goods and services, unsustainable progression of extremes of wealth and poverty and population and economic growth overtaking environmental gains. Newell states that, despite such acknowledgements, the "managing of global environmental change within International Relations continues to look to international regimes for the answers."

Issues of Scale

Multi-Tier Governance: The literature on governance scale shows how changes in the understanding of environmental issues have led to the movement from a local view to recognising their larger and more complicated scale. This move brought an increase in the diversity, specificity and complexity of initiatives. Meadowcroft pointed out innovations that were layered on top of existing structures and processes, instead of replacing them.

Lafferty and Meadowcroft give three examples of multi-tiered governance: internationalisation, increasingly comprehensive approaches, and involvement of multiple governmental entities. Lafferty and Meadowcroft described the resulting multi-tiered system as addressing issues on both smaller and wider scales.

Institutional Fit

Hans Bruyninckx claimed that a mismatch between the scale of the environmental problem and the level of the policy intervention was problematic. Young claimed that such mismatches reduced the effectiveness of interventions. Most of the literature addresses the level of governance rather than ecological scale.

Elinor Ostrom, amongst others, claimed that the mismatch is often the cause of unsustainable management practices and that simple solutions to the mismatch have not been identified.

Considerable debate has addressed the question of which level(s) should take responsibility for fresh water management. Development workers tend to address the problem at the local level. National governments focus on policy issues. This can create conflicts among states because rivers cross borders, leading to efforts to evolve governance of river basins.

Environmental Governance Issues

Soil Deterioration: Soil and land deterioration reduces its capacity for capturing, storing and recycling water, energy and food. Alliance 21 proposed solutions in the following domains:

- include soil rehabilitation as part of conventional and popular education
- involve all stakeholders, including policymakers and authorities, producers and land users, the scientific community and civil society to manage incentives and enforce regulations and laws
- establish a set of binding rules, such as an international convention
- set up mechanisms and incentives to facilitate transformations
- gather and share knowledge;
- mobilize funds nationally and internationally

Climate Change

The scientific consensus on climate change is expressed in the reports of Intergovernmental Panel on Climate Change (IPCC) and also in the statements by all major scientific bodies in the United States such as National Academy of Sciences.

The drivers of climate change can include - Changes in solar irradiance - Changes in atmospheric trace gas and aerosol concentrations Evidence of climate change can be identified by examining - Atmospheric concentrations of Green House Gases (GHGs) such as Carbon-dioxide (CO_2) - Land and sea surface temperatures - Atmospheric water vapor - Precipitation - The occurrence or strength of extreme weather and climate events - Glaciers -Rapid sea ice loss.

It is suggested by climate models that the changes in temperature and sea level can be the causal effects of human activities such as consumption of fossil fuels, deforestation, increased agricultural production and production of xenobiotic gases.

There has been increasing actions in order to mitigate climate change and reduce its impact at national, regional and international levels. Kyoto protocol and United Nations Framework Convention on Climate Change (UNFCCC) plays the most important role in addressing climate change at an international level.

The goal of combating climate change led to the adoption of the Kyoto Protocol by 191 states, an agreement encouraging the reduction of greenhouse gases, mainly CO2. Since developed economies produce more emissions per capita, limiting emissions in all countries inhibits opportunities for emerging economies, the only major success in efforts to produce a global response to the phenomenon.

Two decades following the Brundtland Report, however, there has been no improvement in the key indicators highlighted.

Biodiversity

Environmental governance for protecting the biodiversity has to act in many levels. Biodiversity is fragile because it is threatened by almost all human actions. To promote conservation of biodiversity, agreements and laws have to be created to regulate agricultural activities, urban growth, industrialization of countries, use of natural resources, control of invasive species, the correct use of water and protection of air quality. In other words before making any decision for a region or country decision makers, politicians and community have to take into account what are the potential impacts for biodiversity, that any project can have.

Population growth and urbanization have been a great contributor for deforestation. Also, population growth requires more intense agricultural areas use, which also results in necessity of new areas to be deforested. This causes habitat loss, which is one of the major threats for biodiversity. Habitat loss and habitat fragmentation affects all species, because they all rely on limited resources, to feed on and to breed.

'Species are genetically unique and irreplaceable their loss is irreversible. Ecosystems vary across a vast range of parameters, and similar ecosystems (whether wetlands, forests, coastal reserves etc) cannot be presumed to be interchangeable, such that the loss of one can be compensated by protection or restoration of another'.

To avoid habitat loss, and consequently biodiversity loss, politicians and lawmakers should be aware of the precautionary principle, which means that before approving a project or law all the pros and cons should be carefully analysed. Sometimes the impacts are not explicit, or not even proved to exist. However if there is any chance of an irreversible impact happen, it should be taken into consideration.

To promote environmental governance for biodiversity protection there has to be a clear articulation between values and interests while negotiating environmental management plans. International agreements are good way to have it done right.

The Convention on Biological Diversity (CBD) was signed in Rio de Janeiro in 1992 human activities. The CBD's objectives are: "to conserve biological diversity, to use biological diversity in a sustainable fashion, to share the benefits of biological diversity fairly and equitably." The Convention is the first global agreement to address all aspects of biodiversity: genetic resources, species and ecosystems. It recognises, for the first time, that the conservation of biological diversity is "a common concern for all humanity". The Convention encourages joint efforts on measures for scientific and technological cooperation, access to genetic resources and the transfer of clean environmental technologies.

The Convention on Biological Diversity most important edition happened in 2010 when the Strategic Plan for Biodiversity 2011-2020 and the Aichi Targets, were launched. These two projects together make the United Nations decade on Biodiversity. It was held in Japan and has the targets of '*halting and eventually reversing the loss of biodiversity of the planet*'. The Strategic Plan for Biodiversity has the goal to '*promote its overall vision of living in harmony with nature*' As result (...) '*mainstream biodiversity at different levels. Throughout the United Nations Decade on Biodiversity, governments are encouraged to develop, implement and communicate the results of national strategies for implementation of the Strategic Plan for Biodiversity*'. According to the CBD the five Aichi targets are: 1. '*Address the underlying causes of biodiversity loss by mainstreaming biodiversity across government and society*; 2. *Reduce the direct pressures on biodiversity and promote sustainable use*; 3. *Improve the status of biodiversity by safeguarding ecosystems, species and genetic diversity*; 4. *Enhance the benefits to all from biodiversity and ecosystem services*; 5. *Enhance implementation through participatory planning, knowledge management and capacity building.*'

Water

The 2003 UN World Water Development Report claimed that the amount of water available over the next twenty years would drop by 30%.

At that time, 40% of the planet's inhabitants did not have access to the minimum necessary for basic hygiene. Over 2.2 million people died in 2000 from diseases linked to contaminated water, or from drowning. In 2004, the UK's WaterAid charity reported that one child died every 15 seconds from water-linked diseases.

According to Alliance 21 "All levels of water supply management are necessary and independent. The integrated approach to the catchment areas must take into account the needs of irrigation and those of towns, jointly and not separately as is often seen to be the case....The governance of a water supply must be guided by the principles of sustainable development."

Australian water resources have always been variable but they are becoming increasingly so with changing climate conditions. Because of how limited water resources are in Australia, there needs to be an effective implementation of environmental governance conducted within the country. Water restrictions are an important policy device used in Australian environmental governance to limit the amount of water used in urban and agricultural environments (Beeton et al. 2006). There is increased pressure on surface water resources in Australia because of the uncontrolled growth in groundwater use and the constant threat of drought. These increased pressures not only affect the quantity and quality of the waterways but they also negatively affect biodiversity. The government needs to create policies that preserve, protect and monitor Australia's inland water. The most significant environmental governance policy imposed by the Australian government is environmental flow allocations that allocate water to the natural environment. The proper implementation of water trading systems could help to conserve water resources in Australia. Over the years there has been an increase in demand for water, making Australia the third largest per capita user of water in the world (Beeton et al. 2006). If this trend continues, the gap between supply and demand will need to be addressed. The government needs to implement more efficient water allocations and raise water rates (UNEP, 2014). By changing public perception to promote the action of reusing and recycling water some of the stress of water shortages can be alleviated. More extensive solutions like desalination plants, building more dams and using aquifer storage are all options that could be taken to conserve water levels but all these methods are controversial. With caps on surface water use, both urban and rural consumers are turning to groundwater use; this has caused groundwater levels to decline significantly. Groundwater use is very hard to monitor and regulate. There is not enough research currently being conducted to accurately determine sustainable yields. Some regions are seeing improvement in groundwater levels by applying caps on bores and the amount of water that consumers are allowed to extract. There have been projects in environmental governance aimed at restoring vegetation in the riparian zone. Restoring riparian vegetation helps increase biodiversity, reduce salinity, prevent soil erosion and prevent riverbank collapse.

Many rivers and waterways are controlled by weirs and locks that control the flow of rivers and also prevent the movement of fish. The government has funded fish-ways on some weirs and locks to allow for native fish to move upstream. Wetlands have significantly suffered under restricted water resources with water bird numbers dropping and a decrease in species diversity. The allocation of water for bird breeding through environmental flows in Macquarie Marshes has led to an increase in breeding (Beeton et al. 2006). Because of dry land salinity throughout Australia there has been an increase in the levels of salt in Australian waterways. There has been funding in salt interception schemes which help to improve in-stream salinity levels but whether river salinity has improved or not is still unclear because there is not enough data available yet.

High salinity levels are dangerous because they can negatively affect larval and juvenile stages of certain fish. The introduction of invasive species into waterways has negatively affected native aquatic species because invasive species compete with native species and alter natural habitats. There has been research in producing daughterless carp to help eradicate carp. Government funding has also gone into building in-stream barriers that trap the carp and prevent them from moving into floodplains and wetlands. Investment in national and regional programmes like the Living Murray (MDBC), Healthy Waterways Partnership and the Clean Up the Swan Programme are leading to important environmental governance. The Healthy Rivers programme promotes restoration and recovery of environmental flows, riparian re-vegetation and aquatic pest control. The Living Murray programme has been crucial for the allocation of water to the environment by creating an agreement to recover 500 billion litres of water to the Murray River environment. Environmental governance and water resource management in Australia must be constantly monitored and adapted to suit the changing environmental conditions within the country (Beeton et al. 2006). If environmental programmes are governed with transparency there can be a reduction in policy fragmentation and an increase in policy efficiency (Mclntyre, 2010).

Ozone Layer

On 16 September 1987 the United Nations General Assembly signed the Montreal Protocol to address the declining ozone layer. Since that time, the use of chlorofluorocarbons (industrial refrigerants and aerosols) and farming fungicides such as methyl bromide has mostly been eliminated, although other damaging gases are still in use.

Nuclear Risk

The Nuclear non-proliferation treaty is the primary multilateral agreement governing nuclear activity.

Transgenic Organisms

Genetically modified organisms are not the subject of any major multilateral agreements. They are the subject of various restrictions at other levels of governance. GMOs are in widespread use in the US, but are heavily restricted in many other jurisdictions.

Controversies have ensued over golden rice, genetically-modified salmon, genetically-modified seeds, disclosure and other topics.

Agreements

Conventions: The main multilateral conventions, also known as Rio Conventions, are as follows:

Convention on Biological Diversity (CBD) (1992–1993): aims to conserve biodiversity. Related agreements include the Cartagena Protocol on biosafety.

United Nations Framework Convention on Climate Change (UNFCC) (1992–1994): aims to stabilize concentrations of greenhouse gases at a level that would stabilize the climate system without threatening food production, and enabling the pursuit of sustainable economic development; it incorporates the Kyoto Protocol.

United Nations Convention to Combat Desertification (UNCCD) (1994–1996): aims to combat desertification and mitigate the effects of drought and desertification, particularly in Africa.

Further Conventions

- Ramsar Convention on Wetlands of International Importance (1971–1975)

- UNESCO World Heritage Convention (1972–1975)
- Convention on International Trade in Endangered Species of Wild Flora and Fauna (CITES) (1973–1975)
- Bonn Convention on the Conservation of Migratory Species (1979–1983)
- Convention on the Protection and Use of Transboundary Watercourses and International Lakes (Water Convention) (1992–1996)
- Basel Convention on the Control of Transboundary Movements of Hazardous Wastes and their Disposal (1989–1992)
- Rotterdam Convention on the Prior Informed Consent Procedures for Certain Hazardous Chemicals and Pesticides in International Trade
- Stockholm Convention on Persistent Organic Pollutants (COP) (2001–2004)

The Rio Conventions are Characterized by

- obligatory execution by signatory states
- involvement in a sector of global environmental governance
- focus on the fighting poverty and the development of sustainable living conditions;
- funding from the Global Environment Facility (GEF) for countries with few financial resources;
- inclusion of a for assessing ecosystem status

Environmental Conventions are Regularly Criticized for their

- rigidity and verticality: they are too descriptive, homogenous and top down, not reflecting the diversity and complexity of environmental issues. Signatory countries struggle to translate objectives into concrete form and incorporate them consistently;
- duplicate structures and aid: the sector-specific format of the conventions produced duplicate structures and procedures. Inadequate cooperation between government ministries;
- contradictions and incompatibility: e.g., "if reforestation projects to reduce CO2 give preference to monocultures of exotic species, this can have a negative impact on biodiversity (whereas natural regeneration can strengthen both biodiversity and the conditions needed for life)."

Until now, the formulation of environmental policies at the international level has been divided by theme, sector or territory, resulting in treaties that overlap or clash. International attempts to coordinate environment institutions, include the Inter-Agency Coordination Committee and the Commission for Sustainable Development, but these institutions are not powerful enough to effectively incorporate the three aspects of sustainable development.

Multilateral Environmental Agreements (MEAs)

MEAs are agreements between several countries that apply internationally or regionally and concern a variety of environmental questions. As of 2013 over 500 Multilateral Environmental Agreements (MEAs), including 45 of global scope involve at least 72 signatory countries. Further agreements cover regional environmental problems, such as deforestation in Borneo or pollution in the Mediterranean. Each agreement has a specific mission and objectives ratified by multiple states.

Many Multilateral Environmental Agreements have been negotiated with the support from the United Nations Environmental Programme and work towards the achievement of the United Nations Millennium Development Goals as a means to instil sustainable practices for the environment and its people. Multilateral Environmental Agreements are considered to present enormous opportunities for greener societies and economies which can deliver numerous benefits in addressing food, energy and water security and in achieving sustainable development. These agreements can be implemented on a global or regional scale, for example the issues surrounding the disposal of hazardous waste can be implemented on a regional level as per the Bamako Convention on the Ban of the Import into Africa and the Control of Transboundary Movement and Management of Hazardous Waste within Africa which applies specifically to Africa, or the global approach to hazardous waste such as the Basel Convention on the Control of Transboundary Movements of Hazardous Wastes and their Disposal which is monitored throughout the world.

"The environmental governance structure defined by the Rio and Johannesburg Summits is sustained by UNEP, MEAs and developmental organisations and consists of assessment and policy development, as well as project implementation at the country level.

"The Governance Structure Consists of a Chain of Phases

- assessment of environment status;
- international policy development;
- formulation of MEAs;

- policy implementation;
- policy assessment;
- enforcement;
- sustainable development.

"Traditionally, UNEP has focused on the normative role of engagement in the first three phases. Phases (d) to (f) are covered by MEAs and the sustainable development phase involves developmental organisations such as UNDP and the World Bank."

Lack of coordination affects the development of coherent governance. The report shows that donor states support development organisations, according to their individual interests. They do not follow a joint plan, resulting in overlaps and duplication. MEAs tend not to become a joint frame of reference and therefore receive little financial support. States and organisations emphasize existing regulations rather than improving and adapting them.

Background

The risks associated with nuclear fission raised global awareness of environmental threats. The 1963 Partial Nuclear Test Ban Treaty prohibiting atmospheric nuclear testing was the beginning of the globalization of environmental issues. Environmental law began to be modernised and coordinated with the Stockholm Conference (1972), backed up in 1980 by the Vienna Convention on the Law of Treaties. The Vienna Convention for the Protection of the Ozone Layer was signed and ratified in 1985. In 1987, 24 countries signed the Montreal Protocol which imposed the gradual withdrawal of CFCs.

The Brundtland Report, published in 1987 by the UN Commission on Environment and Development, stipulated the need for economic development that "meets the needs of the present without compromising the capacity of future generations to meet their needs.

Rio Conference (1992) and Reactions

The United Nations Conference on Environment and Development (UNCED), better known as the 1992 Earth Summit, was the first major international meeting since the end of the Cold War and was attended by delegations from 175 countries. Since then the biggest international conferences that take place every 10 years guided the global governance process with a series of MEAs. Environmental treaties are applied with the help of secretariats.

Governments created international treaties in the 1990s to check global threats to the environment. These treaties are far more restrictive than global protocols and set out to change non-sustainable production and consumption models.

Agenda 21

Agenda 21 is a detailed plan of actions to be implemented at the global, national and local levels by UN organisations, member states and key individual groups in all regions. Agenda 21 advocates making sustainable development a legal principle law. At the local level, local Agenda 21 advocates an inclusive, territory-based strategic plan, incorporating sustainable environmental and social policies.

The Agenda has been accused of using neoliberal principles, including free trade to achieve environmental goals. For example, chapter two, entitled "International Cooperation to Accelerate Sustainable Development in Developing Countries and Related Domestic Policies" states, "The international economy should provide a supportive international climate for achieving environment and development goals by: promoting sustainable development through trade liberalization."

Actors

International Institutions:

United Nations Environment Program: The UNEP has had its biggest impact as a monitoring and advisory body, and in developing environmental agreements. It has also contributed to strengthening the institutional capacity of environment ministries.

In 2002 UNEP held a conference to focus on product lifecycle impacts, emphasizing the fashion, advertising, financial and retail industries, seen as key agents in promoting sustainable consumption.

According to Ivanova, UNEP adds value in environmental monitoring, scientific assessment and information sharing, but cannot lead all environmental management processes. She proposed the following tasks for UNEP:

- initiate a strategic independent overhaul of its mission;
- consolidate the financial information and transparency process;
- restructure organising governance by creating an operative executive council that balances the omnipresence of the overly imposing and fairly ineffectual Governing Council/Global Ministerial Environment Forum (GMEF).

Other proposals offer a new mandate to "produce greater unity amongst social and environmental agencies, so that the concept of 'environment for development' becomes a reality. It needs to act as a platform for establishing standards and for other types of interaction with national and international organisations and the United Nations. The principles of cooperation and common but differentiated responsibilities should be reflected in the application of this revised mandate."

Sherman Proposed Principles to Strengthen UNEP

- obtain a social consensus on a long-term vision;
- analyze the current situation and future scenarios;
- produce a comprehensive plan covering all aspects of sustainable development;
- build on existing strategies and processes;
- multiply links between national and local strategies;
- include all these points in the financial and budget plan;
- adopt fast controls to improve process piloting and identification of progress made;
- implement effective participation mechanisms.

Another group stated, "Consider the specific needs of developing countries and respect of the fundamental principle of 'common but differentiated responsibilities'. Developed countries should promote technology transfer, new and additional financial resources, and capacity building for meaningful participation of developing countries in international environmental governance. Strengthening of international environmental governance should occur in the context of sustainable development and should involve civil society as an important stakeholder and agent of transformation."

Global Environment Facility (GEF)

Created in 1991, the Global Environment Facility is an independent financial organisation initiated by donor governments including Germany and France. It was the first financial organisation dedicated to the environment at the global level. As of 2013 it had 179 members. Donations are used for projects covering biodiversity, climate change, international waters, destruction of the ozone layer, soil degradation and persistent organic pollutants.

GEF's institutional structure includes UNEP, UNDP and the World Bank. It is the funding mechanism for the four environmental conventions: climate change, biodiversity, persistent organic pollutants and desertification. GEF transfers resources from developed countries to developing countries to fund UNDP, UNEP and World Bank projects. The World Bank manages the annual budget of US$561.10 million.

The GEF has been criticized for its historic links with the World Bank, at least during its first phase during the 1990s, and for having favoured certain regions to the detriment of others. Another view sees it as contributing to the emergence of a global "green market". It represents "an adaptation (of the World Bank) to this emerging world order, as a response to the emergence of environmental movements that are becoming a geopolitical force." Developing countries demanded financial transfers to help them protect their environment.

GEF is subject to economic profitability criteria, as is the case for all the conventions. It received more funds in its first three years than the UNEP has since its creation in 1972. GEF funding represents less than 1% of development aid between 1992 and 2002.

United Nations Commission on Sustainable Development (CSD)

This intergovernmental institution meets twice a year to assess follow-up on Rio Summit goals. The CSD is made up of 53 member states, elected every three years and was reformed in 2004 to help improve implementation of Agenda 21. It meets twice a year, focusing on a specific theme during each two-year period: 2004-2005 was dedicated to water and 2006-2007 to climate change. The CSD has been criticized for its low impact, general lack of presence and the absence of Agenda 21 at the state level specifically, according to a report by the World Resources Institute. Its mission focuses on sequencing actions and establishing agreements puts it in conflict with institutions such as UNEP and OECD.

World Environment Organisation (WEO)

A proposed World Environment Organisation, analogous to the World Health Organisation could be capable of adapting treaties and enforcing international standards.

The European Union, particularly France and Germany, and a number of NGOs favour creating a WEO. The United Kingdom, the US and most developing countries prefer to focus on voluntary initiatives. WEO partisans maintain that it could offer better political leadership, improved legitimacy and more efficient coordination. Its detractors argue that existing institutions and missions already provide appropriate environmental governance; however the lack of coherence and coordination between them and the absence of clear division of responsibilities prevents them from greater effectiveness.

World Bank

The World Bank influences environmental governance through other actors, particularly the GEF. The World Bank's mandate is not sufficiently defined in terms of environmental governance despite the fact that it is included in its mission. However, it allocates 5 to 10% of its annual funds to environmental projects. The institution's capitalist vocation means that its investment is concentrated solely in areas which are profitable in terms of cost benefits, such as climate change action and ozone layer protection, whilst neglecting other such as adapting to climate change and desertification. Its financial autonomy means that it can make its influence felt indirectly on the creation of standards, and on international and regional negotiations.

Following intense criticism in the 1980s for its support for destructive projects which, amongst other consequences, caused deforestation of tropical forests, the World Bank drew up its own environment-related standards in the 1990s so it could correct its actions. These standards differ from UNEP's standards, meant to be the benchmark, thus discrediting the institution and sowing disorder and conflict in the world of environmental governance. Other financial institutions, regional development banks and the private sector also drew up their own standards. Criticism is not directed at the World Bank's standards in themselves, which Najam considered as "robust", but at their legitimacy and efficacy.

GEF

The GEF's account of itself as of 2012 [11] is as "the largest public funder of projects to improve the global environment", period, which "provides grants for projects related to biodiversity, climate change, international waters, land degradation, the ozone layer, and persistent organic pollutants." It claims to have provided "$10.5 billion in grants and leveraging $51 billion in co-financing for over 2,700 projects in over 165 countries [and] made more than 14,000 small grants directly to civil society and community based organisations, totaling $634 million." It serves as mechanism for the:

- Convention on Biological Diversity (CBD)
- United Nations Framework Convention on Climate Change (UNFCCC)
- Stockholm Convention on Persistent Organic Pollutants (POPs)
- Convention to Combat Desertification (UNCCD)
- implementation of Montreal Protocol on Substances That Deplete the Ozone Layer in some countries with "economies in transition"

This mandate reflects the restructured GEF as of October 2011.

World Trade Organisation (WTO)

The WTO's mandate does not include a specific principle on the environment. All the problems linked to the environment are treated in such a way as to give priority to trade requirements and the principles of the WTO's own trade system. This produces conflictual situations. Even if the WTO recognises the existence of MEAs, it denounces the fact that around 20 MEAs are in conflict with the WTO's trade regulations. Furthermore, certain MEAs can allow a country to ban or limit trade in certain products if they do not satisfy established environmental protection requirements. In these circumstances, if one country's ban relating to another country concerns two signatories of the same MEA, the principles of the treaty can be used to resolve the disagreement, whereas if the country affected by the trade ban with another country has not signed the agreement, the WTO demands that the dispute be resolved using the WTO's trade principles, in other words, without taking into account the environmental consequences.

Some criticisms of the WTO mechanisms may be too broad. In a recently dispute over labelling of dolphin safe labels for tuna between the US and Mexico, the ruling was relatively narrow and did not, as some critics claimed,

International Monetary Fund (IMF)

The IMF's mission is to encourage growth and development. The IMF advocates reduced public expenditure, increased exports and foreign investment. The environment is not a priority for the IMF, leading it to favour projects that may have negative environmental effects.

The IMF Green Fund proposal of Dominique Strauss-Kahn specifically to address "climate-related shocks in Africa", despite receiving serious attention was rejected. Strauss-Kahn's proposal, backed by France and Britain, was that "developed countries would make an initial capital injection into the fund using some of the $176 billion worth of SDR allocations from last year in exchange for a stake in the green fund." However, "most of the 24 directors ... told Strauss-Kahn that climate was not part of the IMF's mandate and that SDR allocations are a reserve asset never intended for development issues."

UN ICLEI

The UN's main body for coordinating municipal and urban decision-making is named the International Council for Local Environmental Initiatives. Its slogan is "Local Governments for Sustainability". This body sponsored the concept of full cost accounting that makes environmental governance the foundation of other governance.

ICLEIs Projects and Achievements include

- Convincing thousands of municipal leaders to sign the World Mayors and Municipal Leaders Declaration on Climate Change (2005) which notably requests of other levels of government that:

Global trade regimes, credits and banking reserve rules be reformed to advance debt relief and incentives to implement polices and practices that reduce and mitigate climate change.

- Starting national councils to implement this and other key agreements, e.g., ICLEI Local Governments for Sustainability USA
- Spreading ecoBudget (2008) and Triple Bottom Line (2007) "tools for embedding sustainability into council operations", e.g. Guntur's Municipal Corporation, one of the first four to implement the entire framework.
- Sustainability Planning Toolkit (launched 2009) integrating these and other tools
- Cities Climate Registry (launched 2010) - part of UNEP Campaign on Cities and Climate Change

ICLEI promotes best practice exchange among municipal governments globally, especially green infrastructure, sustainable procurement.

Other Secretariats

Other international institutions incorporate environmental governance in their action plans, including:

- United Nations Development Programme (UNDP), promoting development;
- World Meteorological Organisation (WMO) which works on the climate and atmosphere;
- Food and Agriculture Organisation (FAO) working on the protection of agriculture, forests and fishing;
- International Atomic Energy Agency (IAEA) which focuses on nuclear security.

Over 30 UN agencies and programmes support environmental management, according to Najam. This produces a lack of coordination, insufficient exchange of information and dispersion of responsibilities. It also results in proliferation of initiatives and rivalry between them.

Criticism

According to Bauer, Busch and Siebenhüner, the different conventions and multilateral agreements of global environmental regulation is increasing their secretariats' influence. Influence varies according to bureaucratic and leadership efficiency, choice of technical or client-centred.

The United Nations is often the target of criticism, including from within over the multiplication of secretariats due to the chaos it produces. Using a separate secretariat for each MEA creates enormous overhead given the 45 international-scale and over 500 other agreements.

States

Environmental Governance at the State Level: Environmental protection has created opportunities for mutual and collective monitoring among neighbouring states. The European Union provides an example of the institutionalization of joint regional and state environmental governance. Key areas include information, led by the European Environment Agency (EEA), and the production and monitoring of norms by states or local institutions.

State Participation in Global Environmental Governance: US refusal to ratify major environment agreements produced tensions with ratifiers in Europe and Japan.

The World Bank, IMF and other institutions are dominated by the developed countries and do not always properly consider the requirements of developing countries.

Business

Environmental governance applies to business as well as government. Considerations are typical of those in other domains:

- values (vision, mission, principles);
- policy (strategy, objectives, targets);
- oversight (responsibility, direction, training, communication);
- process (management systems, initiatives, internal control, monitoring and review, stakeholder dialogue, transparency, environmental accounting, reporting and verification);
- performance (performance indicators, benchmarking, eco-efficiency, reputation, compliance, liabilities, business development).

White and Klernan among others discuss the correlation between environmental governance and financial performance. This correlation is higher in sectors where environmental impacts are greater.

Business environmental issues include emissions, biodiversity, historical liabilities, product and material waste/recycling, energy use/ supply and many others.

Environmental governance has become linked to traditional corporate governance as an increasing number of shareholders are corporate environmental impacts. Corporate governance is the set of processes, customs, policies, laws, and institutions affecting the way a corporation (or company) is managed. Corporate governance is affected by the relationships among stakeholders. These stakeholders research and quantify performance to compare and contrast the environmental performance of thousands of companies.

Large corporations with global supply chains evaluate the environmental performance of business partners and suppliers for marketing and ethical reasons. Some consumers seek environmentally friendly and sustainable products and companies.

Non-Governmental Organisations

According to Bäckstrand and Saward, "broader participation by non-state actors in multilateral environmental decisions (in varied roles such as agenda setting, campaigning, lobbying, consultation, monitoring, and implementation) enhances the democratic legitimacy of environmental governance."

Local activism is capable of gaining the support of the people and authorities to combat environmental degradatation. In Cotacachi, Ecuador, a social movement used a combination of education, direct action, the influence of local public authorities and denunciation of the mining company's plans in its own country, Canada, and the support of international environmental groups to influence mining activity.

Fisher cites cases in which multiple strategies were used to effect change. She describes civil society groups that pressure international institutions and also organise local events. Local groups can take responsibility for environmental governance in place of governments.

According to Bengoa, "social movements have contributed decisively to the creation of an institutional platform wherein the fight against poverty and exclusion has become an inescapable benchmark." But despite successes in this area, "these institutional changes have not produced the processes for transformation that could have made substantial changes to the opportunities available to rural inhabitants, particularly the poorest and those excluded from society." He cites several reasons:

- conflict between in-group cohesion and openness to outside influence;
- limited trust between individuals;
- contradiction between social participation and innovation;
- criticisms without credible alternatives to environmentally damaging activities

A successful initiative in Ecuador involved the establishment of stakeholder federations and management committees (NGOs, communities, municipalities and the ministry) for the management of a protected forest.

Proposals

The International Institute for Sustainable Development proposed an agenda for global governance. These objectives are:

- expert leadership;
- positioning science as the authoritative basis of sound environmental policy;
- coherence and reasonable coordination;
- well-managed institutions;
- incorporate environmental concerns and actions within other areas of international policy and action

Coherence and Coordination

Despite the increase in efforts, actors, agreements and treaties, the global environment continue to degrade at a rapid rate. From the big hole in Earth's ozone layer to over-fishing to the uncertainties of climate change, the world is confronted by several intrinsically global challenges. However, as the environmental agenda becomes more complicated and extensive, the current system has proven ineffective in addressing and tackling problems related to trans-boundary externalities and the environment is still experiencing degradation at unprecedented levels.

Inforesources identifies four major obstacles to global environmental governance, and describes measures in response. The four obstacles are:

- parallel structures and competition, without a coherent strategy
- contradictions and incompatibilities, without appropriate compromise
- competition between multiple agreements with incompatible objectives, regulations and processes
- integrating policy from macro- to micro- scales.

Recommended Measures

- MDGs (Milenium Development Goals) and conventions, combining sustainability and reduction of poverty and equity;
- country-level approach linking global and local scales
- coordination and division of tasks in a multilateral approach that supports developing countries and improves coordination between donor countries and institutions
- use of Poverty Reduction Strategy Papers (PRSPs) in development planning
- transform conflicts into tradeoffs, synergies and win-win options

Contemporary debates surrounding global environmental governance have converged on the idea of developing a stronger and more effective institutional framework. The views on how to achieve this, however, still hotly debated. Currently, rather than teaming up with the United Nations Environment Programme (UNEP), international environmental responsibilities have been spread across many different agencies including: a) specialised agencies within the UN system such as the World Meteorological Organisation, the International Maritime Organisation and others; b) the programs in the UN system such as the UN Development Program; c) the UN regional economic and social commission; d) the Bretton Woods institutions; e) the World Trade Organisation and; f) the environmentally focused mechanisms such as the Global Environment Facility and close to 500 international environmental agreements.

Some analysts also argue that multiple institutions and some degree of overlap and duplication in policies is necessary to ensure maximum output from the system. Others, however, claim that institutions have become too dispersed and lacking in coordination which can be damaging to their effectiveness in global environmental governance. Whilst there are various arguments for and against a WEO, the key challenge, however, remains the same: how to develop a rational and effective framework that will protect the global environment efficiently.

Democratization

Starting in 2002, Saward and others began to view the Earth Summit process as capable opening up the possibility of stakeholder democracy. The summits were deliberative rather than simply participative, with NGOs, women, men, indigenous peoples and businesses joining the decision-making process alongside states and international organisations, characterized by:

- the importance given to scientific and technical considerations
- the official and unofficial participation of many actors with heterogeneous activity scopes
- growing uncertainty
- a new interpretation of international law and social organisation models

As of 2013, the absence of joint rules for composing such fora leads to the development of non-transparent relations that favour the more powerful stakeholders. Criticisms assert that they act more as a lobbying platform, wherein specific interest groups attempt to influence governments.

Institutional Reform

Actors inside and outside the United Nations are discussing possibilities for global environmental governance that provides a solution to current problems of fragility, coordination and coherence. Deliberation is focusing on the goal of making UNEP more efficient. A 2005 resolution recognises "the need for more efficient environmental activities in the United Nations system, with enhanced coordination, improved policy advice and guidance, strengthened scientific knowledge, assessment and cooperation, better treaty compliance, while respecting the legal autonomy of the treaties, and better integration of environmental activities in the broader sustainable development framework."

Proposals Include

- greater and better coordination between agencies;
- strengthen and acknowledge UNEP's scientific role;
- identify MEA areas to strengthen coordination, cooperation and team work between different agreements;
- increase regional presence;
- implement the Bali Strategic Plan on improving technology training and support for the application of environmental measures in poor countries;
- demand that UNEP and MEAs participate formally in all relevant WTO committees as observers.
- strengthen its financial situation;
- improve secretariats' efficiency and effectiveness.

One of the Main Studies Addressing This Issue Proposes

- clearly divide tasks between development organisations, UNEP and the MEAs

- adopt a political direction for environmental protection and sustainable development
- authorize the UNEP Governing Council/Global Ministerial Environment Forum to adopt the UNEP medium-term strategy
- allow Member States to formulate and administer MEAs an independent secretariat for each convention
- support UNEP in periodically assessing MEAs and ensure coordination and coherence
- establish directives for setting up national/regional platforms capable of incorporating MEAs in the Common Country Assessment (CCA) process and United Nations Development Assistance Framework (UNDAF)
- establish a global joint planning framework
- study the aptitude and efficiency of environmental activities' funding, focusing on differential costs
- examine and redefine the concept of funding differential costs as applicable to existing financial mechanisms
- reconsider remits, division of tasks and responsibilities between entities that provide services to the multipartite conferences. Clearly define the services that UN offices provide to MEA secretariats
- propose measures aiming to improve personnel provision and geographic distribution for MEA secretariats
- improve transparency resource use for supporting programmes and in providing services to MEAs. Draw up a joint budget for services supplied to MEAs.

Education

A 2001 Alliance 21 report proposes six fields of action:

- strengthen citizens' critical faculties to ensure greater democratic control of political orientations
- develop a global and critical approach
- develop civic education training for teachers
- develop training for certain socio-professional groups
- develop environmental education for the entire population;
- assess the resulting experiences of civil society

Transform Daily Life

Individuals can modify consumption, based on voluntary simplicity: changes in purchasing habits, simplified lifestyles (less work, less consumption, more socialization and constructive leisure time). But individual actions must not replace vigilance and pressure on policies. Notions of responsible consumption developed over decades, revealing the political nature of individual purchases, according to the principle that consumption should satisfy the population's basic needs. These needs comprise the physical wellbeing of individuals and society, a healthy diet, access to drinking water and plumbing, education, healthcare and physical safety. The general attitude centres on the need to reduce consumption and reuse and recycle materials. In the case of food consumption, local, organic and fair trade products which avoid ill treatment of animals has become a major trend.

Alternatives to the personal automobile are increasing, including public transport, car sharing and bicycles and alternative propulsion systems. Alternative energy sources are becoming less costly. Ecological industrial processes turn the waste from one industry into raw materials for another. Governments can reduce subsidies/increase taxes/tighten regulation on unsustainable activities.

The Community Environmental governance Global Alliance encourages holistic approaches to environmental and economic challenges, incorporating indigenous knowledge. Okotoks, Alberta capped population growth based on the carrying capacity of the Sheep River. The Fraser Basin Council Watershed Governance in British Columbia, Canada, manages issues that span municipal jurisdictions. Smart Growth is an international movement that employs key tenets of Environmental governance in urban planning.

Policies and Regulations

Establish policies and regulations that promote "infrastructures for well being" whilst addressing the political, physical and cultural levels. Eliminate subsidies that have a negative environmental impact and tax pollution Promoting workers' personal and family development.

Coordination

A programme of national workshops on synergies between the three Rio Conventions launched in late 2000, in collaboration with the relevant secretariats. The goal was to strengthen coordination at the local level by:

- sharing information
- promoting political dialogue to obtain financial support and implement programmes
- enabling the secretariats to update their joint work programmes.

According to Campbell, “In the context of globalization, the question of linking up environmental themes with other subjects, such as trade, investment and conflict resolution mechanisms, as well as the economic incentives to participate in and apply agreements would seem to provide an important lesson for the effective development of environmental governance structures.” Environmental concerns would become part of the global economic system. “These problems also contain the seeds of a new generation of international conflicts that could affect both the stability of international relations and collective security. Which is why the concept of ‘collective security’ has arisen.”

Moving local decisions to the global level is as important as the way in which local initiatives and best practices are part of a global system. Kanie points out that NGOs, scientists, international institutions and stakeholder partnerships can reduce the distance that separates the local and international levels.

Policies

Sustainable Tourism

“Sustainable tourism is the concept of visiting a place as a tourist and trying to make only a positive impact on the environment, society and economy.” Tourism can involve primary transportation to the general location, local transportation, accommodations, entertainment, recreation, nourishment and shopping. It can be related to travel for leisure, business and what is called VFR (visiting friends and relatives). There is now broad consensus that tourism development should be sustainable; however, the question of how to achieve this remains an object of debate.

Without travel there is no tourism, so the concept of sustainable tourism is tightly linked to a concept of sustainable mobility. Two relevant considerations are tourism’s reliance on fossil fuels and tourism’s effect on climate change. 72 percent of tourism’s CO_2 come from transportation, 24 percent from accommodations, and 4 percent from local activities. Aviation accounts for 55% of those transportation CO_2 emissions (or 40% of tourism’s total). However, when considering the impact of all greenhouse gas emissions from tourism and that aviation emissions are made at high altitude where their effect on climate is amplified, aviation alone accounts for 75% of tourism’s climate impact.

The International Air Transport Association (IATA) considers an annual increase in aviation fuel efficiency of 2 percent per year through

2050 to be realistic. However, both Airbus and Boeing expect the passenger-kilometres of air transport to increase by about 5 percent yearly through at least 2020, overwhelming any efficiency gains. By 2050, with other economic sectors having greatly reduced their CO_2 emissions, tourism is likely to be generating 40 percent of global carbon emissions. The main cause is an increase in the average distance travelled by tourists, which for many years has been increasing at a faster rate than the number of trips taken. "Sustainable transportation is now established as the critical issue confronting a global tourism industry that is palpably unsustainable, and aviation lies at the heart of this issue (Gossling et al., 2010)."

Social & Economic Aspects

Global economists forecast continuing international tourism growth, the amount depending on the location. As one of the world's largest and fastest growing industries, this continuous growth will place great stress on remaining biologically diverse habitats and indigenous cultures, which are often used to support mass tourism. Tourists who promote sustainable tourism are sensitive to these dangers and seek to protect tourist destinations, and to protect tourism as an industry.

Sustainable tourists can reduce the impact of tourism in many ways:

- informing themselves of the culture, politics, and economy of the communities visited
- anticipating and respecting local cultures, expectations and assumptions
- supporting the integrity of local cultures by favouring businesses which conserve cultural heritage and traditional values
- supporting local economies by purchasing local goods and participating with small, local businesses
- conserving resources by seeking out businesses that are environmentally conscious, and by using the least possible amount of non-renewable resources

Increasingly, destinations and tourism operations are endorsing and following "responsible tourism" as a pathway towards sustainable tourism. Responsible tourism and sustainable tourism have an identical goal, that of sustainable development. The pillars of responsible tourism are therefore the same as those of sustainable tourism – environmental integrity, social justice and economic development. The major difference between the two is that, in responsible tourism, individuals, organisations and businesses are asked to take responsibility for their actions and the impacts of their actions. This shift in emphasis has taken place because some stakeholders feel that insufficient progress towards realising sustainable tourism has been made since the Earth Summit in Rio. This is partly because everyone has been expecting others to behave in a sustainable manner. The emphasis on responsibility in responsible tourism means that everyone involved in tourism – government, product owners and operators, transport operators, community services, NGOs and Community-based organisation CBOs, tourists, local communities, industry associations – are responsible for achieving the goals of responsible tourism.

Stakeholders

Stakeholders of sustainable tourism play a role in continuing this form of tourism. This can include organisations as well as individuals, to be specific, ECOFIN. "A stakeholder in the tourism industry is deemed to be anyone who is impacted on by development positively or negatively, and as a result it reduces potential conflict between the tourists and host community by involving the latter in shaping the way in which tourism develops.

The Global Sustainable Tourism Council (GSTC) serves as the international body for fostering increased knowledge and understanding of sustainable tourism practices, promoting the adoption of universal sustainable tourism principles and building demand for sustainable travel. It has a number of programmes including the setting of international standards for accreditation agencies (the organisations that would inspect a tourism product, and certify them as a sustainable company).

Governments

The values and ulterior motives of governments often need to be taken into account when assessing the motives for sustainable tourism. One important factor to consider in any ecologically sensitive or remote area or an area new to tourism is that of carrying capacity. This is the capacity of tourists of visitors an area can sustainably tolerate without damaging the environment or culture of the surrounding area. This can be altered and revised in time and with changing perceptions and values. For example, originally the sustainable carrying capacity of the Galapagos Islands was set at 12,000 visitors per annum but was later changed by the Ecuadorian government to 50,000 for economic reasons and objectives.

Non-Governmental Organisations

Non-governmental organisations are one of the stakeholders in advocating sustainable tourism. Their roles can range from spearheading sustainable tourism practices to simply doing research. University research teams and scientists can be tapped to aid in the process of planning. Such solicitation of research can be observed in the planning of Cát Bà National Park in Vietnam.

Dive resort operators in Bunaken National Park, Indonesia, play a crucial role by developing exclusive zones for diving and fishing respectively, such that both tourists and locals can benefit from the venture.

Large conventions, meetings and other major organised events drive the travel, tourism and hospitality industry. Cities and convention centres compete to attract such commerce, commerce which has heavy impacts on resource use and the environment. Major sporting events, such as the Olympic Games, present special problems regarding environmental burdens and degradation. But burdens imposed by the regular convention industry can be vastly more significant.

Green conventions and events are a new but growing sector and marketing point within the convention and hospitality industry. More environmentally aware organisations, corporations and government agencies are now seeking more sustainable event practices, greener hotels, restaurants and convention venues, and more energy efficient or climate neutral travel and ground transportation. However, the convention trip not taken can be the most sustainable option: "With most international conferences having hundreds if not thousands of participants, and the bulk of these usually travelling by plane, conference travel is an area where significant reductions in air-travel-related GHG emissions could be made. ... This does not mean non-attendance" (Reay, 2004), since modern Internet communications are now ubiquitous and remote audio/visual participation. For example, by 2003 Access Grid technology had already successfully hosted several international conferences,. A particular example is the large American Geophysical Union's annual meeting, which has used livestreaming several years. This provides live streams and recordings of keynotes, named lectures and oral sessions, and provides opportunities to submit questions and interact with authors and peers. Following the live-stream, the recording of each session is posted on-line within 24 hours.

Some convention centres have begun to take direct action in reducing the impact of the conventions they host. One example is the Moscone Centre in San Francisco, which has a very aggressive recycling program, a large solar power system, and other programs aimed at reducing impact and increasing efficiency.

Local Communities

Local communities benefit from sustainable tourism through economic development, job creation, and infrastructure development.

Tourism revenues bring economic growth and prosperity to attractive tourist destinations which can raise the standard of living in destination communities. Sustainable tourism operators commit themselves to creating jobs for local community members. Increase in tourism revenue to an area acts as a driver for the development of increased infrastructure. As tourist demands increase in a destination, a more robust infrastructure is needed to support the needs of both the tourism industry and the local community.

Sustainable Tourism in Developing Nations

Expansion of Tourism in the LEDC's: The renewed emphasis on outward-orientated growth which accompanied the rise in neoliberal development strategies in the 1990s in the south also focused attention on international tourism as an import potential growth sector for many countries, particularly in LEDC's as many of the world's most beautiful and 'untouched' places are located in the Third World.

Prior to the 1960s studies tended to assume that the extension of the tourism industry to LEDC's was a good thing. In the 1970s this changed as academics started to take a much more negative view on tourism's consequences, particularly criticising the industry as an effective contributor towards development. International tourism is a volatile industry with visitors quick to abandon destinations that were formerly popular because of threats to health or security.

Problems with Sustainable Tourism in the Third World

Displacement and Resettlement: One common issue with tourism in a place where there was none prior to First World companies arriving is that of the displacement and resettlement of local communities. The Maasai tribes in Tanzania have been a victim of this problem. After the second World War First World conservationists with the intent of making such areas accessible to tourists as well as preserving the areas natural beauty and ecology moved into the areas where the Maasai tribes lived. This was often achieved through the setting up of national parks and conservation areas (Monbiot 1994; Olerokonga, 1992:7).

It has been claimed that Maasai activities did not threaten the wildlife and the First World knowledge was blurred by 'colonial disdain' and misunderstandings of savannah wildlife Monbiot 1994. As the Maasai have been displaced the area within the Ngorongoro Conservation Area (NCA) has been modified to allow easier access for tourists by actions such as building campsites, tracks and the removal of stone objects such as stones for souvenirs Olerokonga, 1992:7).

This kind of 'sustainable tourism' is viewed by many as an oxymoron and that many things done in the name of sustainability are actually masking the desire to allow extra profits Monbiot 1994. There is often alienation of local populations from the tourists Olerokonga, 1992:7).

Environmental Impacts

Coastal Tourism: Many coastal areas are experiencing particular pressure from growth in lifestyles and growing numbers of tourists. Coastal environments are limited in extent consisting of only a narrow strip along the edge of the ocean. Coastal areas are often the first environments to experience the detrimental impacts of tourism. A detailed study of the impact on coastal areas, with reference to western India can be an example.

The inevitable change is on the horizon as holiday destinations put more effort into sustainable tourism. Planning and management controls can reduce the impact on coastal environments and ensure that investment into tourism products supports sustainable coastal tourism. Some of the recent studies have led to some interesting conceptual models applicable for coastal tourism. The 'inverted funnel model' and the 'embedded model' can be good metaphors for understanding the interplay of different stake-holders like government, local community, tourists and business community in developing tourist destinations.

Mountain Tourism

Mount Everest attracts many tourist climbers wanting to summit the peak of the highest mountain in the world each year. Everest is a UNESCO World Heritage site. Over the years, carelessness and excessive consumption of resources by mountaineers, as well as overgrazing by livestock, have damaged the habitats of snow leopards, lesser pandas, Tibetan bears, and scores of bird species. To counteract past abuses, various reforestation programs have been carried out by local communities and the Nepalese government.

Expeditions have removed supplies and equipment left by climbers on Everest's slopes, including hundreds of oxygen containers. A large quantity of the litter of past climbers—tons of items such as tents, cans, crampons, and human waste—has been hauled down from the mountain and recycled or discarded. However, the bodies of most of the more than 260 climbers who have died on Everest (notably on its upper slopes) have not been removed, as they are unreachable or—for those that are accessible—their weight makes carrying them down extremely difficult. Notable in the cleanup endeavour have been the efforts of the Eco Everest Expeditions, the first of which was organised in 2008 to commemorate the death that January of Everest-climbing pioneer Sir Edmund Hillary. Those expeditions also have publicized ecological issues (in particular, concerns about the effects of climate change in the region through observations that the Khumbu Icefall has been melting).

Sustainable Tourism as Part of a Development Strategy

Third World countries are especially interested in international tourism, and many believe it brings countries a large selection of economic benefits including employment opportunities, small business development, and increased in payments of foreign exchange. Many assume that more money is gained through developing luxury goods and services in spite of the fact that this increases a countries dependency on imported products, foreign investments and expatriate skills. This classic 'trickle down' financial strategy rarely makes its way down to benefit people at a grassroots level.

It has been said that the economic benefits of large-scale tourism are not doubted but that the backpacker or budget traveller sector is often neglected as a potential growth sector by Third World governments. This sector brings significant non-economic benefits which could help to empower and educate the communities involved in this sector. "Aiming 'low' builds upon the skills of the local population, promotes self-reliance, and develops the confidence of community members in dealing with outsiders, all signs of empowerment" and all of which aid in the overall development of a nation.

Improvements to Sustainable Tourism in the Third World

Management of Sustainable Tourism: There has been the promotion of sustainable tourism practices surrounding the management of tourist locations by locals or the community. This form of tourism is based on the premise that the people living next to a resource are the ones best suited to protecting it. This means that the tourism activities and businesses are developed and operated by local community members, and certainly with their consent and support. Sustainable tourism typically involves the conservation of resources that are capitalized upon for tourism purposes. Locals run the businesses and are responsible for promoting the conservation messages to protect their environment.

Community-based sustainable tourism (CBST) associates the success of the sustainability of the ecotourism location to the management practices of the communities who are directly or indirectly dependent on the location for their livelihoods. A salient feature of CBST is that local knowledge is usually utilised alongside wide general frameworks of ecotourism business models. This allows the participation of locals at the management level and typically allows a more intimate understanding of the environment.

The use of local knowledge also means an easier entry level into a tourism industry for locals whose jobs or livelihoods are affected by the use of their environment as tourism locations. Environmentally sustainable development crucially depends on the presence of local support for a project. It has also been noted that in order for success projects must provide direct benefits for the local community.

However, recent research has found that economic linkages generated by CBST may only be sporadic, and that the linkages with agriculture are negatively affected by seasonality and by the small scale of the cultivated areas. This means that CBST may only have small-scale positive effects for these communities.

It has also been said that partnerships between governments and tourism agencies with smaller communities is not particularly effective because of the disparity in aims between the two groups, i.e. true sustainability versus mass tourism for maximum profit. In Honduras such a divergence can be demonstrated where consultants from the World Bank and officials from the Institute of tourism wanted to set up a selection of 5-star hotels near various ecotourism destinations. But another operating approach in the region by USAID and APROECOH (an ecotourism association) promotes community-based efforts which has trained many local Hondurans. Mader concluded that the grassroot organisations were more successful in Honduras.

Confusion Surrounding Governmental Management of Sustainable Tourism

There has been some discussion regarding the told of inter-governmental organisations and the development of sustainable tourism practices in the third world. In Mowforth and Munt's book 'Tourism and Sustainability: New Tourism in the Third World, they criticised a document that was written by the World Travel and Tourism Council (WTTC), the World Tourism Organisation and the Earth Council, which was included in Agenda 21. It was entitled 'Agenda 21 for the Travel and Tourism Industry: Towards Environmentally Sustainable Development'. Mowforth and Munt commented on the language used to describe the environment and local culture in such documents because the preservation of the environment and local culture are the two main objectives when practising sustainable tourism. They pointed out that some of the key words used were 'core asset', 'core product', 'product quality' and 'preserve'. They argued that the treatment of the environment as a marketable product was clear and that such documents provide a good list of advice for Third World governments regarding sustainable tourism but do not actually provide the resources to incorporate them into the development of their tourism industries.

It is arguments such as these that postulate that there is a gap between the advice given by non-governmental or inter-governmental organisations to Third World governments and what can actually be brought to realisation. These arguments try and persuade readers that documents like the one released by the WTTC that the development of sustainable tourism actually 'bypasses the interests of local people'.

Responsible Tourism

Responsible tourism is regarded as a behaviour. It is more than a form of tourism as it represents an approach to engaging with tourism, be that as a tourist, a business, locals at a destination or any other tourism stakeholder. It emphasizes that all stakeholders are responsible for the kind of tourism they develop or engage in. Whilst different groups will see responsibility in different ways, the shared understanding is that responsible tourism should entail an improvement in tourism. Tourism should become 'better' as a result of the responsible tourism approach.

Within the notion of betterment resides the acknowledgement that conflicting interests need to be balanced. However, the objective is to create better places for people to live in and to visit. Importantly, there is no blueprint for responsible tourism: what is deemed responsible may differ depending on places and cultures. Responsible Tourism is an aspiration that can be realised in different ways in different originating markets and in the diverse destinations of the world (Goodwin, 2002).

Focusing in particular on businesses, according to the Cape Town Declaration on Responsible Tourism, it will have the following characteristics:

- minimises negative economic, environmental, and social impacts
- generates greater economic benefits for local people and enhances the well-being of host communities, improves working conditions and access to the industry

- involves local people in decisions that affect their lives and life chances
- makes positive contributions to the conservation of natural and cultural heritage, to the maintenance of the world's diversity
- provides more enjoyable experiences for tourists through more meaningful connections with local people, and a greater understanding of local cultural, social and environmental issues
- provides access for people with disabilities and
- is culturally sensitive, engenders respect between tourists and hosts, and builds local pride and confidence.

Sustainable tourism is where tourists can enjoy their holiday and at the same time respect the culture of people and also respect the environment. It also means that local people (such as the Masaai) get a fair say about tourism and also receive some money from the profit which the game reserve make. The environment is being damaged quite a lot by tourists and part of Sustainable tourism is to make sure that the damaging does not carry on.

There arc many private companies who are working into embracing the principles and aspects of Responsible Tourism, some for the purpose of Corporate Social Responsibility activities, and others such as responsibletravel.com and WorldHotel-Link, which was originally a project of the International Finance Corporation, have built their entire business model around responsible tourism, local capacity building and increasing market access for small and medium tourism enterprises.

Humane Tourism

Humane tourism is part of the movement of responsible tourism. The idea is to empower local communities through travel related businesses around the world, first and foremost in developing countries. The idea of humane travel or humane tourism is to connect travelers from Europe, North America, Australia and New Zealand seeking new adventures and authentic experiences directly, to local businesses in the specific locations they wish to visit – thus, giving economic advantages to local businesses and giving travelers authentic and truly unique travel experiences. Humane travel or humane tourism focuses on the people, the local community. The idea is to enable travelers to experience the world through the eyes of its local people while contributing directly to those people, ensuring that tourist dollars benefit the local community directly.

Humane tourism is about giving opportunity to the local people, empower them, enable them to enjoy the fruits of tourism directly.

The Internet is changing tourism. More and more travelers are planning their travels and vacations via the net. The Internet enables people to cut off commissions. The traveler can search for new destinations to visit, talk or read about other people experience, and buy the services directly. The Internet platform can encourage local people to start new businesses and that already existing small businesses will begin to promote themselves through the net and receive the economic advantages of this directly in their communities. The world is now in a new tourism age, with globalization and the Internet playing a key role.

The new travelers have travelled the world, they have seen the classic sites. Staying at a Western hotel is not attractive enough, and they are excited by the prospect of experiencing the authentic local way of life: to go fishing with a local fisherman, to eat the fish with his family, to sleep in a typical village house. These tourists or travelers, are happy to know that while doing so they promote the economic well-being of those same people they spend time with.

Humane tourism is part of Responsible tourism. The concept of Responsible Tourism originated in the work of Jost Krippendorf in The Holiday Makers called for "rebellious tourists and rebellious locals" to create new forms of tourism. His vision was "to develop and promote new forms of tourism, which will bring the greatest possible benefit to all the participants – travelers, the host population and the tourist business, without causing intolerable ecological and social damage." As one can see he already talked, back in the 80s about benefits for the host population and used the term human tourism. Humane travel focuses on that host local population.

The South African national tourism policy (1996) used the term "responsible tourism" and mentioned the well-being of the local community as a main factor.

The Cape Town Declaration on Responsible Tourism in Destinations, agreed in 2002, that Responsible Tourism is about "making better places for people to live in and better places for people to visit." The declaration focused on "places" but did mention the local population.

From the Rio summit or earth summit on 1992 until the UN Commission on Sustainable Development in 1999, the main focus of the tourism industry was the earth, the planet, the places, "green" or "eco" tourism. Now there is a trend to include the local population. This trend or branch of responsible tourism is called humane tourism or humane travel.

Responsible Hospitality

As with the view of responsible tourism, responsible hospitality is essentially about creating better places for people to live in, and better places for people to visit. This does not mean all forms of hospitality are also forms of tourism although hospitality is the largest sector of the tourism industry. As such we should not be surprised at overlaps between responsible hospitality and responsible tourism. In the instance where place of permanent residence is also the place where the hospitality service is consumed, if for example a meal is consumed in a local restaurant, this does not obviate the requirement to improve the place of residence. As such, the essence of Responsible Hospitality is not contingent upon touristic forms of hospitality.

While Friedman (1962) famously argued that, admittedly within legal parameters, the sole responsibility of business was to generate profit for shareholders the idea that businesses' responsibility extends beyond this has existed for decades and is most frequently encountered in the concept of corporate social responsibility. There are numerous ways businesses can and do engage in activities that are not intended to benefit shareholders and management, at least not in the short term. However, often acts of corporate social responsibility are undertaken because of the perceived benefit to business. Usually in hospitality this relates to the cost reductions associated with improved energy efficiency but may also relate to, for example, the rise in ethical consumerism and the view that being seen to be a responsible business is beneficial to revenue growth.

As per the Cape Town Declaration on Responsible Tourism, responsible hospitality is culturally sensitive. Instead of then calling for the unachievable, responsible hospitality simply makes the case for more responsible forms of hospitality, hospitality that benefits locals first, and visitors second. Certainly, all forms of hospitality can be improved and managed so that negative impacts are minimized whilst striving for a maximization of positive impacts.

Ecotax

Ecotax (short for Ecological taxation) refers to taxes intended to promote environmentally friendly activities via economic incentives. Such a policy can complement or avert the need for regulatory (command and control) approaches. Often, an ecotax policy proposal may attempt to maintain overall tax revenue by proportionately reducing other taxes (e.g. taxes on human labour and renewable resources); such proposals are known as a green tax shift towards ecological taxation.

Ecotaxes are examples of Pigouvian taxes, which are *taxes that attempt to make the private parties involved feel the social burden of their actions.* An example might be philosopher Thomas Pogge's proposed Global Resources Dividend.

Taxes Affected

Examples of taxes which could be lowered or eliminated by a green tax shift are:

- Payroll, income, and, to a lesser extent, sales taxes.
- Corporate taxes (taxes on investment and entrepreneurship).
- Property taxes on buildings and other infrastructure.

Examples of ecotaxes which could be implemented or increased are:

- Carbon taxes on the use of fossil fuels by greenhouse gases produced. Old hydrocarbon taxes don't penalize green house gas (GHG) production.
- Duties on imported goods containing significant non-ecological energy input (to a level necessary to treat fairly local manufacturers)
- Severance taxes on the extraction of mineral, energy, and forestry products.
- License fees for camping, hiking, fishing and hunting and associated equipment.
- Specific taxes on technologies and products which are associated with substantial negative externalities.
- Waste disposal taxes and refundable fees.
- Steering taxes on effluents, pollution and other hazardous wastes.
- Site value taxes on the unimproved value of land.

Economic Frameworks and Strategies Employing Tax Shifting and Ecotaxes

The object of a green tax shift is often to implement a "full cost accounting" or "true cost accounting", using fiscal policy to internalize market distorting externalities, which leads to sustainable wealth creation. The broader measures required for this are also sometimes called ecological fiscal reform, especially in Canada, where the government has generally employed this terminology. In some countries the name is eco-social market economy.

Tax shifting usually includes balancing taxation levels to be revenue-neutral for government and to maintain overall progressiveness. It also usually includes measures to protect the most vulnerable, such as raising the minimum income to file income tax at all, or an increase to pension and social assistance levels to offset increased costs of fuel consumption.

Basic economic theory recognises the existence of externalities and their potential negative effects. To the extent that green taxes correct for externalities such as pollution, they correspond with mainstream economic theory. In practice, however, setting the correct taxation level or the tax collection system needed to do so is difficult, and may lead to further distortions or unintended consequences. Taxes on consumption may take the "feebate" approach advocated by Amory Lovins, in which additional fees on less sustainable products — such as sport utility vehicles — are pooled to fund subsidies on more sustainable alternatives, such as hybrid electric vehicles.

However, they may simply act as incentives to change habits and make capital investments in newer more efficient vehicles or appliances or to upgrade buildings. Small changes in corporate tax rates for instance can radically change return on investment of capital projects, especially if the averted costs of future fossil fuel use are taken into account. The same logic applies to major consumer purchases. A "green mortgage" such as a Location Efficient Mortgage, for example, recognises that persons who do not drive cars and live generally energy-efficient lifestyles pay far less per month than others and accordingly have more to pay a heftier mortgage bill with. This justifies lending them much more money to upgrade a house to use even less energy overall. The result is a bank taking more per month from a consumer's income as utilities and car insurance companies take less, and housing stock upgraded to use the minimum energy feasible with current technology.

Aside from energy, the refits will generally be those required to be maximally accommodating to telework, permaculture gardens (for example green roofs), and a lifestyle that is generally localized in the community not based on commuting. The last, especially, raises real state valuations for not only the neighbourhood but the entire surrounding region. Consumers living sustainable lifestyles in upgraded housing will generally be unwilling to drive around aimlessly shopping, for instance, to save a few dollars on their purchases. Instead, they'll stay nearer to home and create jobs in grocery delivery and small organic grocers, spending substantially less money on gasoline and car operation costs even if they pay more for food.

Progressive or Regressive?

Some green tax shift proposals have been criticized as being fiscally regressive (a tax with an average tax rate that decreases as the taxpayer's income increases). Taxing negative externalities usually entails exerting a burden on consumption, and since the poor consume more and save or invest less as a share of their income, any shift towards consumption taxes can be regressive. In 2004, research by the Policy Studies Institute and Joseph Rowntree Foundation indicated that flat rate taxes on domestic rubbish, energy, water and transport use would have a relatively higher impact on poorer households.

However, conventional regulatory approaches can affect prices in much the same way, while lacking the revenue-recycling potential of ecotaxes. Moreover, correctly assessing distributive impact of any tax shift requires an analysis of the specific instrument design features. For example, tax revenue could be redistributed on a per capita basis as part of a basic income scheme; in this case, the poorest would gain what the average citizen pays as ecotaxes, minus their own small contribution (no car, small apartment, ...). This design would be highly progressive. Alternatively, an ecotax can have a "lifeline" design, in which modest consumption levels are priced relatively low (even zero, in the case of water), and higher consumption levels are priced at a higher rate. Furthermore, an ecotax policy package can include revenue recycling to reduce or eliminate any regressivity; an increase in an ecotax could be more than offset by a decrease in a (regressive) payroll or consumption tax. Some proponents claim a second benefit of increased employment or lower health care costs as the market and society adjust to the new fiscal policy (these claims, as with the claim "tax cuts create jobs," are often difficult to prove or disprove even after the fact).

Furthermore, pollution and other forms of environmental harm are often felt more acutely by the poor, who cannot "buy their way out" of being receptors of air pollution, water pollution, etc. Such losses, although externalities, have real economic welfare impacts. Thus by reducing environmental harm, such instruments have a progressive effect.

Ecotax policies Enacted

An ecotax has been enacted in Germany by means of three laws in 1998, 1999 and 2002. The first introduced a tax on electricity and petroleum, at variable rates based on environmental considerations; renewable sources of electricity were not taxed. The second adjusted the taxes to favour efficient conventional power plants. The third increased the tax on petroleum. At the same time, income taxes were reduced proportionally so that the total tax burden remained constant.

The regional government of Balearic Islands (then held by an ecosocialist coalition) established an ecotax in 1999. The Balearic Island suffer a high human pressure from tourism, that at the same time provides the main source of income. The tax (€1.00 per person per day) would be paid by visitors staying at tourist resorts. This was criticized by the conservative opposition as contrary to business interests, and they abolished the tax in 2003 after seizing back the government.

A variety of ecotaxes (often called "severance taxes") have been enacted by various states in the United States. The Supreme Court of the United States held in *Commonwealth Edison Co. v. Montana*, 453 U.S. 609 (1981), that in the absence of federal law to the contrary, states may set ecotaxes as high as they wish without violating the Commerce Clause or the Supremacy Clause of the United States Constitution.

Registration Taxes

The Netherlands, Portugal, Canada, Spain and Finland have introduced differentiations into their car registration taxes to encourage car buyers to opt for the cleanest car models.

In the Netherlands, the new registration taxes, payable when a car is sold to its first buyer, can earn the owner of a hybrid a discount up to €6000. Spain reduced taxes for cars that produced less CO2 (some of which will be exempted), while the more consuming, like SPV and 4WD saw their taxes increased.

Austria has had a registration tax based on fuel consumption for several years.

Worldwide Implementation

United Kingdom: In 1993, the conservative government introduced the Fuel Price Escalator, featuring a small but steady increase of fuel taxes, as proposed by Weizsäcker and Jesinghaus in 1992. The FPE was stopped in 2000, following nationwide protests; while fuel was relatively cheap in 1993, fuel prices were then among the highest in Europe. Under the Blair-Brown government, despite Gordon Brown's promise to the contrary, green taxes as a percentage of overall taxes have actually fallen from 9.4% to 7.7%, according to calculations by Friends of the Earth.

In a 2006 proposal, the U.K.'s then-Environment Secretary David Miliband had the government in discussions on the use of various green taxes to reduce climate-changing pollution. Of the proposed taxes, which were meant to be revenue-neutral, Miliband stated: *"They're not fundamentally there to raise revenue."*

Miliband provided additional comments on their need, saying: *"Changing people's behaviour is only achieved by "market forces and price signals"*, and *"As our understanding of climate change increases, it is clear more needs to be done."*

Ukraine

Starting in 1999, the Ukrainian government has been collecting an ecological tax, officially known as Environmental Pollution Fee, which is collected from all polluting entities, whether it's one-time or ongoing pollution and regardless of whether the polluting act was legal or illegal at the time.

India

The Ministry of Environment and Forests, Government of India, asked Madras School of Economics, Chennai, to udertake a study of taxes on polluting inputs and outputs in 2001. Raja Chelliah, Paul Appasamy, U.Sankar and Rita Pandey (Academic Foundation, 2007, New Delhi) recommended eco taxes on coal, automobiles, chlorine, phosphate detergents, chemical pesticides, chemical fertilizers, lead acid batteries and plastics. The Finance Minister introduced a coal cess at the rate of Rs 50 per ton in 2010.

Environmental Tariff

An Environmental tariff, also known as a green tariff or eco-tariff, is an import or export tax placed on products being imported from, or also being sent to countries with substandard environmental pollution controls. They can be used as controls on global pollution and can also be considered as corrective measures against "environmental races to the bottom" and "eco-dumping".

International Trade vs. Environmental Degradation: There has been debate on the role that increased international trade has played in increasing pollution. While some maintain that increases in pollution which result in both local environmental degradation and a global *tragedy of the commons* are intimately linked to increases in international trade, others have argued that as citizens become more affluent they'll also advocate for cleaner environments. According to a World Bank paper:

> *"Since freer trade raises income, it directly contributes to increasing pollution levels via the scale effect. However,*

> *it thereby induces the composition (and) technique effects of increased income, both of which tend to reduce pollution levels".*

Early Tariff Implementation Proposal

Although the United States has in the past been accused of dragging its feet on implementing tough new anti-pollution measures, it was the originator of a legislative proposal suggesting an environmental tariff be applied against exporting countries whose exports gained significant cost advantages due to less stringent environmental regulations. The proposed legislation was tabled as the International Pollution Deterrence Act of 1991 and was introduced in its Senate in April of that year.

Proposed International Pollution Control Index

A notable feature of the proposed U.S. *International Pollution Deterrence Act* was the international pollution control index it cited within its Section 5, which read:

International Pollution Control Index

Section 8002 of the Solid Waste Disposal Act (42 U.S.C. 6982) is amended by adding the following new subsections at the end thereof:

> *'(t) The Administrator shall prepare, within one hundred and twenty days of the enactment of this section and yearly thereafter, a pollution control index for each of the top fifty countries identified by the Office of Trade and Investment of the Department of Commerce based on the value of exports to the United States from that country's attainment of pollution control standards in the areas of air, water, hazardous waste and solid waste as compared to the United States. The purpose of this index is to measure the level of compliance within each country with standards comparable to or greater than those in the United States. The Administrator shall analyze, in particular, the level of technology employed and actual costs incurred for pollution control in the major export sectors of each country in formulating the index.*

Agitation against Use of Environmental Tariffs

Environment tariffs were not implemented in the past, in part, because they were not sanctioned by multilateral trade regimes such as the World Trade Organisation and within the General Agreement on Tariffs and Trade (GATT), a fact which generated considerable criticism and calls for reform.

Additionally, many foreign factory owners in newly industrialized countries and underdeveloped countries saw the attempts to impose pollution controls on them as suspicious...

> *"...seeing it as a threat to their growth and fearing that developed countries would attempt to export their preferences for pollution control or to place 'environmental' tariffs on imports from countries with lower standards."*

Ecolabel

Eco-labels and Green Stickers are labelling systems for food and consumer products. Ecolabels are voluntary, but green stickers are mandated by law; for example, in North America major appliances and automobiles use Energy Star. They are a form of sustainability measurement directed at consumers, intended to make it easy to take environmental concerns into account when shopping. Some labels quantify pollution or energy consumption by way of index scores or units of measurement; others simply assert compliance with a set of practices or minimum requirements for sustainability or reduction of harm to the environment.

Ecolabelling systems exist for both food and consumer products. Both systems were started by NGOs, since then the European Union have developed legislation for conduct of ecolabelling and also have created their own ecolabels, one for food and one for consumer products. At least for food, the ecolabel is nearly identical with the common NGO definition of the rules for ecolabelling. Label trust is an issue for consumers because as manufacturers and manufacturing associations have set up "rubber stamp" labels to greenwash their products with fake ecolabels. High trust levels can be created when ecolabels apply for Governmental recognition as formal Certification Marks [recognised by logos or names with 'CTM', CM or 'CertTM']. Typically this means schemes approved as a Certification Mark, have had the Government Department responsible declare that the scheme has a standard and certifies that they are 'Competent to Certify'. The highest trust levels would be a government recognised certification mark that was also compliant with key ISO standards especially ISO 14024- Type 1 Ecolabels that undertake ISO 14040 compliant life cycle analysis as part of their assessment.

ISO Participation

The last few years have seen two key trends in the ecolabels space. There is an explosion in the numbers of different ecolabelling programs across the world and across business sectors and secondly the proliferation of umbrella labelling programs. The International Organisation for Standardization ISO has created standards for labelling practices within the ISO 14000 schema. ISO 14020 to 14025 series deals with environmental labels and declarations.

Environmental Governance

Consumer desires for sustainable consumption is driving the global marketplace with desire to regulate product production. The globalization of economies is shifting control of sustainability away from traditional command and control measures imposed by governments towards market governance which is a self-regulatory new environmental policy instrument, ecolabelling.

Eco-labelling standardization is a new form of regulation which is voluntary in nature, but impose upon large companies market forces in order to harmonize production of goods and services with stronger ecological practices. Recently, it has turned into a new form of non-state authority at both national and international levels. This idea of entrepreneurial democracy based on the success of the ISO 14000 standards on the management of environmental quality and the ISO 9000 standards on quality production control. Once an industry sector decides to get this certification, it has to provide evidences of documented proof of compliance required. In terms of ISO 14042 standard, it is obligatorily for all applicants to respect environmental legislation and related legislation; breaching of any laws may result in licensing suspension.

Sustainable Initiatives

During the UN Earth Summit Conference in 1992, an international consensus was generated to integrate environmental issues into manufacturing procedures. The idea was to manipulate consumption patterns in order to achieve sustainable development. The result of this is as follows.

Currently in the developed world: Eco-labels and green stickers have evolved to play a vital role. They provide a verifiable link between products and informed consumer wishes. This approach applies market pressure on industries to minimize their environmental impact; this is evidenced by growth in population of informed consumers. Marketing strategists are responding with Green Certifications and its abuse, Greenwashing. Currently in the developing world: First consumers became concerned about the quality, safety and environmental sustainability of food and supported demand for green foods, then focused on the environmental effects of agriculture and globalization of food production, which lead to the exposure of globally controlled food regimes. Consumer advocate groups responded with a call for [Alternative Food Networks]. This gives a new dimension to consumer demands and corporate competitiveness. Australian Consumer Association CHOICE confronted corporate interests with their concerns about growing interests in green consumption, food production, use of pesticides, organic production, and genetic modification, etc...

History

Green Stickers on consumer goods have been evolving since the 1970s. The main drivers have been energy and fuel consumption. These stickers first started appearing on major appliances after government agencies in the United States and Canada legislated their requirement. Manufacturers are also required to meet minimum standards of energy use. The automobile industry in North America is required to meet a minimum emissions standard. This led to fuel efficiency labels being placed on new automobiles sold. The major appliance manufactures were required to use standard testing practices and place clear labels on products. The International Organisation for Standardization has developed standards for addressing environmental labelling with the ISO 14000 family which grew out of ISO's commitment to support the objective of sustainable development discussed at the United Nations Conference on Environment and Development, in Rio de Janeiro, in 1992.

Green Labelling worldwide is moving beyond traditional country borders. Most of these initiatives are voluntary Eco-labels, however there is an initiative under way in North America to broaden the scope of Green Stickers to include other consumer goods.

Programs by Region

Governments of many countries have environmental protection agencies. These agencies are mandated watchdogs of industry and regulate releasing chemical pollution into the environment. Some of them administer labelling standards; other set minimum requirements for manufacturers.

Canada: The Office of Energy Efficiency (OEE) run by the Department of Natural Resources Canada regulates both the automobile and appliance manufacturers. EnerGuide label for vehicles found on all new passenger cars, light-duty vans, pickup trucks and special purpose vehicles not exceeding a gross vehicle weight of 3855 kg (8500 lb). The label shows the city and highway fuel consumption ratings and an estimated annual fuel cost for that particular vehicle.

Federal law in Canada, under Canada's Energy Efficiency Regulations, requires that the EnerGuide label be placed on all new electrical appliances manufactured in or imported into Canada and that the label indicate the amount of electricity used by that appliance. This information is determined by standardized test procedures. A third-party agency verifies that an appliance meets Canada's minimum energy performance levels.

United States: All major home appliances must meet the Appliance Standards Program set by the US Department of Energy (DOE) on cooperation with the US Federal Trade Commission. Manufacturers must use standard test procedures developed by DOE to prove the energy use and efficiency of their products. Test results are printed on yellow EnergyGuide label, which manufacturers are required to display on many appliances. This label estimates how much energy the appliance uses, compares energy use of similar products, and lists approximate annual operating costs. Appliances that meet strict energy efficiency criteria set by the U.S. Environmental Protection Agency are eligible for the blue Energy Star label. The Energy Star label is also available on energy-efficient televisions, computers, audio visual equipment and electronics, office equipment, heating and cooling equipment, and many more products. Energy Star is also available on energy efficient homes and buildings in the United States. American automobile manufacturers are required to use certified U.S. Environmental Protection Agency fuel economy test results and cannot use any other fuel mileage results to advertise vehicle fuel efficiency. The state of California has green sticker license plates issued to OHVs is introducing green stickers for all new automobiles in 2009.

European Union: The EU Ecolabel was established in 1992 by the European Commission. The EU Ecolabel helps to identify products and services that have a reduced environmental impact throughout their life cycle. Recognised throughout Europe, EU Ecolabel is a voluntary label promoting environmental excellence which can be trusted. It is the only pan-European Type I official ecolabel. The EU Ecolabel is awarded according to ecological criteria agreed on by experts, industry, consumer organisations and environmental NGOs and verified by independent third parties. The implementation of the EU Ecolabel is set through the Regulation (EC) No 66/2010 of the European Parliament and of the Council.

Northern Europe: The Nordic swan is the official ecolabel in Nordic countries. It uses a system of standards, applications for licenses, and independent verification.

ASEAN: In Asia ASEAN is moving towards adopting the ISO's TC 207 environmental management system. Anyone can contribute verifiable sources substantiating it's adoption and implementation by member countries as this information is not easily accessible.

Australasia: A number of ecolabels operate in Australia and New Zealand mostly as separate schemes operating in one country only. Global GreenTag operates and is recognised in both countries as is GECA whereas GECNZ operates only within NZ. All 3 ecolabels are ISO 14024 compliant. GreenTag is also an Australian Competition and Consumer Commission (ACCC) approved Certification Mark.

Seafood

There are a plethora of sustainable seafood ecolabels, many conservationists feel that the increasing number of labels is further confusing consumers in regard to what seafood is sustainable. As of 2010, ecolabels that can be found on seafood include Marine Stewardship Council, Friend of the Sea, KRAV (Sweden), Naturland (Germany), Thai Quality Shrimp, Global Aquaculture Alliance's Best Aquaculture Practices standard, Label Rouge (France), among still others, and the Aquaculture Stewardship Council (ASC) is in development. Seafood is also labelled "organic" but USDA standards for organic seafood are still in development.

There are a variety of dolphin safe labels, asserting that tuna is caught in a manner that does not harm dolphins.

Marine Stewardship Council

The Marine Stewardship Council (MSC) is an independent non-profit organisation which sets a standard for sustainable fishing. Fisheries that wish to demonstrate they are well managed and sustainable against the science-based MSC standard are assessed by a team of experts who are independent of both the fishery and the MSC. Seafood products can display the blue MSC ecolabel only if that seafood can be traced back to a fishery that has been certified against the MSC standard.

The MSC was founded in 1997 by the World Wide Fund for Nature and Unilever, and became fully independent in 1999. The MSC standard is consistent with the 'Guidelines for the Eco-labelling of Fish and Fishery Products from Marine Wild Capture Fisheries' adopted by the UN Food and Agriculture Organisation (FAO) in 2005.

As of February 2012, there are over 13,000 seafood products available with the MSC ecolabel, sold in 74 countries around the world. At present uptake of MSC labelled products in the UK is mixed; some of the more ethical supermarkets such as Sainsbury's source a significant number of MSC labelled seafood products, whilst Tesco lags behind.

Friend of the Sea

The Friend of the Sea is an NGO founded in December 2006 to conserve marine habitat and resources by means of market incentives and specific conservation projects. It is the only scheme which certifies as sustainable, with the same seal of approval, both farmed and wild-caught products. Certified products from all continents include anchovies, caviar, clams, cuttlefish, halibut, kingfish, mackerel, mulloway, mussels, prawns, salmon, seabass, seabream, shrimps, squid, sturgeon, trout, tuna, turbot. Fishmeal, fishfeed and Omega-3 Fish oil have also been certified. Sustainable seafood, products and their origins are audited onsite by international certification bodies, against Friend of the Sea criteria. Certification bodies currently auditing against Friend of the Sea criteria are Aqa, Bureau Veritas, IFQC and SGS .

Sustainable Timber

Ecolabels indicating that timber in wood-based products originates from forests that are sustainably managed in compliance with internationally recognised standards include at a global level labels by the Programme for the Endorsement of Forest Certification and the Forest Stewardship Council, at regional and national levels labels by the Sustainable Forestry Initiative and the Malaysian Timber Certification System (both internationally recognised by PEFC) or the Lembaga Ekolabel Indonesia (LEI).

The timber is tracked through the supply chain to the end product, so that consumers can choose to buy sustainably harvested wood over alternatives that may be contributing to deforestation worldwide.

Energy Labels

Many consumer appliances have labels indicating whether or not they are energy efficient compared to similar products. Common labels include yellow EnergyGuide tags found in North America as part of the Energy Star program, European Union energy labels, and the Energy Saving Trust Recommended logo administrated by the Energy Saving Trust in the United Kingdom. These labels document how much energy an appliance consumes while being used; energy input labelling documents how much energy was used to *manufacture* the product, an additional consideration in the full life cycle energy use of product.

Carbon emission labels are an alternative methodology for certification, examining impact on greenhouse gas emissions rather than direct energy use.

Chapter 3

Preempting Future Regulation

Toxic Waste

Toxic waste is waste material that can cause death, injury or birth defects to living creatures. It spreads quite easily and can contaminate lakes, rivers, and the atmosphere. The term is often used interchangeably with "hazardous waste", or discarded material that can pose a long-term risk to health or environment.

Hazardous wastes are poisonous byproducts of manufacturing, farming, city septic systems, construction, automotive garages, laboratories, hospitals and other industries. The waste may be liquid, solid, or sludge and contain chemicals, heavy metals, radiation, dangerous pathogens, or other toxins. Even households generate hazardous waste from items such as batteries, used computer equipment, and leftover paints or pesticides.

In the United States, the Environmental Protection Agency (EPA) and the state departments oversee the rules that regulate hazardous waste. The EPA requires that toxic waste be handled with special precautions and be disposed of in designated facilities around the country. Also, many cities in the United States have collection days where household toxic waste is gathered. Some materials that may not be accepted at regular landfills are ammunition, commercially generated waste, explosives/shock sensitive items, hypodermic needles/ syringes, medical waste, radioactive materials, and smoke detectors.

Health Effects

Toxic wastes often contain carcinogens, and exposure to these by some route, such as leakage or evaporation from the storage, causes cancer to appear at increased frequency in exposed individuals. For example, a cluster of the rare blood cancer polycythemia vera was found around a toxic waste dump site in northeast Pennsylvania in 2008.

The Human & Ecological Risk Assessment Journal conducted a study which focused on the health of individuals living near municipal landfills to see if it would be as harmful as living near hazardous landfills. They conducted a 7-year study that specifically tested for 18 types of cancers to see if the participants had higher rates than those that don't live around landfills. They conducted this study in western Massachusetts within a 1-mile radius of the North Hampton Regional Landfill.

People encounter these toxins buried in the ground, in stream runoff, in groundwater that supplies drinking water, or in floodwaters, as happened after Hurricane Katrina. Some toxins, such as mercury, persist in the environment and accumulate. As a result of the bioaccumulation of mercury in both freshwater and marine ecosystems, predatory fish are a significant source of mercury in human and animal diets.

Handling and Disposal

Disposal is the placement of waste into or on the land. Disposal facilities are usually designed to permanently contain the waste and prevent the release of harmful pollutants to the environment. The most common hazardous waste disposal practice is placement in a land disposal unit such as a landfill, surface impoundment, waste pile, land treatment unit, or injection well. Land disposal is subject to requirements under EPA's Land Disposal Restrictions Program.

Organic wastes can be destroyed by incineration at high temperatures; however, if the waste contains heavy metals or radioactive isotopes, these must be separated and stored, as they cannot be destroyed. The method of storage will seek to immobilize the toxic components of the waste, possibly through storage in sealed containers, inclusion in a stable medium such as glass or a cement mixture, or burial under an impermeable clay cap. Waste transporters and waste facilities may charge fees; consequently, improper methods of disposal may be used to avoid paying these fees. Where the handling of toxic waste is regulated, the improper disposal of toxic waste may be punishable by fines or prison terms. Burial sites for toxic waste and other contaminated brownfield land may eventually be used as greenspace or redeveloped for commercial or industrial use.

History of US Toxic Waste Regulation

Resource Conservation and Recovery Act (RCRA) Enforcement,. The Act gives the United States Environmental Protection Agency the authority to control the generation, transportation, treatment, storage, and disposal of hazardous waste The Resource Conservation and Recovery Act was followed by the Toxic Substances Control Act, which took effect on January 1, 1977. The Act authorized the EPA to secure information on all new and existing chemical substances, as well as to control any substances that were determined to cause unreasonable risk to public health or the environment.

The Superfund Act is another act administered by the EPA. It contains rules about cleaning up toxic waste that was dumped illegally.

There has been a long ongoing battle between communities and environmentalists versus governments and corporations about how strict and how fairly the regulations and laws are written and enforced. That battle began in North Carolina in the late summer of 1979, as EPA's TSCA regulations were being implemented. In North Carolina, 31,000 gallons of PCB-contaminated oil were deliberately dripped in a 3-foot swath along some 240 miles of rural Piedmont highways, creating the largest PCB spills in American history and a public health crisis that would have repercussions for generations to come. The PCB-contaminated material was eventually collected and buried in a landfill in Warren County, but citizens' opposition, including large public demonstrations, exposed the dangers of toxic waste, the fallibility of landfills then in use, and EPA regulations allowing landfills to be built on marginal, but politically acceptable sites.

Warren County citizens argued that the toxic waste landfill regulations were based on the fundamental assumption that the EPA's conceptual dry-tomb landfill would contain the toxic waste. This assumption informed the siting of toxic waste landfills and waivers to regulations that were included in EPA's *Federal Register*. For example, in 1978, the base of a major toxic waste landfill could be no closer than five feet from ground water, but this regulation and others could be waived. The waiver to the regulation concerning the distance between the base of a toxic waste landfill and groundwater allowed the base to be only a foot above ground water if the owner/operator of the facility could demonstrate to the EPA regional administrator that a leachate collection system could be installed and that there would be no hydraulic connection between the base of the landfill and groundwater. Citizens argued that the waivers to the siting regulations were discriminatory mechanisms facilitating the shift from scientific to political considerations concerning the siting decision and that in the South this would mean a discriminatory proliferation of dangerous waste management facilities in poor black and other minority communities. They also argued that the scientific consensus was that permanent containment could not be assured. As resistance to the siting of the PCB landfill in Warren County continued and studies revealed that EPA dry-tomb landfills were failing, EPA stated in its *Federal Register* that all landfills would eventually leak and should only be used as a stopgap measure.

Years of research and empirical knowledge of the failures of the Warren County PCB landfill led citizens of Warren County to conclude that the EPA's dry-tomb landfill design and regulations governing the disposal of toxic and hazardous waste were not based on sound science and adequate technology. Citizens concluded also that North Carolina's *1981 Waste Management Act* was scientifically and constitutionally unacceptable because it authorized the siting of toxic, hazardous and nuclear waste facilities prior to public hearings, preempted local authority over the siting of the facilities, and authorized the use of force if needed.

In the aftermath of the Warren County protests, the 1984 Federal Hazardous and Solid Waste Amendments to the Resource Conservation and Recovery Act focused on waste minimization and phasing out land disposal of hazardous waste as well as corrective action for releases of hazardous materials. Other measures included in the 1984 amendments included increased enforcement authority for EPA, more stringent hazardous waste management standards, and a comprehensive underground storage tank program.

The disposal of toxic waste continues to be a source of conflict in the U.S. Due to the hazards associated with toxic waste handling and disposal, communities often resist the siting of toxic waste landfills and other waste management facilities; however, determining where and how to dispose of waste is a necessary part of economic and environmental policy-making.

Mapping of Toxic Waste in the United States

TOXMAP is a Geographic Information System (GIS) from the Division of Specialised Information Services of the United States National Library of Medicine (NLM) that uses maps of the United States to help users visually explore data from the United States Environmental Protection Agency's (EPA) Superfund and Toxics Release Inventory programs. TOXMAP is a resource funded by the US

Federal Government. TOXMAP's chemical and environmental health information is taken from NLM's Toxicology Data Network (TOXNET) and PubMed, and from other authoritative sources.

Hazardous Waste

Hazardous waste is waste that poses substantial or potential threats to public health or the environment. In the United States, the treatment, storage and disposal of hazardous waste is regulated under the Resource Conservation and Recovery Act (RCRA). Hazardous wastes are defined under RCRA in 40 CFR 261 where they are divided into two major categories: characteristic wastes and listed wastes.

- Characteristic hazardous wastes are materials that are known or tested to exhibit one or more of the following four hazardous traits:
  - ignitability (i.e., flammable)
  - reactivity
  - corrosivity
  - toxicity
- Listed hazardous wastes are materials specifically listed by regulatory authorities as a hazardous waste which are from non-specific sources, specific sources, or discarded chemical products.

The requirements of RCRA apply to all the companies that generate hazardous waste as well as those companies that store or dispose of hazardous waste in the United States. Many types of businesses generate hazardous waste. For example, dry cleaners, automobile repair shops, hospitals, exterminators, and photo processing centres may all generate hazardous waste. Some hazardous waste generators are larger companies such as chemical manufacturers, electroplating companies, and oil refineries.

These wastes may be found in different physical states such as gaseous, liquids, or solids. A hazardous waste is a special type of waste because it cannot be disposed of by common means like other by-products of our everyday lives. Depending on the physical state of the waste, treatment and solidification processes might be required.

Worldwide, The United Nations Environmental Programme (UNEP) estimated that more than 400 million tons of hazardous wastes are produced universally each year, mostly by industrialized countries (schmit, 1999). About 1- percent of this total is shipped across international boundaries, with the majority of the transfers occurring between countries in the Organisation for the Economic Cooperation and Development(OECD) (Krueger, 1999). Some of the reasons for industrialized countries to ship the hazardous waste to industrializing countries for disposal are the rising cost of disposing hazardous waste in the home country.

Regulatory History

Resource Conservation and Recovery Act (RCRA): Hazardous waste is a waste with properties that make it dangerous or potentially harmful to human health or the environment. Hazardous wastes can be liquids, solids, contained gases, or sludges. They can be the by-products of manufacturing processes or simply discarded commercial products, like cleaning fluids or pesticides. In regulatory terms, a RCRA hazardous waste is a waste that appears on one of the four hazardous wastes lists (F-list, K-list, P-list, or U-list), or exhibits at least one of four characteristics-ignitability, corrosivity, reactivity, or toxicity. Hazardous waste is regulated under the Resource Conservation and Recovery Act (RCRA) Subtitle C.

By definition, EPA determined that some specific wastes are hazardous. These wastes are incorporated into lists published by the Agency. These lists are organised into three categories: F-list (non-specific source wastes) found in the regulations at 40 CFR §261.31, K-list (source-specific wastes) found in the regulations at 40 CFR §261.32, and P-list and the U-list (discarded commercial chemical products) found in the regulations at 40 CFR §261.33.

RCRA's record keeping system helps to track the life cycle of hazardous waste and reduces the amount of hazardous waste illegally disposed.

Comprehensive Environmental Response, Compensation, and Liability Act

The Comprehensive Environmental Response, Compensation, and Liability Act (CERCLA), was enacted in 1980. The primary contribution of CERCLA was to create a "Superfund" and provided for the clean-up and remediation of closed and abandoned hazardous waste sites. CERCLA addresses historic releases of hazardous materials, but does not specifically manage hazardous wastes.

Hazardous Wastes in the United States of America

A U.S. facility that treats, stores or disposes of hazardous waste must obtain a permit for doing so under the Resource Conservation and Recovery Act. Generators of and transporters of hazardous waste must meet specific requirements for handling, managing, and tracking waste. Through the RCRA, Congress directed the United States Environmental Protection Agency (EPA) to create regulations to manage hazardous waste. Under this mandate, the EPA developed strict requirements for all aspects of hazardous waste management including the treatment, storage, and disposal of hazardous waste. In addition to these federal requirements, states may develop more stringent requirements that are broader in scope than the federal regulations. Furthermore, RCRA allows states to develop regulatory programs that are at least as stringent as RCRA and, after review by EPA, the states may take over responsibility for the implementation of the requirements under RCRA. Most states take advantage of this authority, implementing their own hazardous waste programs that are at least as stringent, and in some cases are more stringent than the federal program.

Hazardous Waste Mapping Systems

The US government provides several tools for mapping hazardous wastes to particular locations. These tools also allow the user to view additional information.

- TOXMAP is a Geographic Information System (GIS) from the Division of Specialised Information Services [3] of the United States National Library of Medicine (NLM) that uses maps of the United States to help users visually explore data from the United States Environmental Protection Agency's (EPA) Toxics Release Inventory and Superfund Basic Research Programs. TOXMAP is a resource funded by the US Federal Government. TOXMAP's chemical and environmental health information is taken from NLM's Toxicology Data Network (TOXNET) [4] and PubMed, and from other authoritative sources.
- The US Environmental Protection Agency (EPA) "Where You Live" allows users to select a region from a map to find information about Superfund sites in that region.

Universal Wastes

Universal wastes are special category of hazardous wastes that (in the U.S.):

- generally pose a lower threat relative to other hazardous wastes
- are ubiquitous and produced in very large quantities by a large number of generators.

Some of the most common "universal wastes" are: fluorescent light bulbs, some speciality batteries (e.g. lithium or lead containing batteries), cathode ray tubes, and mercury-containing devices. Universal wastes are subject to somewhat less stringent regulatory requirements and small quantity generators of universal wastes may be classified as "conditionally exempt small quantity generators" (CESQGs) which releases them from some of the regulatory requirements for the handling and storage hazardous wastes.

Final Disposal of Hazardous Waste

Historically, some hazardous wastes were disposed of in regular landfills. This resulted in unfavourable amounts of hazardous materials seeping into the ground. These chemicals eventually entered natural hydrologic systems. Many landfills now require countermeasures against groundwater contamination, an example being installing a barrier along the foundation of the landfill to contain the hazardous substances that may remain in the disposed waste. Currently, hazardous wastes must often be stabilized and solidified in order to enter a landfill and many hazardous wastes undergo different treatments in order to stabilize and dispose of them. Most flammable materials can be recycled, used as industrial fuel. Some materials with hazardous constituents can be recycled, lead acid batteries are one example.

Recycling

Many hazardous wastes can be recycled into new products. Examples might include lead-acid batteries or electronic circuit boards where the heavy metals these types of ashes go though the proper treatment, they could bind to other pollutants and convert them into easier-to- dispose solids, or they could be used as pavement filling. Such treatments reduce the level of threat of harmful chemicals, like fly and bottom ash, while also recycling the safe product.

Portland Cement

Another commonly used treatment is cement based solidification and stabilization. Cement is used because it can treat a range of hazardous wastes by improving physical characteristics and decreasing the toxicity and transmission of contaminants. The cement produced is categorized into 5 different divisions, depending on its strength and components. This process of converting sludge into cement might include the addition of pH adjustment agents, phosphates, or sulfur reagents to reduce the settling or curing time, increase the compressive strength, or reduce the leach ability of contaminants.

Incineration, Destruction and Waste-to-Energy

A HW may be "destroyed" for example by incinerating it at a high temperature. Flammable wastes can sometimes be burned as energy sources. For example many cement kilns burn HWs like used oils or solvents. Today incineration treatments not only reduce the amount of hazardous waste, but also they also generate energy throughout the gases released in the process. It is known that this particular waste treatment releases toxic gases produced by the combustion of byproduct or other materials and this can affect the environment. However, current technology has developed more efficient incinerator units that control these emissions to a point that this treatment is considered a more beneficial option. There are different types of incinerators and they vary depending on the characteristics of the waste. Starved air incineration is another method used to treat hazardous wastes. Just like in common incineration, burning occurs, however controlling the amount of oxygen allowed proves to be significant to reduce the amount of harmful byproducts produced. Starved Air Incineration is an improvement of the traditional incinerators in terms of air pollution. Using this technology it is possible to control the combustion rate of the waste and therefore reduce the air pollutants produced in the process.

Hazardous Waste Landfill (Sequestering, Isolation, etc.)

A HW may be sequestered in a HW landfill or permanent disposal facility. "In terms of hazardous waste, a landfill is defined as a disposal facility or part of a facility where hazardous waste is placed or on land and which is not a pile, a land treatment facility, a surface impoundment, an underground injection well, a salt dome formation, a salt bed formation, an underground mine, a cave, or a corrective action management unit (40 CFR 260.10)."

Pyrolysis

Some hazardous waste types may be eliminated using pyrolysis in an ultra high temperature electrical arc, in inert conditions to avoid combustion. This treatment method may be preferable to high temperature incineration in some circumstances such as in the destruction of concentrated organic waste types, including PCBs, pesticides and other persistent organic pollutants.

Chemical Waste

Chemical waste is a waste that is made from harmful chemicals (mostly produced by large factories). Chemical waste may fall under regulations such as COSHH in the United Kingdom, or the Clean Water Act and Resource Conservation and Recovery Act in the United States. In the U.S., the Environmental Protection Agency (EPA) and the Occupational Safety and Health Administration (OSHA), as well as state and local regulations also regulate chemical use and disposal. Chemical waste may or may not be classed as hazardous waste.

Laboratory

In the laboratory, chemical wastes are usually segregated on-site into appropriate waste carboys, and disposed by a specialist contractor in order to meet safety, health, and legislative requirements. Waste organic solvents are separated into chlorinated and non-chlorinated solvent waste. Chlorinated solvent waste is usually incinerated at high temperature to minimize the formation of dioxins. Non-chlorinated solvent waste can be burned for energy recovery. Innocuous aqueous waste (such as solutions of sodium chloride) may be poured down the sink; aqueous waste containing toxic compounds are collected separately.

Waste elemental mercury, spent acids and bases may be collected separately for recycling. Broken glassware are usually collected in plastic-lined cardboard boxes for landfilling. Due to contamination, they are usually not suitable for recycling. Similarly, used hypodermic needles are collected as sharps and are incinerated as medical waste.

Mapping of Chemical Waste in the United States

TOXMAP is a Geographic Information System (GIS) from the Division of Specialised Information Services of the United States National Library of Medicine (NLM) that uses maps of the United States to help users visually explore data from the United States Environmental Protection Agency's (EPA) Toxics Release Inventory and Superfund Basic Research Programs. TOXMAP is a resource funded by the US Federal Government. TOXMAP's chemical and environmental health information is taken from NLM's Toxicology Data Network (TOXNET) and PubMed, and from other authoritative sources.

Construction Waste

Construction waste consists of unwanted material produced directly or incidentally by the construction or industries. This includes building materials such as insulation, nails, electrical wiring, and rebar, as well as waste originating from site preparation such as dredging materials, tree stumps, and rubble. Construction waste may contain lead, asbestos, or other hazardous substances.

Much building waste is made up of materials such as bricks, concrete and wood damaged or unused for various reasons during construction. Observational research has shown that this can be as high as 10 to 15% of the materials that go into a building, a much higher percentage than the 2.5-5% usually assumed by quantity surveyors and the construction industry. Since considerable variability exists between construction sites, there is much opportunity for reducing this waste.

Certain components of construction waste such as plasterboard are hazardous once landfilled. Plasterboard is broken down in landfill conditions releasing hydrogen sulfide, a toxic gas. There is the potential to recycle many elements of construction waste. Often roll-off containers are used to transport the waste. Rubble can be crushed and reused in construction projects. Waste wood can also be recovered and recycled.

Government or local authorities often make rules about how much waste should be sorted before it is hauled away to landfills or other waste treatment facilities. Some hazardous materials may not be moved, before the authorities have ascertained that safety guidelines and restrictions have been followed. Among their concerns would be the proper handling and disposal of such toxic elements as lead, asbestos or radioactive materials.

In Kuwait, The Ministry of Finance granted a BOT (Build Operate and Transfer) contract to the Environmental Preservation Industries Company to build the first construction waste recycle plant in the middle east with a daily production of 2,500 tonnes. The government pays tipping fee to the company for waste removal as an incentive to relieve the stress on the environment. The construction waste is recycled to several sizes of gravels that can be reused in construction beside the screened sand can be used in ancillary construction uses.

Industrial Waste

Industrial waste is the waste produced by industrial activity which includes any material that is rendered useless during a manufacturing process such as that of factories, mills and mining operations or excavation. It has existed since the outset of the industrial revolution. Some examples of industrial waste are chemical solvents, paints, sand paper, paper products, industrial by-products, metals, and radioactive wastes.

Toxic waste, chemical waste, industrial solid waste and municipal solid waste are designations of industrial waste. Sewage treatment plants can treat some industrial wastes, i.e. those consisting of conventional pollutants such as biochemical oxygen demand (BOD). Industrial wastes containing toxic pollutants require specialised treatment systems.

Industrial Waste Management in Thailand

In Thailand the roles in Municipal solid waste (MSW) management and Industrial waste management is organised by the Royal Thai Government which is then divided into central government, regional government, and local government. Each government is responsible for different tasks such as the central government is responsible to stimulate regulation, policies, and standard, the regional government is to be responsible for coordinated between central and local government, and the local government is responsible for waste management in their governed area. However, the local government does not dispose of the waste by their own but instead hired the private company that has been granted the right from the Pollution Control Department (PCD) in Thailand. These companies are namely Bangpoo Industrial Waste Management Centre, General Environmental Conservation Public Company Limited (GENCO), SGS Thailand, Waste Management Siam LTD (WMS), and Better World Green Public Company Limited (BGW) . These companies will be responsible for the waste they have received from their customers before releasing to the environment, buried, and reused as energy.

For example, BGW has provided services range from contacting the industries, analyze the waste in the lab so that the waste is treated safely. After the analysis of waste, if they are able to manage the waste safely, BGW will provide the truck for transportation of waste. Lastly, all of the wastes will be classified at BGW. After the classification, the industrial wastes which are hazardous will be dispose or put into the landfill for hazardous waste, and the non-hazardous waste will be put into a separate landfill . On the other hand, the waste waster is being treated on the operated chemical and biological waste water treatment. Some of the large contaminated waste including solid and liquid waste will be burnt in the incinerator with high-technology that is acceptable that it can ensure that incomplete combustion will not occur. BGW also developed a way to reduce waste materials by using solid and liquid blending that is used to make material and fuel substitutes respectively. Furthermore, BGW also provide the waste management consultant for their customer to discuss about the method of waste management and waste disposal, transportation and collection system, management of waste water, waste manifest system, and public activities.

Radioactive Waste

Radioactive wastes are wastes that contain radioactive material. Radioactive wastes are usually by-products of nuclear power generation and other applications of nuclear fission or nuclear technology, such as research and medicine. Radioactive waste is hazardous to most forms of life and the environment, and is regulated by government agencies in order to protect human health and the environment.

Radioactivity naturally decays over time, so radioactive waste has to be isolated and confined in appropriate disposal facilities for a sufficient period of time until it no longer poses a hazard. The period of time waste must be stored depends on the type of waste and radioactive isotopes. It can range from a few days for very short-lived isotopes to millions of years if one chooses to waste the unspent portions of "spent nuclear fuel". Current major approaches to managing radioactive waste have been segregation and storage for short-lived waste, near-surface disposal for low and some intermediate level waste, and deep burial or partitioning / transmutation for the high-level waste.

A summary of the amounts of radioactive waste and management approaches for most developed countries are presented and reviewed periodically as part of the International Atomic Energy Agency (IAEA) Joint Convention on the Safety of Spent Fuel Management and on the Safety of Radioactive Waste Management.

Nature and Significance of Radioactive Waste

Radioactive waste typically comprises a number of radioisotopes: unstable configurations of elements that decay, emitting ionizing radiation which can be harmful to humans and the environment. Those isotopes emit different types and levels of radiation, which last for different periods of time.

Physics

The radioactivity of all nuclear waste diminishes with time. All radioisotopes contained in the waste have a half-life—the time it takes for any radionuclide to lose half of its radioactivity—and eventually all radioactive waste decays into non-radioactive elements (i.e., stable isotopes). Certain radioactive elements (such as plutonium-239) in "spent" fuel will remain hazardous to humans and other creatures for hundreds or thousands of years. Other radioisotopes remain radioactive for millions of years (though most of these products have so little activity as a result of their long half-lives that their radiation is lost in the background level). Thus, these wastes must be shielded for centuries and isolated from the living environment for millennia. Since radioactive decay follows the half-life rule, the rate of decay is inversely proportional to the duration of decay. In other words, the radiation from a long-lived isotope like iodine-129 will be much less intense than that of a short-lived isotope like iodine-131. The two tables show some of the major radioisotopes, their half-lives, and their radiation yield as a proportion of the yield of fission of uranium-235.

The energy and the type of the ionizing radiation emitted by a radioactive substance are also important factors in determining its threat to humans. The chemical properties of the radioactive element will determine how mobile the substance is and how likely it is to spread into the environment and contaminate humans. This is further complicated by the fact that many radioisotopes do not decay immediately to a stable state but rather to radioactive decay products within a decay chain before ultimately reaching a stable state.

Legend for superscript symbols¡ has thermal neutron capture cross section in the range of 8–50 barns*ƒ* fissilem metastable isomer[1] naturally occurring radioactive material (NORM)þ neutron poison (thermal neutron capture cross section greater than 3k barns)† range 4a–97a: Medium-lived fission product‡ over 200ka: Long-lived fission product

Pharmacokinetics

Exposure to high levels of radioactive waste may cause serious harm or death. Treatment of an adult animal with radiation or some other mutation-causing effect, such as a cytotoxic anti-cancer drug, may cause cancer in the animal. In humans it has been calculated that a 5 sievert dose is usually fatal, and the lifetime risk of dying from radiation-induced cancer from a single dose of 0.1 sievert is 0.8%, increasing by the same amount for each additional 0.1 sievert increment of dosage. Ionizing radiation causes deletions in chromosomes. If a developing organism such as an unborn child is irradiated, it is possible a birth defect may be induced, but it is unlikely this defect will be in a gamete or a gamete-forming cell. The incidence of radiation-induced mutations in humans is small, as in most mammals, because of natural cellular-repair mechanisms, many just now coming to light. These mechanisms range from DNA, mRNA and protein repair, to internal lysosomic digestion of defective proteins, and even induced cell suicide—apoptosis.

Depending on the decay mode and the pharmacokinetics of an element (how the body processes it and how quickly), the threat due to exposure to a given activity of a radioisotope will differ. For instance iodine-131 is a short-lived beta and gamma emitter, but because it concentrates in the thyroid gland, it is more able to cause injury than caesium-137 which, being water soluble, is rapidly excreted in urine. In a similar way, the alpha emitting actinides and radium are considered very harmful as they tend to have long biological half-lives and their radiation has a high relative biological effectiveness, making it far more damaging to tissues per amount of energy deposited. Because of such differences, the rules determining biological injury differ widely according to the radioisotope, time of exposure and sometimes also the nature of the chemical compound which contains the radioisotope.

Sources of Waste

Radioactive waste comes from a number of sources. The majority of waste originates from the nuclear fuel cycle and nuclear weapons reprocessing. Other sources include medical and industrial wastes, as well as naturally occurring radioactive materials (NORM) that can be concentrated as a result of the processing or consumption of coal, oil and gas, and some minerals, as discussed below.

Front End

Waste from the front end of the nuclear fuel cycle is usually alpha-emitting waste from the extraction of uranium. It often contains radium and its decay products.

Uranium dioxide (UO_2) concentrate from mining is not very radioactive – only a thousand or so times as radioactive as the granite used in buildings. It is refined from yellowcake (U_3O_8), then converted to uranium hexafluoride gas (UF_6). As a gas, it undergoes enrichment to increase the U-235 content from 0.7% to about 4.4% (LEU). It is then turned into a hard ceramic oxide (UO_2) for assembly as reactor fuel elements.

The main by-product of enrichment is depleted uranium (DU), principally the U-238 isotope, with a U-235 content of ~0.3%. It is stored, either as UF_6 or as U_3O_8. Some is used in applications where its extremely high density makes it valuable such as anti-tank shells, even sailboat keels on at least one occasion. It is also used with plutonium for making mixed oxide fuel (MOX) and to dilute, or downblend, highly enriched uranium from weapons stockpiles which is now being redirected to become reactor fuel.

Back End

The back end of the nuclear fuel cycle, mostly spent fuel rods, contains fission products that emit beta and gamma radiation, and actinides that emit alpha particles, such as uranium-234, neptunium-237, plutonium-238 and americium-241, and even sometimes some neutron emitters such as californium (Cf). These isotopes are formed in nuclear reactors.

It is important to distinguish the processing of uranium to make fuel from the reprocessing of used fuel. Used fuel contains the highly radioactive products of fission. Many of these are neutron absorbers, called neutron poisons in this context. These eventually build up to a level where they absorb so many neutrons that the chain reaction stops, even with the control rods completely removed. At that point the fuel has to be replaced in the reactor with fresh fuel, even though there is still a substantial quantity of uranium-235 and plutonium present. In the United States, this used fuel is stored, while in countries such as Russia, the United Kingdom, France, Japan and India, the fuel is reprocessed to remove the fission products, and the fuel can then be reused. This reprocessing involves handling highly radioactive materials, and the fission products removed from the fuel are a concentrated form of high-level waste as are the chemicals used in the process. While these countries reprocess the fuel carrying out single plutonium cycles, India is the only country known to be planning multiple plutonium recycling schemes.

Fuel Composition and Long Term Radioactivity

Long-lived radioactive waste from the back end of the fuel cycle is especially relevant when designing a complete waste management plan for spent nuclear fuel (SNF). When looking at long term radioactive decay, the actinides in the SNF have a significant influence due to their characteristically long half-lives. Depending on what a nuclear reactor is fuelled with, the actinide composition in the SNF will be different.

An example of this effect is the use of nuclear fuels with thorium. Th-232 is a fertile material that can undergo a neutron capture reaction and two beta minus decays, resulting in the production of fissile U-233. The SNF of a cycle with thorium will contain U-233. Its radioactive decay will strongly influence the long-term activity curve of the SNF around 1 million years. A comparison of the activity associated to U-233 for three different SNF types can be seen in the figure on the top right.

The burnt fuels are thorium with reactor-grade plutonium (RGPu), thorium with weapons-grade plutonium (WGPu) and Mixed Oxide fuel (MOX). For RGPu and WGPu, the initial amount of U-233 and its decay around 1 million years can be seen. This has an effect in the total activity curve of the three fuel types. The absence of U-233 and its daughter products in the MOX fuel results in a lower activity in region 3 of the figure on the bottom right, whereas for RGPu and WGPu the curve is maintained higher due to the presence of U-233 that has not fully decayed.

The use of different fuels in nuclear reactors results in different SNF composition, with varying activity curves.

Proliferation Concerns

Since uranium and plutonium are nuclear weapons materials, there have been proliferation concerns. Ordinarily (in spent nuclear fuel), plutonium is reactor-grade plutonium. In addition to plutonium-239, which is highly suitable for building nuclear weapons, it contains large amounts of undesirable contaminants: plutonium-240, plutonium-241, and plutonium-238. These isotopes are extremely difficult to separate, and more cost-effective ways of obtaining fissile material exist (e.g. uranium enrichment or dedicated plutonium production reactors).

High-level waste is full of highly radioactive fission products, most of which are relatively short-lived. This is a concern since if the waste is stored, perhaps in deep geological storage, over many years the fission products decay, decreasing the radioactivity of the waste and making the plutonium easier to access. The undesirable contaminant Pu-240 decays faster than the Pu-239, and thus the quality of the bomb material increases with time (although its quantity decreases during that time as well). Thus, some have argued, as time passes, these deep storage areas have the potential to become "plutonium mines", from which material for nuclear weapons can be acquired with relatively little difficulty. Critics of the latter idea point out that the half-life of Pu-240 is 6,560 years and Pu-239 is 24,110 years, and thus the relative enrichment of one isotope to the other with time occurs with a half-life of 9,000 years (that is, it takes 9000 years for the *fraction* of Pu-240 in a sample of mixed plutonium isotopes, to spontaneously decrease by half—a typical enrichment needed to turn reactor-grade into weapons-grade Pu). Thus "weapons grade plutonium mines" would be a problem for the very far future (>9,000 years from now), so that there remains a great deal of time for technology to advance to solve it.

Pu-239 decays to U-235 which is suitable for weapons and which has a very long half-life (roughly 10^9 years). Thus plutonium may decay and leave uranium-235. However, modern reactors are only moderately enriched with U-235 relative to U-238, so the U-238 continues to serve as a denaturation agent for any U-235 produced by plutonium decay.

One solution to this problem is to recycle the plutonium and use it as a fuel e.g. in fast reactors. In pyrometallurgical fast reactors, the separated plutonium and uranium are contaminated by actinides and cannot be used for nuclear weapons.

Nuclear Weapons Decommissioning

Waste from nuclear weapons decommissioning is unlikely to contain much beta or gamma activity other than tritium and americium.

It is more likely to contain alpha-emitting actinides such as Pu-239 which is a fissile material used in bombs, plus some material with much higher specific activities, such as Pu-238 or Po.

In the past the neutron trigger for an atomic bomb tended to be beryllium and a high activity alpha emitter such as polonium; an alternative to polonium is Pu-238. For reasons of national security, details of the design of modern bombs are normally not released to the open literature.

Some designs might contain a radioisotope thermoelectric generator using Pu-238 to provide a long lasting source of electrical power for the electronics in the device.

It is likely that the fissile material of an old bomb which is due for refitting will contain decay products of the plutonium isotopes used in it, these are likely to include U-236 from Pu-240 impurities, plus some U-235 from decay of the Pu-239; due to the relatively long half-life of these Pu isotopes, these wastes from radioactive decay of bomb core material would be very small, and in any case, far less dangerous (even in terms of simple radioactivity) than the Pu-239 itself.

The beta decay of Pu-241 forms Am-241; the in-growth of americium is likely to be a greater problem than the decay of Pu-239 and Pu-240 as the americium is a gamma emitter (increasing external-exposure to workers) and is an alpha emitter which can cause the generation of heat. The plutonium could be separated from the americium by several different processes; these would include pyrochemical processes and aqueous/organic solvent extraction. A truncated PUREX type extraction process would be one possible method of making the separation. Naturally occurring uranium is not fissile because it contains 99.3% of U-238 and only 0.7% of U-235.

Legacy Waste

Due to historic activities typically related to radium industry, uranium mining, and military programs, there are numerous sites that contain or are contaminated with radioactivity. In the United States alone, the Department of Energy states there are "millions of gallons of radioactive waste" as well as "thousands of tons of spent nuclear fuel and material" and also "huge quantities of contaminated soil and water." Despite copious quantities of waste, the DOE has stated a goal of cleaning all presently contaminated sites successfully by 2025. The Fernald, Ohio site for example had "31 million pounds of uranium product", "2.5 billion pounds of waste", "2.75 million cubic yards of contaminated soil and debris", and a "223 acre portion of the underlying

Great Miami Aquifer had uranium levels above drinking standards." The United States has at least 108 sites designated as areas that are contaminated and unusable, sometimes many thousands of acres. DOE wishes to clean or mitigate many or all by 2025, using the recently developed method of geomelting, however the task can be difficult and it acknowledges that some may never be completely remediated. In just one of these 108 larger designations, Oak Ridge National Laboratory, there were for example at least "167 known contaminant release sites" in one of the three subdivisions of the 37,000-acre (150 km^2) site. Some of the U.S. sites were smaller in nature, however, cleanup issues were simpler to address, and DOE has successfully completed cleanup, or at least closure, of several sites.

Medical

Radioactive medical waste tends to contain beta particle and gamma ray emitters. It can be divided into two main classes. In diagnostic nuclear medicine a number of short-lived gamma emitters such as technetium-99m are used. Many of these can be disposed of by leaving it to decay for a short time before disposal as normal waste. Other isotopes used in medicine, with half-lives in parentheses, include:

- Y-90, used for treating lymphoma (2.7 days)
- I-131, used for thyroid function tests and for treating thyroid cancer (8.0 days)
- Sr-89, used for treating bone cancer, intravenous injection (52 days)
- Ir-192, used for brachytherapy (74 days)
- Co-60, used for brachytherapy and external radiotherapy (5.3 years)
- Cs-137, used for brachytherapy, external radiotherapy (30 years)

Industrial

Industrial source waste can contain alpha, beta, neutron or gamma emitters. Gamma emitters are used in radiography while neutron emitting sources are used in a range of applications, such as oil well logging.

Naturally Occurring Radioactive Material (NORM)

Substances containing natural radioactivity are known as NORM. After human processing that exposes or concentrates this natural radioactivity (such as mining bringing coal to the surface or burning it to produce concentrated ash), it becomes technologically-enhanced naturally-occurring radioactive material (TENORM). A lot of this waste is alpha particle-emitting matter from the decay chains of uranium and thorium. The main source of radiation in the human body is potassium-40 (^{40}K), typically 17 milligrams in the body at a time and 0.4 milligrams/day intake. Most rocks, due to their components, have a low level of radioactivity. Usually ranging from 1 millisievert (mSv) to 13 mSv annually depending on location, average radiation exposure from natural radioisotopes is 2.0 mSv per person a year worldwide. This makes up the majority of typical total dosage (with mean annual exposure from other sources amounting to 0.6 mSv from medical tests averaged over the whole populace, 0.4 mSv from cosmic rays, 0.005 mSv from the legacy of past atmospheric nuclear testing, 0.005 mSv occupational exposure, 0.002 mSv from the Chernobyl disaster, and 0.0002 mSv from the nuclear fuel cycle).

TENORM is not regulated as restrictively as nuclear reactor waste, though there are no significant differences in the radiological risks of these materials.

Coal

Coal contains a small amount of radioactive uranium, barium, thorium and potassium, but, in the case of pure coal, this is significantly less than the average concentration of those elements in the Earth's crust. The surrounding strata, if shale or mudstone, often contain slightly more than average and this may also be reflected in the ash content of 'dirty' coals. The more active ash minerals become concentrated in the fly ash precisely because they do not burn well. The radioactivity of fly ash is about the same as black shale and is less than phosphate rocks, but is more of a concern because a small amount of the fly ash ends up in the atmosphere where it can be inhaled. According to U.S. NCRP reports, population exposure from 1000-MWe power plants amounts to 490 person-rem/year for coal power plants, 100 times as great as nuclear power plants (4.8 person-rem/year). (The exposure from the complete nuclear fuel cycle from mining to waste disposal is 136 person-rem/year; the corresponding value for coal use from mining to waste disposal is "probably unknown".)

Oil and Gas

Residues from the oil and gas industry often contain radium and its decay products. The sulfate scale from an oil well can be very radium rich, while the water, oil and gas from a well often contain radon. The radon decays to form solid radioisotopes which form coatings on the inside of pipework. In an oil processing plant the area of the plant where propane is processed is often one of the more contaminated areas of the plant as radon has a similar boiling point to propane.

Classification of Radioactive Waste

Classifications of nuclear waste varies by country. The IAEA, which publishes the Radioactive Waste Safety Standards (RADWASS), also plays a significant role.

Uranium Tailings

Uranium tailings are waste by-product materials left over from the rough processing of uranium-bearing ore. They are not significantly radioactive. Mill tailings are sometimes referred to as 11(e)2 wastes, from the section of the Atomic Energy Act of 1946 that defines them. Uranium mill tailings typically also contain chemically hazardous heavy metal such as lead and arsenic. Vast mounds of uranium mill tailings are left at many old mining sites, especially in Colorado, New Mexico, and Utah.

Low-Level Waste

Low level waste (LLW) is generated from hospitals and industry, as well as the nuclear fuel cycle. Low-level wastes include paper, rags, tools, clothing, filters, and other materials which contain small amounts of mostly short-lived radioactivity. Materials that originate from any region of an Active Area are commonly designated as LLW as a precautionary measure even if there is only a remote possibility of being contaminated with radioactive materials. Such LLW typically exhibits no higher radioactivity than one would expect from the same material disposed of in a non-active area, such as a normal office block.

Some high-activity LLW requires shielding during handling and transport but most LLW is suitable for shallow land burial. To reduce its volume, it is often compacted or incinerated before disposal. Low-level waste is divided into four classes: class A, class B, class C, and Greater Than Class C (GTCC).

Intermediate-Level Waste

Intermediate-level waste (ILW) contains higher amounts of radioactivity and in general require shielding, but not cooling. Intermediate-level wastes includes resins, chemical sludge and metal nuclear fuel cladding, as well as contaminated materials from reactor decommissioning. It may be solidified in concrete or bitumen for disposal. As a general rule, short-lived waste (mainly non-fuel materials from reactors) is buried in shallow repositories, while long-lived waste (from fuel and fuel reprocessing) is deposited in geological repository.

U.S. regulations do not define this category of waste; the term is used in Europe and elsewhere.

High-Level Waste

High-level waste (HLW) is produced by nuclear reactors. The exact definition of HLW differs internationally. After a nuclear fuel rod serves one fuel cycle and is removed from the core, it is considered HLW. Fuel rods contain fission products and transuranic elements generated in the reactor core. Spent fuel is highly radioactive and often hot. HLW accounts for over 95 percent of the total radioactivity produced in the process of nuclear electricity generation. The amount of HLW worldwide is currently increasing by about 12,000 metric tons every year, which is the equivalent to about 100 double-decker buses or a two-story structure with a footprint the size of a basketball court. A 1000-MW nuclear power plant produces about 27 tonnes of spent nuclear fuel (unreprocessed) every year.

The ongoing controversy over high-level nuclear waste disposal is a major constraint on the nuclear power's global expansion. Most scientists agree that the main proposed long-term solution is deep geological burial, either in a mine or a deep borehole. However, almost six decades after commercial nuclear energy began, no government has succeeded in opening such a repository for civilian high-level nuclear waste. Reprocessing or recycling spent nuclear fuel options already available or under active development still generate waste and so are not a total solution. Deep geological burial remains the only responsible way to deal with high-level nuclear waste. The Morris Operation is currently the only de facto high-level radioactive waste storage site in the United States.

Transuranic Waste

Transuranic waste (TRUW) as defined by U.S. regulations is, without regard to form or origin, waste that is contaminated with alpha-emitting transuranic radionuclides with half-lives greater than 20 years and concentrations greater than 100 nCi/g (3.7 MBq/kg), excluding high-level waste. Elements that have an atomic number greater than uranium are called transuranic ("beyond uranium"). Because of their long half-lives, TRUW is disposed more cautiously than either low- or intermediate-level waste. In the U.S., it arises mainly from weapons production, and consists of clothing, tools, rags, residues, debris and other items contaminated with small amounts of radioactive elements (mainly plutonium).

Under U.S. law, transuranic waste is further categorized into "contact-handled" (CH) and "remote-handled" (RH) on the basis of the radiation dose rate measured at the surface of the waste container. CH TRUW has a surface dose rate not greater than 200 mrem per hour (2 mSv/h), whereas RH TRUW has a surface dose rate of 200 mrem/h (2 mSv/h) or greater. CH TRUW does not have the very high radioactivity of high-level waste, nor its high heat generation, but RH TRUW can be highly radioactive, with surface dose rates up to 1,000,000 mrem/h (10,000 mSv/h). The U.S. currently disposes of TRUW generated from military facilities at the Waste Isolation Pilot Plant (WIPP) in a deep salt formation in New Mexico.

Prevention of Waste

A theoretical way to reduce waste accumulation is to phase out current reactors in favour of Generation IV Reactors or Liquid Fluoride Thorium Reactors, which output less waste per power generated. Fast reactors can theoretically consume some existing waste, but the UK's Nuclear Decommissioning Authority described this technology as immature and commercially unproven, and unlikely to start before 2050.

Management of Waste

Of particular concern in nuclear waste management are two long-lived fission products, Tc-99 (half-life 220,000 years) and I-129 (half-life 15.7 million years), which dominate spent fuel radioactivity after a few thousand years. The most troublesome transuranic elements in spent fuel are Np-237 (half-life two million years) and Pu-239 (half-life 24,000 years). Nuclear waste requires sophisticated treatment and management to successfully isolate it from interacting with the biosphere. This usually necessitates treatment, followed by a long-term management strategy involving storage, disposal or transformation of the waste into a non-toxic form. Governments around the world are considering a range of waste management and disposal options, though there has been limited progress toward long-term waste management solutions.

In second half of 20th century, several methods of disposal of radioactive waste were investigated by nuclear nations. Which are;

- "Long term above ground storage", not implemented.
- "Disposal in outer space", not implemented.
- "Deep borehole disposal", not implemented.
- "Rock-melting", not implemented.

- "Disposal at subduction zones", not implemented.
- "Ocean disposal", done by the USSR, the United Kingdom, Switzerland, the United States, Belgium, France, The Netherlands, Japan, Sweden, Russia, Germany, Italy and South Korea. (1954–93) This is no longer permitted by international agreements.
- "Sub seabed disposal", not implemented, not permitted by international agreements.
- "Disposal in ice sheets", rejected in Antarctic Treaty
- "Direct injection", done by USSR and USA.

Initial Treatment of Waste

Vitrification: Long-term storage of radioactive waste requires the stabilization of the waste into a form which will neither react nor degrade for extended periods of time. One way to do this is through vitrification. Currently at Sellafield the high-level waste (PUREX first cycle raffinate) is mixed with sugar and then calcined. Calcination involves passing the waste through a heated, rotating tube. The purposes of calcination are to evaporate the water from the waste, and de-nitrate the fission products to assist the stability of the glass produced.

The 'calcine' generated is fed continuously into an induction heated furnace with fragmented glass. The resulting glass is a new substance in which the waste products are bonded into the glass matrix when it solidifies. This product, as a melt, is poured into stainless steel cylindrical containers ("cylinders") in a batch process. When cooled, the fluid solidifies ("vitrifies") into the glass. Such glass, after being formed, is highly resistant to water.

After filling a cylinder, a seal is welded onto the cylinder. The cylinder is then washed. After being inspected for external contamination, the steel cylinder is stored, usually in an underground repository. In this form, the waste products are expected to be immobilized for thousands of years.

The glass inside a cylinder is usually a black glossy substance. All this work (in the United Kingdom) is done using hot cell systems. The sugar is added to control the ruthenium chemistry and to stop the formation of the volatile RuO_4 containing radioactive ruthenium isotopes. In the West, the glass is normally a borosilicate glass (similar to Pyrex), while in the former Soviet bloc it is normal to use a phosphate glass. The amount of fission products in the glass must be limited because some (palladium, the other Pt group metals, and tellurium) tend to form metallic phases which separate from the glass. Bulk vitrification uses electrodes to melt soil and wastes, which are then buried underground. In Germany a vitrification plant is in use; this is treating the waste from a small demonstration reprocessing plant which has since been closed down.

Ion Exchange

It is common for medium active wastes in the nuclear industry to be treated with ion exchange or other means to concentrate the radioactivity into a small volume. The much less radioactive bulk (after treatment) is often then discharged. For instance, it is possible to use a ferric hydroxide floc to remove radioactive metals from aqueous mixtures. After the radioisotopes are absorbed onto the ferric hydroxide, the resulting sludge can be placed in a metal drum before being mixed with cement to form a solid waste form. In order to get better long-term performance (mechanical stability) from such forms, they may be made from a mixture of fly ash, or blast furnace slag, and Portland cement, instead of normal concrete (made with Portland cement, gravel and sand).

Synroc

The Australian Synroc (synthetic rock) is a more sophisticated way to immobilize such waste, and this process may eventually come into commercial use for civil wastes (it is currently being developed for US military wastes). Synroc was invented by the late Prof Ted Ringwood (a geochemist) at the Australian National University. The Synroc contains pyrochlore and cryptomelane type minerals. The original form of Synroc (Synroc C) was designed for the liquid high level waste (PUREX raffinate) from a light water reactor. The main minerals in this Synroc are hollandite ($BaAl_2Ti_6O_{16}$), zirconolite ($CaZrTi_2O_7$) and perovskite ($CaTiO_3$). The zirconolite and perovskite are hosts for the actinides. The strontium and barium will be fixed in the perovskite. The caesium will be fixed in the hollandite.

Long Term Management of Waste

The time frame in question when dealing with radioactive waste ranges from 10,000 to 1,000,000 years, according to studies based on the effect of estimated radiation doses. Researchers suggest that forecasts of health detriment for such periods should be examined critically. Practical studies only consider up to 100 years as far as effective planning and cost evaluations are concerned. Long term behaviour of radioactive wastes remains a subject for ongoing research projects in geoforecasting.

Above-Ground Disposal

Dry cask storage typically involves taking waste from a spent fuel pool and sealing it (along with an inert gas) in a steel cylinder, which is placed in a concrete cylinder which acts as a radiation shield. It is a relatively inexpensive method which can be done at a central facility or adjacent to the source reactor. The waste can be easily retrieved for reprocessing.

Geologic Disposal

The process of selecting appropriate deep final repositories for high level waste and spent fuel is now under way in several countries with the first expected to be commissioned some time after 2010. The basic concept is to locate a large, stable geologic formation and use mining technology to excavate a tunnel, or large-bore tunnel boring machines (similar to those used to drill the Channel Tunnel from England to France) to drill a shaft 500 metres (1,600 ft) to 1,000 metres (3,300 ft) below the surface where rooms or vaults can be excavated for disposal of high-level radioactive waste. The goal is to permanently isolate nuclear waste from the human environment. Many people remain uncomfortable with the immediate stewardship cessation of this disposal system, suggesting perpetual management and monitoring would be more prudent.

Because some radioactive species have half-lives longer than one million years, even very low container leakage and radionuclide migration rates must be taken into account. Moreover, it may require more than one half-life until some nuclear materials lose enough radioactivity to cease being lethal to living things. A 1983 review of the Swedish radioactive waste disposal program by the National Academy of Sciences found that country's estimate of several hundred thousand years—perhaps up to one million years—being necessary for waste isolation "fully justified." Aside from dilution, chemically toxic stable elements in some waste such as arsenic remain toxic for up to billions of years or indefinitely.

Ocean floor disposal of radioactive waste has been suggested by the finding that deep waters in the North Atlantic Ocean do not present an exchange with shallow waters for about 140 years based on oxygen content data recorded over a period of 25 years. They include burial beneath a stable abyssal plain, burial in a subduction zone that would slowly carry the waste downward into the Earth's mantle, and burial beneath a remote natural or human-made island. While these approaches all have merit and would facilitate an international solution to the problem of disposal of radioactive waste, they would require an amendment of the Law of the Sea.

Article 1 (Definitions), 7., of the 1996 Protocol to the Convention on the Prevention of Marine Pollution by Dumping of Wastes and Other Matter, (the London Dumping Convention) states:

> *"Sea" means all marine waters other than the internal waters of States, as well as the seabed and the subsoil thereof; it does not include sub-seabed repositories accessed only from land."*

The proposed land-based subductive waste disposal method disposes of nuclear waste in a subduction zone accessed from land, and therefore is not prohibited by international agreement. This method has been described as the most viable means of disposing of radioactive waste, and as the state-of-the-art as of 2001 in nuclear waste disposal technology. Another approach termed Remix & Return would blend high-level waste with uranium mine and mill tailings down to the level of the original radioactivity of the uranium ore, then replace it in inactive uranium mines. This approach has the merits of providing jobs for miners who would double as disposal staff, and of facilitating a cradle-to-grave cycle for radioactive materials, but would be inappropriate for spent reactor fuel in the absence of reprocessing, due to the presence in it of highly toxic radioactive elements such as plutonium.

Deep borehole disposal is the concept of disposing of high-level radioactive waste from nuclear reactors in extremely deep boreholes. Deep borehole disposal seeks to place the waste as much as 5 kilometres (3.1 mi) beneath the surface of the Earth and relies primarily on the immense natural geological barrier to confine the waste safely and permanently so that it should never pose a threat to the environment. The Earth's crust contains 120 trillion tons of thorium and 40 trillion tons of uranium (primarily at relatively trace concentrations of parts per million each adding up over the crust's 3 * 10 ton mass), among other natural radioisotopes. Since the fraction of nuclides decaying per unit of time is inversely proportional to an isotope's half-life, the relative radioactivity of the lesser amount of human-produced radioisotopes (thousands of tons instead of trillions of tons) would diminish once the isotopes with far shorter half-lives than the bulk of natural radioisotopes decayed.

In January 2013, Cumbria county council rejected UK central government proposals to start work on an underground storage dump for nuclear waste near to the Lake District National Park. "For any host community, there will be a substantial community benefits package and worth hundreds of millions of pounds" said Ed Davey, Energy Secretary, but nonetheless, the local elected body voted 7-3 against research continuing, after hearing evidence from independent geologists that "the fractured strata of the county was impossible to entrust with such dangerous material and a hazard lasting millennia."

Transmutation

There have been proposals for reactors that consume nuclear waste and transmute it to other, less-harmful nuclear waste. In particular, the Integral Fast Reactor was a proposed nuclear reactor with a nuclear fuel cycle that produced no transuranic waste and in fact, could consume transuranic waste. It proceeded as far as large-scale tests, but was then cancelled by the US Government. Another approach, considered safer but requiring more development, is to dedicate subcritical reactors to the transmutation of the left-over transuranic elements.

An isotope that is found in nuclear waste and that represents a concern in terms of proliferation is Pu-239. The estimated world total of plutonium in the year 2000 was of 1,645 MT, of which 210 MT had been separated by reprocessing. The large stock of plutonium is a result of its production inside uranium-fuelled reactors and of the reprocessing of weapons-grade plutonium during the weapons program. An option for getting rid of this plutonium is to use it as a fuel in a traditional Light Water Reactor (LWR). Several fuel types with differing plutonium destruction efficiencies are under study.

Transmutation was banned in the US in April 1977 by President Carter due to the danger of plutonium proliferation, but President Reagan rescinded the ban in 1981. Due to the economic losses and risks, construction of reprocessing plants during this time did not resume. Due to high energy demand, work on the method has continued in the EU. This has resulted in a practical nuclear research reactor called Myrrha in which transmutation is possible. Additionally, a new research program called ACTINET has been started in the EU to make transmutation possible on a large, industrial scale. According to President Bush's Global Nuclear Energy Partnership (GNEP) of 2007, the US is now actively promoting research on transmutation technologies needed to markedly reduce the problem of nuclear waste treatment.

There have also been theoretical studies involving the use of fusion reactors as so called "actinide burners" where a fusion reactor plasma such as in a tokamak, could be "doped" with a small amount of the "minor" transuranic atoms which would be transmuted (meaning fissioned in the actinide case) to lighter elements upon their successive bombardment by the very high energy neutrons produced by the fusion of deuterium and tritium in the reactor. A study at MIT found that only 2 or 3 fusion reactors with parameters similar to that of the International Thermonuclear Experimental Reactor (ITER) could transmute the entire annual minor actinide production from all of the light water reactors presently operating in the United States fleet while simultaneously generating approximately 1 gigawatt of power from each reactor.

Reuse of Waste

Another option is to find applications for the isotopes in nuclear waste so as to re-use them. Already, caesium-137, strontium-90 and a few other isotopes are extracted for certain industrial applications such as food irradiation and radioisotope thermoelectric generators. While re-use does not eliminate the need to manage radioisotopes, it reduces the quantity of waste produced.

The Nuclear Assisted Hydrocarbon Production Method, Canadian patent application 2,659,302, is a method for the temporary or permanent storage of nuclear waste materials comprising the placing of waste materials into one or more repositories or boreholes constructed into an unconventional oil formation. The thermal flux of the waste materials fracture the formation, alters the chemical and/or physical properties of hydrocarbon material within the subterranean formation to allow removal of the altered material. A mixture of hydrocarbons, hydrogen, and/or other formation fluids are produced from the formation. The radioactivity of high-level radioactive waste affords proliferation resistance to plutonium placed in the periphery of the repository or the deepest portion of a borehole.

Breeder reactors can run on U-238 and transuranic elements, which comprise the majority of spent fuel radioactivity in the 1000-100000 year time span.

Space Disposal

Space disposal is attractive because it removes nuclear waste from the planet. It has significant disadvantages, such as the potential for catastrophic failure of a launch vehicle, which could spread radioactive material into the atmosphere and around the world. A high number of launches would be required because no individual rocket would be able to carry very much of the material relative to the total amount that needs to be disposed of. This makes the proposal impractical economically and it increases the risk of at least one or more launch failures. To further complicate matters, international agreements on the regulation of such a program would need to be established. Costs and inadequate reliability of modern rocket launch systems for space disposal has been one of the motives for interest in non-rocket space launch systems such as mass drivers, space elevators, and other proposals.

National Management Plans

Most countries are considerably ahead of the United States in developing plans for high-level radioactive waste disposal. Sweden and Finland are furthest along in committing to a particular disposal technology, while many others reprocess spent fuel or contract with France or Great Britain to do it, taking back the resulting plutonium and high-level waste. "An increasing backlog of plutonium from reprocessing is developing in many countries... It is doubtful that reprocessing makes economic sense in the present environment of cheap uranium."

In many European countries (e.g., Britain, Finland, the Netherlands, Sweden and Switzerland) the risk or dose limit for a member of the public exposed to radiation from a future high-level nuclear waste facility is considerably more stringent than that suggested by the International Commission on Radiation Protection or proposed in the United States. European limits are often more stringent than the standard suggested in 1990 by the International Commission on Radiation Protection by a factor of 20, and more stringent by a factor of ten than the standard proposed by the US Environmental Protection Agency (EPA) for Yucca Mountain nuclear waste repository for the first 10,000 years after closure.

The U.S. EPA's proposed standard for greater than 10,000 years is 250 times more permissive than the European limit. The U.S. EPA proposed a legal limit of a maximum of 3.5 millisieverts (350 millirem) each annually to local individuals after 10,000 years, which would be up to several percent of the exposure currently received by some populations in the highest natural background regions on Earth, though the U.S. DOE predicted that received dose would be much below that limit. Over a timeframe of thousands of years, after the most active short half-life radioisotopes decayed, burying U.S. nuclear waste would increase the radioactivity in the top 2000 feet of rock and soil in the United States (10 million km^2) by H" 1 part in 10 million over the cumulative amount of natural radioisotopes in such a volume, but the vicinity of the site would have a far higher concentration of artificial radioisotopes underground than such an average.

Mongolia

After serious opposition had risen about plans and negotiations between Mongolia with Japan and the United States of America to build nuclear waste facilities in Mongolia, Mongolia stopped all negotiations in September 2011. These negotiations started after U.S. Deputy Secretary of Energy Daniel B. Poneman visited Mongolia in September, 2010. Talks were held in Washington DC between officials of Japan, the United States and Mongolia in February 2011. After this the United Arab Emirates (UAE), which wanted to buy nuclear fuel from Mongolia, joined in the negotiations. The talks were kept secret, and although The Mainichi Daily News reported on it in May, Mongolia officially denied the existence of these negotiations. But alarmed by this news, Mongolian citizens protested against the plans, and demanded the government withdraw the plans and disclose information. The Mongolian President Tsakhia Elbegdorj issued a presidential order on Sept. 13 banning all negotiations with foreign governments or international organisations on nuclear waste storage plans in Mongolia. The Mongolian government has accused the newspaper of distributing false claims around the world. After the presidential order, the Mongolian president fired the individual that was supposedly involved in these conversations.

Illegal Dumping

Authorities in Italy are investigating a 'Ndrangheta mafia clan accused of trafficking and illegally dumping nuclear waste. According to a whistleblower, a manager of the Italy's state energy research agency Enea paid the clan to get rid of 600 drums of toxic and radioactive waste from Italy, Switzerland, France, Germany, and the US, with Somalia as the destination, where the waste was buried after buying off local politicians. Former employees of Enea are suspected of paying the criminals to take waste off their hands in the 1980s and 1990s. Shipments to Somalia continued into the 1990s, while the 'Ndrangheta clan also blew up shiploads of waste, including radioactive hospital waste, and sending them to the sea bed off the Calabrian coast. According to the environmental group Legambiente, former members of the 'Ndrangheta have said that they were paid to sink ships with radioactive material for the last 20 years.

Accidents Involving Radioactive Waste

A few incidents have occurred when radioactive material was disposed of improperly, shielding during transport was defective, or when it was simply abandoned or even stolen from a waste store. In the Soviet Union, waste stored in Lake Karachay was blown over the area during a dust storm after the lake had partly dried out. At Maxey Flat, a low-level radioactive waste facility located in Kentucky, containment trenches covered with dirt, instead of steel or cement, collapsed under heavy rainfall into the trenches and filled with water. The water that invaded the trenches became radioactive and had to be disposed of at the Maxey Flat facility itself. In other cases of radioactive waste accidents, lakes or ponds with radioactive waste accidentally overflowed into the rivers during exceptional storms. In Italy, several radioactive waste deposits let material flow into river water, thus contaminating water for domestic use. In France, in the summer of 2008 numerous incidents happened; in one, at the Areva plant in Tricastin, it was reported that during a draining operation, liquid containing untreated uranium overflowed out of a faulty tank and about 75 kg of the radioactive material seeped into the ground and, from there, into two rivers nearby; in another case, over 100 staff were contaminated with low doses of radiation.

Scavenging of abandoned radioactive material has been the cause of several other cases of radiation exposure, mostly in developing nations, which may have less regulation of dangerous substances (and sometimes less general education about radioactivity and its hazards) and a market for scavenged goods and scrap metal. The scavengers and those who buy the material are almost always unaware that the material is radioactive and it is selected for its aesthetics or scrap value. Irresponsibility on the part of the radioactive material's owners, usually a hospital, university or military, and the absence of regulation concerning radioactive waste, or a lack of enforcement of such regulations, have been significant factors in radiation exposures.

Transportation accidents involving spent nuclear fuel from power plants are unlikely to have serious consequences due to the strength of the spent nuclear fuel shipping casks.

On 15 December 2011 top government spokesman Osamu Fujimura of the Japanese government admitted that nuclear substances were found in the waste of Japanese nuclear facilities. Although Japan did commit itself in 1977 to these inspections in the safeguard agreement with the IAEA, the reports were kept secret for the inspectors of the International Atomic Energy Agency. Japan did start discussions with the IAEA about the large quantities of enriched uranium and plutonium that were discovered in nuclear waste cleared away by Japanese nuclear operators. At the press conference Fujimura said: "Based on investigations so far, most nuclear substances have been properly managed as waste, and from that perspective, there is no problem in safety management," But according to him, the matter was at that moment still being investigated.

Wastewater

Wastewater, also written as waste water, is any water that has been adversely affected in quality by anthropogenic influence. Municipal wastewater is usually conveyed in a combined sewer or sanitary sewer, and treated at a wastewater treatment plant. Treated wastewater is discharged into receiving water via an effluent sewer. Wastewaters generated in areas without access to centralized sewer systems rely on on-site wastewater systems. These typically comprise a septic tank, drain field, and optionally an on-site treatment unit.

Sewage is the subset of wastewater that is contaminated with feces or urine, but is often used to mean any wastewater. Sewage includes domestic, municipal, or industrial liquid waste products disposed of, usually via a pipe or sewer (sanitary or combined), sometimes in a cesspool emptier.

Sewerage is the physical infrastructure, including pipes, pumps, screens, channels etc. used to convey sewage from its origin to the point of eventual treatment or disposal. It is found in all types of sewage treatment, with the exception of septic systems, which treat sewage on site.

Origin

Wastewater or sewage can come from (text in brackets indicates likely inclusions or contaminants):

- Human waste (feces, used toilet paper or wipes, urine, or other bodily fluids), also known as blackwater, usually from lavatories;
- Cesspit leakage;
- Septic tank discharge;
- Sewage treatment plant discharge;
- Washing water (personal, clothes, floors, dishes, etc.), also known as greywater or sullage;
- Rainfall collected on roofs, yards, hard-standings, etc. (generally clean with traces of oils and fuel);
- Groundwater infiltrated into sewage;
- Surplus manufactured liquids from domestic sources (drinks, cooking oil, pesticides, lubricating oil, paint, cleaning liquids, etc.);

- Urban rainfall runoff from roads, carparks, roofs, sidewalks/ pavements (contains oils, animal feces, litter, gasoline/petrol, diesel or rubber residues, soapscum, metals from vehicle exhausts, etc.);
- Seawater ingress (high volumes of salt and microbes);
- Direct ingress of river water (high volumes of micro-biota);
- Direct ingress of manmade liquids (illegal disposal of pesticides, used oils, etc.);
- Highway drainage (oil, de-icing agents, rubber residues);
- Storm drains (almost anything, including cars, shopping trolleys, trees, cattle, etc.);
- Blackwater (surface water contaminated by sewage);
- Industrial waste
- Industrial site drainage (silt, sand, alkali, oil, chemical residues);
  - Industrial cooling waters (biocides, heat, slimes, silt);
  - Industrial process waters;
  - Organic or biodegradable waste, including waste from abattoirs, creameries, and ice cream manufacture;
  - Organic or non bio-degradable/difficult-to-treat waste (pharmaceutical or pesticide manufacturing);
  - Extreme pH waste (from acid/alkali manufacturing, metal plating);
  - Toxic waste (metal plating, cyanide production, pesticide manufacturing, etc.);
  - Solids and emulsions (paper manufacturing, foodstuffs, lubricating and hydraulic oil manufacturing, etc.);
  - Agricultural drainage, direct and diffuse.
  - Hydraulic fracturing
  - Produced water from oil & natural gas production

Wastewater Constituents

The composition of wastewater varies widely. This is a partial list of what it may contain:

- Water (more than 95 percent), which is often added during flushing to carry waste down a drain;
- Pathogens such as bacteria, viruses, prions and parasitic worms;
- Non-pathogenic bacteria;

- Organic particles such as feces, hairs, food, vomit, paper fibres, plant material, humus, etc.;
- Soluble organic material such as urea, fruit sugars, soluble proteins, drugs, pharmaceuticals, etc.;
- Inorganic particles such as sand, grit, metal particles, ceramics, etc.;
- Soluble inorganic material such as ammonia, road-salt, sea-salt, cyanide, hydrogen sulfide, thiocyanates, thiosulfates, etc.;
- Animals such as protozoa, insects, arthropods, small fish, etc.;
- Macro-solids such as sanitary napkins, nappies/diapers, condoms, needles, children's toys, dead animals or plants, etc.;
- Gases such as hydrogen sulfide, carbon dioxide, methane, etc.;
- Emulsions such as paints, adhesives, mayonnaise, hair colorants, emulsified oils, etc.;
- Toxins such as pesticides, poisons, herbicides, etc.
- Pharmaceuticals and hormones.

Wastewater Quality Indicators

Any oxidizable material present in a natural waterway or in an industrial wastewater will be oxidized both by biochemical (bacterial) or chemical processes. The result is that the oxygen content of the water will be decreased. Basically, the reaction for biochemical oxidation may be written as:

Oxidizable material + bacteria + nutrient + $O_2 \rightarrow CO_2 + H_2O$ + oxidized inorganics such as NO^-_3 or SO_4^{--}

Oxygen consumption by reducing chemicals such as sulfides and nitrites is typified as follows:

$$S^{--} + 2\,O_2 \rightarrow SO_4^{--}$$

$$NO_2^- + \tfrac{1}{2}\,O_2 \rightarrow NO_3^-$$

Since all natural waterways contain bacteria and nutrients, almost any waste compounds introduced into such waterways will initiate biochemical reactions (such as shown above). Those biochemical reactions create what is measured in the laboratory as the biochemical oxygen demand (BOD). Such chemicals are also liable to be broken down using strong oxidizing agents and these chemical reactions create what is measured in the laboratory as the chemical oxygen demand (COD). Both the BOD and COD tests are a measure of the relative oxygen-depletion effect of a waste contaminant. Both have been widely adopted as a measure of pollution effect. The BOD test measures the oxygen demand of biodegradable pollutants whereas the COD test measures the oxygen demand of oxidizable pollutants.

The so-called 5-day BOD measures the amount of oxygen consumed by biochemical oxidation of waste contaminants in a 5-day period. The total amount of oxygen consumed when the biochemical reaction is allowed to proceed to completion is called the Ultimate BOD. Because the Ultimate BOD is so time consuming, the 5-day BOD has been almost universally adopted as a measure of relative pollution effect.

There are also many different COD tests of which the 4-hour COD is probably the most common.

There is no generalized correlation between the 5-day BOD and the ultimate BOD. Similarly there is no generalized correlation between BOD and COD. It is possible to develop such correlations for specific waste contaminants in a specific wastewater stream but such correlations cannot be generalized for use with any other waste contaminants or wastewater streams. This is because the composition of any wastewater stream is different. As an example an effluent consisting of a solution of simple sugars that might discharge from a confectionery factory is likely to have organic components that degrade very quickly. In such a case, the 5 day BOD and the ultimate BOD would be very similar since there would be very little organic material left after 5 days. However a final effluent of a sewage treatment works serving a large industrialised area might have a discharge where the ultimate BOD was much greater than the 5 day BOD because much of the easily degraded material would have been removed in the sewage treatment process and many industrial processes discharge difficult to degrade organic molecules.

The laboratory test procedures for the determining the above oxygen demands are detailed in many standard texts. American versions include the "Standard Methods for the Examination of Water and Wastewater."

Sewage Disposal

In some urban areas, sewage is carried separately in sanitary sewers and runoff from streets is carried in storm drains. Access to either of these is typically through a manhole. During high precipitation periods a combined sewer overflow can occur, forcing untreated sewage to flow back into the environment. This can pose a serious threat to public health and the surrounding environment.

Sewage may drain directly into major watersheds with minimal or no treatment. When untreated, sewage can have serious impacts on the quality of an environment and on the health of people. Pathogens can cause a variety of illnesses. Some chemicals pose risks even at very low concentrations and can remain a threat for long periods of time because of bioaccumulation in animal or human tissue.

Treatment

There are numerous processes that can be used to clean up wastewaters depending on the type and extent of contamination. There are two basic approaches: to use the waste in the water as a resource (such as constructed wetlands) or strictly as a pollution (such as the majority of today's treatment plants). Most wastewater is treated in industrial-scale energy intensive wastewater treatment plants (WWTPs) which include physical, chemical and biological treatment processes. However, the use of septic tanks and other On-Site Sewage Facilities (OSSF) is widespread in rural areas, serving up to 20 percent of the homes in the U.S.

The most important aerobic treatment system is the activated sludge process, based on the maintenance and recirculation of a complex biomass composed by micro-organisms able to absorb and adsorb the organic matter carried in the wastewater. Anaerobic wastewater treatment processes (UASB, EGSB) are also widely applied in the treatment of industrial wastewaters and biological sludge. Some wastewater may be highly treated and reused as reclaimed water. Increasingly, for most wastewaters ecological approaches using reed bed systems such as constructed wetlands are being used. Tertiary treatment is being increasingly applied and most common technologies are micro filtration or synthetic membranes. After membrane filtration, the treated wastewater is indistinguishable from waters of natural origin of drinking quality (without its minerals). Nitrates can be removed from wastewater by natural processes in wetlands but also via intensive microbial denitrification, for which a small amount of methanol is typically added to provide the bacteria with a source of carbon. Ozone wastewater treatment is also growing in popularity, and requires the use of an ozone generator, which decontaminates the water as ozone bubbles percolate through the tank but is energy intensive. Latest, and very promising treatment technology is the use aerobic granulation.

Disposal of wastewaters from an industrial plant is a difficult and costly problem. Most petroleum refineries, chemical and petrochemical plants have onsite facilities to treat their wastewaters so that the pollutant concentrations in the treated wastewater comply with the local and/or national regulations regarding disposal of wastewaters into community treatment plants or into rivers, lakes or oceans. Constructed wetlands are being used in an increasing number of cases as they provided high quality and productive on-site treatment. Other industrial processes that produce a lot of waste-waters such as paper and pulp production has created environmental concern, leading to development of processes to recycle water use within plants before they have to be cleaned and disposed.

Reuse

Treated wastewater can be reused as drinking water, in industry (cooling towers), in artificial recharge of aquifers, in agriculture (70 percent of Israel's irrigated agriculture is based on highly purified wastewater) and in the rehabilitation of natural ecosystems (Florida's Everglades).

Recycled Wastewater Irrigation in Heterogeneous Urban Vegetation

There are numerous benefits of using recycled water for irrigation, including the low cost (when compared to other sources, particularly in an urban area), consistency of sup- ply (regardless of season, climatic conditions and associated water restrictions), and general consistency of quality. Irrigation of recycled wastewater is also considered as a means for plant fertilization and particularly nutrient supplementation. This approach carries with it a risk of soil and water pollution through excessive wastewater application. Hence, a detailed understanding of soil water conditions is essential for effective utilisation of wastewater for irrigation.

Use of Untreated Wastewater by Agriculture

Around 90% of wastewater produced globally remains untreated, causing widespread water pollution, especially in low-income countries. Increasingly, agriculture is using untreated wastewater for irrigation. Cities provide lucrative markets for fresh produce, so are attractive to farmers. However, because agriculture has to compete for increasingly scarce water resources with industry and municipal users, there is often no alternative for farmers but to use water polluted with urban waste directly to water their crops.

Health Hazards of Polluted Irrigation Water

There can be significant health hazards related to using the water in this way. Wastewater from cities can contain a mixture of chemical and biological pollutants. In low-income countries, there are often high levels of pathogens from excreta, while in emerging nations, where industrial development is outpacing environmental regulation, there are increasing risks from inorganic and organic chemicals. The World Health Organisation, in collaboration with the Food and Agriculture Organisation of the United Nations (FAO) and the United Nations Environmental Program (UNEP), has developed guidelines for safe use of wastewater.

The International Water Management Institute has worked in India, Pakistan, Vietnam, Ghana, Ethiopia, Mexico and other countries on various projects aimed at assessing and reducing risks of wastewater irrigation. They advocate a 'multiple-barrier' approach to wastewater use, where farmers are encouraged to adopt various risk-reducing behaviours. These include ceasing irrigation a few days before harvesting to allow pathogens to die off in the sunlight, applying water carefully so it does not contaminate leaves likely to be eaten raw, cleaning vegetables with disinfectant or allowing fecal sludge used in farming to dry before being used as a human manure.

Industrial Wastewater Treatment

Industrial wastewater treatment covers the mechanisms and processes used to treat waters that have been contaminated in some way by anthropogenic industrial or commercial activities prior to its release into the environment or its re-use.

Most industries produce some wet waste although recent trends in the developed world have been to minimise such production or recycle such waste within the production process. However, many industries remain dependent on processes that produce wastewaters.

Sources of Industrial Wastewater

Iron and Steel Industry

The production of iron from its ores involves powerful reduction reactions in blast furnaces. Cooling waters are inevitably contaminated with products especially ammonia and cyanide. Production of coke from coal in coking plants also requires water cooling and the use of water in by-products separation. Contamination of waste streams includes gasification products such as benzene, naphthalene, anthracene, cyanide, ammonia, phenols, cresols together with a range of more complex organic compounds known collectively as polycyclic aromatic hydrocarbons (PAH).

The conversion of iron or steel into sheet, wire or rods requires hot and cold mechanical transformation stages frequently employing water as a lubricant and coolant. Contaminants include hydraulic oils, tallow and particulate solids. Final treatment of iron and steel products before onward sale into manufacturing includes *pickling* in strong mineral acid to remove rust and prepare the surface for tin or chromium plating or for other surface treatments such as galvanisation or painting. The two acids commonly used are hydrochloric acid and sulfuric acid. Wastewaters include acidic rinse waters together with waste acid. Although many plants operate acid recovery plants (particularly those using hydrochloric acid), where the mineral acid is boiled away from the iron salts, there remains a large volume of highly acid ferrous sulfate or ferrous chloride to be disposed of. Many steel industry wastewaters are contaminated by hydraulic oil, also known as *soluble oil.*

Mines and Quarries

The principal waste-waters associated with mines and quarries are slurries of rock particles in water. These arise from rainfall washing exposed surfaces and haul roads and also from rock washing and grading processes. Volumes of water can be very high, especially rainfall related arisings on large sites. Some specialised separation operations, such as coal washing to separate coal from native rock using density gradients, can produce wastewater contaminated by fine particulate haematite and surfactants. Oils and hydraulic oils are also common contaminants. Wastewater from metal mines and ore recovery plants are inevitably contaminated by the minerals present in the native rock formations. Following crushing and extraction of the desirable materials, undesirable materials may become contaminated in the wastewater. For metal mines, this can include unwanted metals such as zinc and other materials such as arsenic. Extraction of high value metals such as gold and silver may generate slimes containing very fine particles in where physical removal of contaminants becomes particularly difficult.

Mining Processing Chemicals

Food Industry

Wastewater generated from agricultural and food operations has distinctive characteristics that set it apart from common municipal wastewater managed by public or private sewage treatment plants throughout the world: it is biodegradable and nontoxic, but that has high concentrations of biochemical oxygen demand (BOD) and suspended solids (SS). The constituents of food and agriculture wastewater are often complex to predict due to the differences in BOD and pH in effluents from vegetable, fruit, and meat products and due to the seasonal nature of food processing and postharvesting. Processing of food from raw materials requires large volumes of high grade water. Vegetable washing generates waters with high loads of particulate matter and some dissolved organic matter. It may also contain surfactants.

Animal slaughter and processing produces very strong organic waste from body fluids, such as blood, and gut contents. This wastewater is frequently contaminated by significant levels of antibiotics and growth hormones from the animals and by a variety of pesticides used to control external parasites. Insecticide residues in fleeces is a particular problem in treating waters generated in wool processing.

Processing food for sale produces wastes generated from cooking which are often rich in plant organic material and may also contain salt, flavourings, colouring material and acids or alkali. Very significant quantities of oil or fats may also be present.

Pulp and Paper Industry

Effluent from the pulp and paper industry is generally high in suspended solids and BOD. Stand alone paper mills using imported pulp may only require simple primary treatment, such as sedimentation or dissolved air flotation. Increased BOD or chemical oxygen demand (COD) loadings, as well as organic pollutants, may require biological treatment such as activated sludge or upflow anaerobic sludge blanket reactors. For mills with high inorganic loadings like salt, tertiary treatments may be required, either general membrane treatments like ultrafiltration or reverse osmosis or treatments to remove specific contaminants, such as nutrients.

Complex Organic Chemicals Industry

A range of industries manufacture or use complex organic chemicals. These include pesticides, pharmaceuticals, paints and dyes, petrochemicals, detergents, plastics, paper pollution, etc. Waste waters can be contaminated by feedstock materials, by-products, product material in soluble or particulate form, washing and cleaning agents, solvents and added value products such as plasticisers. Treatment facilities that do not need control of their effluent typically opt for a type of aerobic treatment, i.e. aerated lagoons.

Nuclear Industry

The waste production from the nuclear and radio-chemicals industry is dealt with as *Radioactive waste.*

Water Treatment

Many industries have a need to treat water to obtain very high quality water for demanding purposes. Water treatment produces organic and mineral sludges from filtration and sedimentation. Ion exchange using natural or synthetic resins removes calcium, magnesium and carbonate ions from water, replacing them with hydrogen and hydroxyl ions. Regeneration of ion exchange columns with strong acids and alkalis produces a wastewater rich in hardness ions which are readily precipitated out, especially when in admixture with other wastewater.

Treatment of Industrial Wastewater

The various types of contamination of wastewater require a variety of strategies to remove the contamination.

Brine Treatment

Brine treatment involves removing dissolved salt ions from the waste stream. Although similarities to seawater or brackish water desalination exist, industrial brine treatment may contain unique combinations of dissolved ions, such as hardness ions or other metals, necessitating specific processes and equipment.

Brine treatment systems are typically optimized to either reduce the volume of the final discharge for more economic disposal (as disposal costs are often based on volume) or maximize the recovery of fresh water or salts. Brine treatment systems may also be optimized to reduce electricity consumption, chemical usage, or physical footprint.

Brine treatment is commonly encountered when treating cooling tower blowdown, produced water from steam assisted gravity drainage (SAGD), produced water from natural gas extraction such as coal seam gas, frac flowback water, acid mine or acid rock drainage, reverse osmosis reject, chlor-alkali wastewater, pulp and paper mill effluent, and waste streams from food and beverage processing.

Brine treatment technologies may include: membrane filtration processes, such as reverse osmosis; ion exchange processes such as electrodialysis or weak acid cation exchange; or evaporation processes, such as brine concentrators and crystallizers employing mechanical vapour recompression and steam.

Reverse osmosis may not be viable for brine treatment, due to the potential for fouling caused by hardness salts or organic contaminants, or damage to the reverse osmosis membranes from hydrocarbons.

Evaporation processes are the most widespread for brine treatment as they enable the highest degree of concentration, as high as solid salt. They also produce the highest purity effluent, even distillate-quality. Evaporation processes are also more tolerant of organics, hydrocarbons, or hardness salts. However, energy consumption is high and corrosion may be an issue as the prime mover is concentrated salt water. As a result, evaporation systems typically employ titanium or duplex stainless steel materials.

Brine Management

Brine management examines the broader context of brine treatment and may include consideration of government policy and regulations, corporate sustainability, environmental impact, recycling, handling and transport, containment, centralized compared to on-site treatment, avoidance and reduction, technologies, and economics. Brine management shares some issues with leachate management and more general waste management.

Solids Removal

Most solids can be removed using simple sedimentation techniques with the solids recovered as slurry or sludge. Very fine solids and solids with densities close to the density of water pose special problems. In such case filtration or ultrafiltration may be required. Although, flocculation may be used, using alum salts or the addition of polyelectrolytes.

Oils and Grease Removal

Many oils can be recovered from open water surfaces by skimming devices. Considered a dependable and cheap way to remove oil, grease and other hydrocarbons from water, oil skimmers can sometimes achieve the desired level of water purity. At other times, skimming is also a cost-efficient method to remove most of the oil before using membrane filters and chemical processes. Skimmers will prevent filters from blinding prematurely and keep chemical costs down because there is less oil to process.

Because grease skimming involves higher viscosity hydrocarbons, skimmers must be equipped with heaters powerful enough to keep grease fluid for discharge. If floating grease forms into solid clumps or mats, a spray bar, aerator or mechanical apparatus can be used to facilitate removal.

However, hydraulic oils and the majority of oils that have degraded to any extent will also have a soluble or emulsified component that will require further treatment to eliminate. Dissolving or emulsifying oil using surfactants or solvents usually exacerbates the problem rather than solving it, producing wastewater that is more difficult to treat.

The wastewaters from large-scale industries such as oil refineries, petrochemical plants, chemical plants, and natural gas processing plants commonly contain gross amounts of oil and suspended solids. Those industries use a device known as an API oil-water separator which is designed to separate the oil and suspended solids from their wastewater effluents. The name is derived from the fact that such separators are designed according to standards published by the American Petroleum Institute (API).

The API separator is a gravity separation device designed by using Stokes Law to define the rise velocity of oil droplets based on their density and size. The design is based on the specific gravity difference between the oil and the wastewater because that difference is much smaller than the specific gravity difference between the suspended solids and water. The suspended solids settles to the bottom of the separator as a sediment layer, the oil rises to top of the separator and the cleansed wastewater is the middle layer between the oil layer and the solids.

Typically, the oil layer is skimmed off and subsequently re-processed or disposed of, and the bottom sediment layer is removed by a chain and flight scraper (or similar device) and a sludge pump. The water layer is sent to further treatment consisting usually of an electroflotation module for additional removal of any residual oil and then to some type of biological treatment unit for removal of undesirable dissolved chemical compounds.

Parallel plate separators are similar to API separators but they include tilted parallel plate assemblies (also known as parallel packs). The parallel plates provide more surface for suspended oil droplets to coalesce into larger globules. Such separators still depend upon the specific gravity between the suspended oil and the water. However, the parallel plates enhance the degree of oil-water separation. The result is that a parallel plate separator requires significantly less space than a conventional API separator to achieve the same degree of separation. Hydrocyclone Oil Separators Hydrocyclone oil separators operate on the process where wastewater enters the cyclone chamber and is spun under extreme centrifugal forces up to 1000 times the force of gravity. This force causes the water and oil droplets to separate. The separated oil is discharged from one end of the cyclone where treated water is discharged through the opposite end for further treatment, filtration or discharge.

Removal of Biodegradable Organics

Biodegradable organic material of plant or animal origin is usually possible to treat using extended conventional sewage treatment processes such as activated sludge or trickling filter. Problems can arise if the wastewater is excessively diluted with washing water or is highly concentrated such as undiluted blood or milk. The presence of cleaning agents, disinfectants, pesticides, or antibiotics can have detrimental impacts on treatment processes.

Activated Sludge Process

Activated sludge is a biochemical process for treating sewage and industrial wastewater that uses air (or oxygen) and microorganisms to biologically oxidize organic pollutants, producing a waste sludge (or floc) containing the oxidized material. In general, an activated sludge process includes:

- An aeration tank where air (or oxygen) is injected and thoroughly mixed into the wastewater.
- A settling tank (usually referred to as a clarifier or "settler") to allow the waste sludge to settle. Part of the waste sludge is recycled to the aeration tank and the remaining waste sludge is removed for further treatment and ultimate disposal.

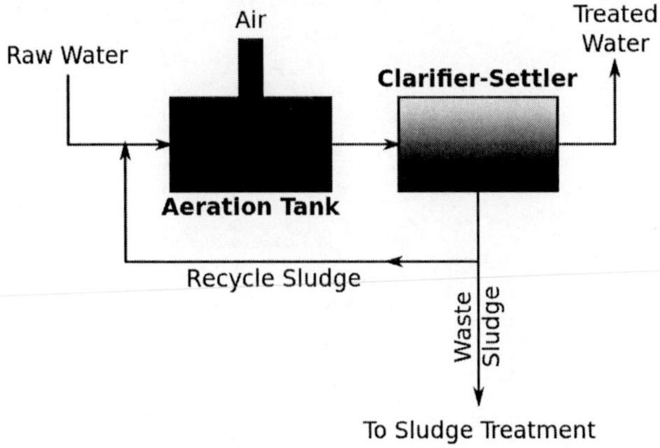

Figure: *A generalized diagram of an activated sludge process.*

Trickling Filter Process

A trickling filter consists of a bed of rocks, gravel, slag, peat moss, or plastic media over which wastewater flows downward and contacts a layer (or film) of microbial slime covering the bed media. Aerobic conditions are maintained by forced air flowing through the bed or by natural convection of air. The process involves adsorption of organic compounds in the wastewater by the microbial slime layer, diffusion of air into the slime layer to provide the oxygen required for the biochemical oxidation of the organic compounds. The end products include carbon dioxide gas, water and other products of the oxidation. As the slime layer thickens, it becomes difficult for the air to penetrate the layer and an inner anaerobic layer is formed.

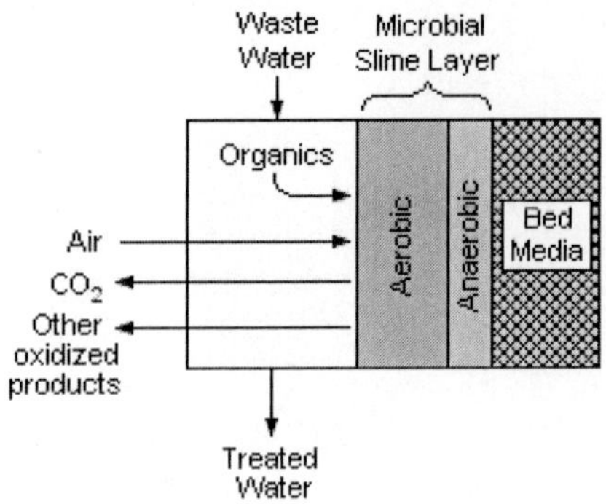

Figure: *Image 1: A schematic cross-section of the contact face of the bed media in a trickling filter*

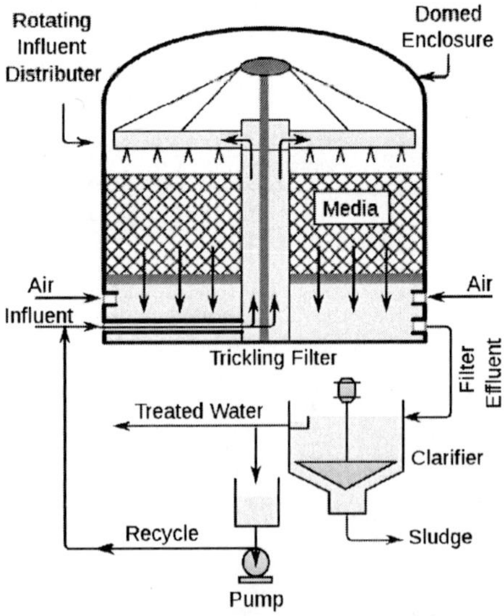

Figure: *A typical complete trickling filter system*

The fundamental components of a complete trickling filter system are:

- A bed of filter medium upon which a layer of microbial slime is promoted and developed.
- An enclosure or a container which houses the bed of filter medium.
- A system for distributing the flow of wastewater over the filter medium.

- A system for removing and disposing of any sludge from the treated effluent.

The treatment of sewage or other wastewater with trickling filters is among the oldest and most well characterized treatment technologies.

A trickling filter is also often called a *trickle filter*, *trickling biofilter*, *biofilter*, *biological filter* or *biological trickling filter*.

Treatment of Other Organics

Synthetic organic materials including solvents, paints, pharmaceuticals, pesticides, coking products and so forth can be very difficult to treat. Treatment methods are often specific to the material being treated. Methods include advanced oxidation processing, distillation, adsorption, vitrification, incineration, chemical immobilisation or landfill disposal. Some materials such as some detergents may be capable of biological degradation and in such cases, a modified form of wastewater treatment can be used.

Treatment of Acids and Alkalis

Acids and alkalis can usually be neutralised under controlled conditions. Neutralisation frequently produces a precipitate that will require treatment as a solid residue that may also be toxic. In some cases, gases may be evolved requiring treatment for the gas stream. Some other forms of treatment are usually required following neutralisation.

Waste streams rich in hardness ions as from de-ionisation processes can readily lose the hardness ions in a buildup of precipitated calcium and magnesium salts. This precipitation process can cause severe *furring* of pipes and can, in extreme cases, cause the blockage of disposal pipes. A 1 metre diameter industrial marine discharge pipe serving a major chemicals complex was blocked by such salts in the 1970s. Treatment is by concentration of de-ionisation waste waters and disposal to landfill or by careful pH management of the released wastewater.

Treatment of Toxic Materials

Toxic materials including many organic materials, metals (such as zinc, silver, cadmium, thallium, etc.) acids, alkalis, non-metallic elements (such as arsenic or selenium) are generally resistant to biological processes unless very dilute. Metals can often be precipitated out by changing the pH or by treatment with other chemicals. Many, however, are resistant to treatment or mitigation and may require concentration followed by landfilling or recycling. Dissolved organics can be *incinerated* within the wastewater by the advanced oxidation process.

Chapter 4

Industrial Ecology

Industrial ecology (IE) is the study of material and energy flows through industrial systems. The global industrial economy can be modelled as a network of industrial processes that extract resources from the Earth and transform those resources into commodities which can be bought and sold to meet the needs of humanity. Industrial ecology seeks to quantify the material flows and document the industrial processes that make modern society function. Industrial ecologists are often concerned with the impacts that industrial activities have on the environment, with use of the planet's supply of natural resources, and with problems of waste disposal. Industrial ecology is a young but growing multidisciplinary field of research which combines aspects of engineering, economics, sociology, toxicology and the natural sciences.

Industrial ecology has been defined as a "systems-based, multidisciplinary discourse that seeks to understand emergent behaviour of complex integrated human/natural systems". The field approaches issues of sustainability by examining problems from multiple perspectives, usually involving aspects of sociology, the environment, economy and technology. The name comes from the idea that the analogy of natural systems should be used as an aid in understanding how to design sustainable industrial systems.

History of Industrial Ecology

The birth of industrial ecology is commonly attributed to an article devoted to industrial ecosystems, written by Frosch and Gallopoulos, which appeared in a 1989 special issue of Scientific American, but the field's fundamentals appeared much earlier. Industrial Ecology emerged from several ideas and concepts, some of which date back to the 19th century. This article is an attempt to outline the historical build-up, which led to the emergence of Industrial Ecology as a concept and as a field of scientific research.

Before the 1960s

The term "Industrial Ecology" has been used alongside "Industrial Symbiosis" at least since the 1940s. Economic geography was perhaps one of the first fields to use these terms. For example, in an article published in 1947, George T. Renner refers to "The General Principle of Industrial Location" as a "Law of Industrial Ecology". Briefly stated this is:

> *Any industry tends to locate at a point which provides optimum access to its ingredients or component elements. If all these component elements be juxtaposed, the location of the industry is predetermined. If, however, they occur widely separated, the industry is so located as to be most accessible to that element which would be the most expensive or difficult to transport and which, therefore, becomes the locative factor for the industry in question.*

In the same article the author defines and describes industrial symbiosis:

> *Often the location of an industry cannot be fully understood solely in terms of its locative ingredient elements. There are relationships between industries, sometimes simple, but often quite complex, which enter into and complicate the analysis. Chief among these is the phenomenon of industrial symbiosis. By this is meant the consorting together of two or more of dissimilar industries. Industrial Symbiosis, when scrutinized, is seen to be of two kinds, disjunctive and conjunctive.*

It appears that the concept of Industrial Symbiosis was not new for the field of economic geography, since the same categorization is used by Walter G. Lezius in his 1937 article "Geography of Glass Manufacture at Toledo, Ohio", also published in the Journal of Economic Geography.

Used in a different context, the term "Industrial Ecology" is also found in a 1958 paper concerned with the relationship between the ecological impact from increasing urbanization and value orientations of related peoples. The case study is in Lebanon:

> *The central ecological variable in the present research is ecological mobility, or the movement of men in space. It*

> *is patent that modern Industrial Ecology requires more such adaptive mobility than does traditional folk-village organisation.*

1960s

In 1963, we find the term Industrial Ecology (defined as the "complex ecology of the modern industrial world") being used to describe the social nature and complexity of (and within) industrial systems:

> ...industrial organisations are social rather than mechanical systems. A firm is not only a working organisation with a working purpose. It is rather a community with its own 'politics', in so far as it is involved in problems concerned with the proper distribution of power between individuals and groups of individuals and with questions of individual and group prestige, influence, status and standing... [and he concludes that] the understanding which the student of management is expected to gain is no less than the attainment of insight into an Industrial Ecology of great complexity.

In 1967, the President of the American association for the advancement of science writes in "The experimental city" that "There are examples of industrial symbiosis where one industry feeds off, or at least neutralizes, the wastes of another..." The same author in 1970 talks about "The Next Industrial Revolution." The concept of material and energy sharing and reuse is central to his proposal for a new industrial revolution and he cites agro-industrial symbiosis as a practical way for achieving this:

> The object of the next industrial revolution is to ensure that there will be no such thing as waste, on the basis that waste is simply some substance that we do not vet have the wit to use... The next industrial revolution is this generating of a huge new [industry that]... will not produce products, it will rather reprocess the things we call wastes so they may be reproduced in the factories into the things we need... Having the city near the rural area will enable waste heat to be used to speed up the biological processes of treating the organic wastes before they go back into the land. This might end in an elegant arrangement-the power plants located close enough to the centre of use, to the people who need the power, but also, within the economics, close enough to the agriculture lands so that the waste heat may be used there. This is an example of agro-industrial symbiosis, if you like to call it that.

In these early articles, "Industrial Ecology" is used in its literal sense - as a system of interacting industrial entities. The relation to natural ecosystems (through either metaphor or analogy) is not explicit.

Industrial Symbiosis on the other hand, is already clearly defined as a type of industrial organisation, and the term symbiosis is borrowed from the ecological sciences to describe an analogous phenomenon in industrial systems.

1970s

Industrial Ecology has been a research subject of the Japan Industrial Policy Research Institute since 1971. Their definition of Industrial Ecology is "research for the prospect of dynamic harmonization between human activities and nature by a systems approach based upon ecology (JIPRI, 1983)". This programme has resulted to a number of reports that are available only in Japanese.

One of the earliest definitions of Industrial Ecology was proposed by Harry Zvi Evan at a seminar of the Economic Commission of Europe in Warsaw (Poland) in 1973 (an article was subsequently published by Evan in the Journal for International Labour Review in 1974 vol. 110 (3), pp. 219–233). Evan defined Industrial Ecology as a systematic analysis of industrial operations including factors like: Technology, environment, natural resources, bio-medical aspects, institutional and legal matters as well as the socio-economic aspects.

In 1974 the term of Industrial Ecology is perhaps for the first time associated with a cyclical production mode (rather than a linear one, resulting to waste). In this article, the necessity for a transition to an "open-world Industrial Ecology", is used as argument for the need to establish lunar industries:

Low living standards provide one strong motive for most developing countries to increase their productivity and grow economically. Population increase (while it lasts) is a still more powerful driver for increased world consumption. Thus the pressure on resources will continue to grow. Instead of deploring it, we better grow with it. Only through transition to an open-world Industrial Ecology - which includes both benign industrial revolution on Earth and extraterrestrial industrialization - can the present apparent limits to growth be overcome.

Many elements of modern Industrial Ecology were commonplace in the industrial sectors of the former Soviet Union. For example, "kombinirovanaia produksia" (combined production) was present from the earliest years of the Soviet Union and was instrumental in shaping the patterns of Soviet industrialization. "Bezotkhodnoyi tekhnologii" (waste-free technology) was introduced in the final decades of the USSR as a way to increase industrial production while limiting environmental impact. Fiodor Davitaya, a Soviet scientist from the Republic of Georgia, described in 1977 the analogy relating industrial systems to natural systems as a model for a desirable transition to cleaner production:

Nature operates without any waste products. What is rejected by some organisms provides food for others. The organisation of industry on this principle—with the waste products of some branches of industry providing raw material for others—means in effect using natural processes as a model, for in them the resolution of all arising contradictions is the motive force of progress.

1980s

By the 80s Industrial Ecology was already "promoted" to a research subject, which several institutes around the globe embraced. In a 1986 article published in the Journal of Ecological Modelling, there is a full description of Industrial Ecology and the analogy to natural ecosystems is clearly stated:

> *The structure and inner-working of an industrial society resemble those of a natural ecosystem. The concepts in ecology such as habitat, succession, trophic level, limiting factors and community metabolism can also apply to the study of the ecology of an industrial society. For instance, an industry in a society may grow or decline as a consequence of dynamic changes in exogenous limiting resources and in the hierarchical and/or metabolic structure of that society. When studying the ecology of an industrial society (henceforth termed 'Industrial Ecology'), these concepts and methodologies employed in ecosystems analyses are useful.*

In fact, in the above article there is an attempt to model an "industrial ecological system". The model is composed of seven major sections: industry, population, labour force, living state, environment and pollution, general health, and occupational health. Notice the rough similarity with Evan's factors as stated in the above section.

During the 80s the emergence of another related term, "industrial metabolism", is observed. The term is used as a metaphor for the organisation and functioning of industrial activity. In an article defending the "biological modulation of terrestrial carbon cycle", the author includes an extraordinary parenthetical note:

Parenthetically, it should be noted that it is an intrinsic property of life to proliferate exponentially until the encounter of limits set by (I) the availability of biologically utilisable reducing power, or (2) the exhaustion of some critical nutrient, or (3) an autotoxic effect imposed by life on its own environment. These limits are universal, applying to microbial ecosystems as well as to the population dynamics of a seemingly unrestricted biological superdominant such as Homo Sapiens (here, the ultimate limit is likely to be placed by an autotoxic effect exerted by the "extrasomatic" (industrial) metabolism of the human race).

1989 – Decisive Articles

In 1989 two articles were released that played a decisive role in the history of industrial ecology. The first one was titled "Industrial Metabolism" by Robert Ayres. Ayres essentially lays the foundations of Industrial Ecology, although the term is not to be found in this article. In the appendix of the article he includes "a theoretical exploration of the biosphere and the industrial economy as material-transformation systems and lessons that might be learned from their comparison". He proposes that:

> *We may think of both the biosphere and the industrial economy as systems for the transformation of materials. The biosphere as it now exists is nearly a perfect system for recycling materials. This was not the case when life on earth began. The industrial system of today resembles the earliest stage of biological evolution, when the most primitive living organisms obtained their energy from a stock of organic molecules accumulated during prebiotic times. It is increasingly urgent for us to learn from the biosphere and modify our industrial metabolism, the energy - and value - yielding process essential to economic development... we should not only postulate, but indeed endorse, a long-run imperative favouring an industrial metabolism that results in reduced extraction of virgin materials, reduced loss of waste materials, and increased recycling of useful ones.*

The term "Industrial Ecology" gains mainstream attention later the same year (1989) through a "Scientific American" article named "Strategies for Manufacturing". In this article, R.Frosch and N.Gallopoulos wonder "why would not our industrial system behave like an ecosystem, where the wastes of a species may be resource to another species? Why would not the outputs of an industry be the inputs of another, thus reducing use of raw materials, pollution, and saving on waste treatment?"

This vision gave birth to the concept of the Eco-industrial Park, the industrial complex that is governed by Industrial Ecology principles.

A notable example resides in a Danish industrial park in the city of Kalundborg. There, several linkages of byproducts and waste heat can be found between numerous entities such as a large power plant, an oil refinery, a pharmaceutical plant, a plasterboard factory, an enzyme manufacturer, a waste company and the city itself.

Frosch's and Gallopoulos' thinking was in certain ways simply an extension of earlier ideas, such as the efficiency and waste-reduction thinking annunciated by Buckminster Fuller and his students (e.g., J. Baldwin), and parallel ideas about energy cogeneration, such as those of Amory Lovins and the Rocky Mountain Institute.

1990s

In 1991, C. Kumar Patel organised a seminal colloquium on Industrial Ecology, held on May 20 and 21, 1991, at the National Academy of Sciences in Washington D.C. The papers were later published in the Proceedings of the National Academy of Sciences USA, and they form an excellent reference on Industrial Ecology. Papers include

- "Industrial Ecology: Concepts and Approaches"
- "Industrial Ecology: A Philosophical Introduction"
- "The Ecology of Markets,"
- "Industrial Ecology: Reflections on a Colloquium"

All twenty three papers are available online.

21st Century

The scientific field Industrial Ecology has grown fast in recent years. The Journal of Industrial Ecology (since 1997), the International Society for Industrial Ecology (since 2001), and the journal Progress in Industrial Ecology (since 2004) give Industrial Ecology a strong and dynamic position in the international scientific community. Industrial Ecology principles are also emerging in various policy realms such as the concept of the Circular Economy that is being promoted in China. Although the definition of the Circular Economy has yet to be formalized, generally the focus is on strategies such as creating a circular flow of materials, and cascading energy flows. An example of this would be using waste heat from one process to run another process that requires a lower temperature. This maximizes the efficiency of exergy use. The hope is that strategy such as this will create a more efficient economy with fewer pollutants and other unwanted by products.

Principles

One of the central principles of Industrial Ecology is the view that societal and technological systems are bounded within the biosphere, and do not exist outside of it. Ecology is used as a *metaphor* due to the observation that natural systems reuse materials and have a largely closed loop cycling of nutrients. Industrial Ecology approaches problems with the hypothesis that by using similar principles as *natural systems, industrial systems* can be improved to reduce their impact on the natural environment as well. The table shows the general metaphor.

Biosphere:

- Environment
- Organism
- Natural Product
- Natural Selection
- Ecosystem
- Ecological Niche
- Anabolism / Catabolism
- Mutation and Selection
- Succession
- Adaptation
- Food Web

Technosphere:

- Market
- Company
- Industrial Product
- Competition
- Eco-Industrial Park
- Market Niche
- Manufacturing / Waste Management
- Design for Environment
- Economic Growth
- Innovation
- Product Life Cycle

The Kalundborg industrial park is located in Denmark. This industrial park is special because companies reuse each other's waste (which then becomes by-products). For example, thc Energy E2 Asnæs

Power Station produces gypsum as a by-product of the electricity generation process; this gypsum becomes a resource for the BPB Gyproc A/S which produces plasterboards. This is one example of a system inspired by the biosphere-technosphere metaphor: in ecosystems, the waste from one organism is used as inputs to other organisms; in industrial systems, waste from a company is used as a resource by others.

Apart from the direct benefit of incorporating waste into the loop, the use of an eco-industrial park can be a means of making renewable energy generating plants, like Solar PV, more economical and environmentally friendly. In essence, this assists the growth of the renewable energy industry and the environmental benefits that come with replacing fossil-fuels.

IE examines societal issues and their relationship with both technical systems and the environment. Through this *holistic view* , IE recognises that solving problems must involve understanding the connections that exist between these systems, various aspects cannot be viewed in isolation. Often changes in one part of the overall system can propagate and cause changes in another part. Thus, you can only understand a problem if you look at its parts in relation to the whole. Based on this framework, IE looks at environmental issues with a *systems thinking* approach.

Take a city for instance. A city can be divided into commercial areas, residential areas, offices, services, infrastructures, etc. These are all sub-systems of the 'big city' system. Problems can emerge in one sub-system, but the solution has to be global. Let's say the price of housing is rising dramatically because there is too high a demand for housing. One solution would be to build new houses, but this will lead to more people living in the city, leading to the need of more infrastructure like roads, schools, more supermarkets, etc. This system is a simplified interpretation of reality whose behaviours can be 'predicted'.

In many cases, the systems IE deals with are complex systems. Complexity makes it difficult to understand the behaviour of the system and may lead to rebound effects. Due to unforeseen behavioural change of users or consumers, a measure taken to improve environmental performance does not lead to any improvement or may even worsen the situation. For instance, in big cities, traffic can become problematic. Let's imagine the government wants to reduce air pollution and makes a policy stating that only cars with an even license plate number can drive on Tuesdays and Thursdays. Odd license plate numbers can drive on Wednesdays and Fridays. Finally, the other days, both cars are allowed on the roads. The first effect could be that people buy a second car, with a specific demand for license plate numbers, so they can drive every day. The rebound effect is that, the days when all cars are allowed to drive, some inhabitants now use both cars (whereas they only had one car to use before the policy). The policy did obviously not lead to environmental improvement but even made air pollution worse.

Moreover, *life cycle thinking* is also a very important principle in industrial ecology. It implies that all environmental impacts caused by a product, system, or project during its life cycle are taken into account. In this context life cycle includes

- Raw material extraction
- Material processing
- Manufacture
- Use
- Maintenance
- Disposal

The transport necessary between these stages is also taken into account as well as, if relevant, extra stages such as reuse, remanufacture, and recycle. Adopting a life cycle approach is essential to avoid shifting environmental impacts from one life cycle stage to another. This is commonly referred to as problem shifting. For instance, during the re-design of a product, one can choose to reduce its weight, thereby decreasing use of resources. However, it is possible that the lighter materials used in the new product will be more difficult to dispose of. The environmental impacts of the product gained during the extraction phase are shifted to the disposal phase. Overall environmental improvements are thus null.

A final and important principle of IE is its *integrated approach* or *multidisciplinarity*. IE takes into account three different disciplines: social sciences (including economics), technical sciences and environmental sciences. The challenge is to merge them into a single approach.

Tools

People:

- Stakeholder analysis
- Strength Weakness Opportunities Threats Analysis (SWOT Analysis)
- Ecolabelling

- ISO 14000
- Environmental management system (EMS)
- Integrated chain management (ICM)
- Technology assessment

Planet:

- Environmental impact assessment (EIA)
- Input-output analysis (IOA)
- Life-cycle assessment (LCA)
- Material flow analysis (MFA)
- Substance flow analysis (SFA)
- MET Matrix

Profit:

- Cost benefit analysis (CBA)
- Full cost accounting (FCA)
- Life cycle costing (LCC)

Modelling:

- Stock and flow analysis
- Agent based modelling

Criticisms

The discipline of industrial ecology is to a large part based on the implicit assumption that if "we just get our technologies right", the problems of environmental pollution and unsustainability will be solved. This is the reason why most current research in industrial ecology is focused on technological innovation (i.e., the T in the IPAT equation), such as improvements in eco-efficiency, design for environment, material flow analysis, etc. This simplistic view has been recently questioned by Huesemann and Huesemann who demonstrate that negative unintended consequences of technology are inherently unpredictable and unavoidable, that most current techno-optimism reflected in industrial ecology is unjustified, and that modern technology, in the presence of continued economic growth, does not promote sustainability, but hastens collapse. Therefore, more than technological tinkering is needed to achieve long-term sustainability. Most importantly, the problem of human overpopulation must be addressed immediately and a transition to a steady state economy is needed to guarantee environmental and societal sustainability.

Future Directions

The ecosystem metaphor popularized by Frosch and Gallopoulos has been a valuable creative tool for helping researchers look for novel solutions to difficult problems. Recently, it has been pointed out that this metaphor is based largely on a model of classical ecology, and that advancements in understanding ecology based on complexity science have been made by researchers such as C. S. Holling, James J. Kay, and others. For industrial ecology, this may mean a shift from a more mechanistic view of systems, to one where sustainability is viewed as an emergent property of a complex system. To explore this further, several researchers are working with agent based modelling techniques.

Exergy analysis is performed in the field of industrial ecology to use energy more efficiently. The term *exergy* was coined by Zoran Rant in 1956, but the concept was developed by J. Willard Gibbs. In recent decades, utilisation of exergy has spread outside of physics and engineering to the fields of industrial ecology, ecological economics, systems ecology, and energetics.

Recently, there has been work advocating for large scale photovoltaic production facilities in an industrial ecology setting. These facilities not only reduce their environmental impact but also decrease the costs of photovoltaic productions to as little as $1 per Watt by economy of scale.

Environmental Impact Assessment

Environmental impact assessment is the formal process used to predict the environmental consequences (positive or negative) of a plan, policy, program, or project prior to the decision to move forward with the proposed action. Formal impact assessments may be governed by rules of administrative procedure regarding public participation and documentation of decisionmaking, and may be subject to judicial review. An impact assessment may propose measures to adjust impacts to acceptable levels or to investigate new technological solutions.

The purpose of the assessment is to ensure that decision makers consider the environmental impacts when deciding whether or not to proceed with a project. The International Association for Impact Assessment (IAIA) defines an environmental impact assessment as "the process of identifying, predicting, evaluating and mitigating the biophysical, social, and other relevant effects of development proposals prior to major decisions being taken and commitments made." EIAs are unique in that they do not require adherence to a predetermined environmental outcome, but rather they require decision -makers to account for environmental values in their decisions and to justify those decisions in light of detailed environmental studies and public comments on the potential environmental impacts.

History

Environmental impact assessments commenced in the 1960s, as part of increasing environmental awareness. EIAs involved a technical evaluation intended to contribute to more objective decision making. In the United States, environmental impact assessments obtained formal status in 1969, with enactment of the National Environmental Policy Act. EIAs have been used increasingly around the world.

The number of "Environmental Assessments" filed every year "has vastly overtaken the number of more rigorous Environmental Impact Statements (EIS)." An Environmental Assessment is a "mini-EIS designed to provide sufficient information to allow the agency to decide whether the preparation of a full-blown Environmental Impact Statement (EIS) is necessary." Eia is an activity that is done to find out the impact that would be done before development will occur.

Methods

General and industry specific assessment methods are available including:

- *Industrial products* - Product environmental life cycle analysis (LCA) is used for identifying and measuring the impact of industrial products on the environment. These EIAs consider activities related to extraction of raw materials, ancillary materials, equipment; production, use, disposal and ancillary equipment.
- *Genetically modified plants* - Specific methods available to perform EIAs of genetically modified organisms include GMP-RAM and INOVA.
- *Fuzzy logic* - EIA methods need measurement data to estimate values of impact indicators. However many of the environment impacts cannot be quantified, e.g. landscape quality, lifestyle quality and social acceptance. Instead information from similar EIAs, expert judgment and community sentiment are employed. Approximate reasoning methods known as fuzzy logic can be used. A fuzzy arithmetic approach has also been proposed and implemented using a software tool (TDEIA). More information can be found at ARAI web site.

Follow-up

At the end of the project, an audit evaluates the accuracy of the EIA by comparing actual to predicted impacts. The objective is to make future EIAs more valid and effective. Two primary considerations are:

- *Scientific* - to examine the accuracy of predictions and explain errors
- *Management* - to assess the success of mitigation in reducing impacts

Audits can be performed either as a rigorous assessment of the null hypothesis or with a simpler approach comparing what actually occurred against the predictions in the EIA document.

After an EIA, the precautionary and polluter pays principles may be applied to decide whether to reject, modify or require strict liability or insurance coverage to a project, based on predicted harms.

Around the World

Australia: The history of EIA in Australia could be linked to the enactment of the U.S. National Environment Policy Act (NEPA) in 1969, which made the preparation of environmental impact statements a requirement. In Australia, one might say that the EIA procedures were introduced at a State Level prior to that of the Commonwealth (Federal), with a majority of the states having divergent views to the Commonwealth. One of the pioneering states was New South Wales, whose State Pollution Control Commission issued EIA guidelines in 1974. At a Commonwealth (Federal) level, this was followed by passing of the Environment Protection (Impact of Proposals) Act in 1974. The Environment Protection and Biodiversity Conservation Act 1999 (EPBC) superseded the Environment Protection (Impact of Proposals) Act 1974 and is the current central piece for EIA in Australia on a Commonwealth (Federal) level. An important point to note is that this Commonwealth Act does not affect the validity of the States and Territories environmental and development assessments and approvals; rather the EPBC runs as a parallel to the State/Territory Systems. Overlap between federal and state requirements is addressed via bilateral agreements or one off accreditation of state processes, as provided for in the EPBC Act.

The Commonwealth Level

The EPBC Act provides a legal framework to protect and manage nationally and internationally important flora, fauna, ecological communities and heritage places-defined in the EPBC Act as matters of 'national environmental significance'. Following are the eight matters of 'national environmental significance' to which the EPBC ACT applies:

- World Heritage sites
- National Heritage places
- RAMSAR wetlands of international significance
- Listed threatened species and ecological communities
- Migratory species protected under international agreements
- The Commonwealth marine environment
- Nuclear actions (including uranium mining)
- National Heritage.

In addition to this, the EPBC Act aims at providing a streamlined national assessment and approval process for activities. These activities could be by the Commonwealth, or its agents, anywhere in the world or activities on Commonwealth land; and activities that are listed as having a 'significant impact' on matters of 'national environment significance'.

The EPBC Act comes into play when a person (a 'proponent') wants an action (often called a 'proposal' or 'project') assessed for environmental impacts under the EPBC Act, he or she must refer the project to the Department of Environment, Water, Heritage and the Arts (Australia). This 'referral' is then released to the public, as well as relevant state, territory and Commonwealth ministers, for comment on whether the project is likely to have a significant impact on matters of national environmental significance. The Department of Environment, Water, Heritage and the Arts assess the process and makes recommendation to the minister or the delegate for the feasibility. The final discretion on the decision remains of the minister, which is not solely based on matters of 'national environmental significance' but also the consideration of social and economic impact of the project.

The Australian Government environment minister cannot intervene in a proposal if it has no significant impact on one of the eight matters of 'national environmental significance' despite the fact that there may be other undesirable environmental impacts. This is primarily due to the division of powers between the States and the Federal government and due to which the Australian Government environment minister cannot overturn a state decision.

There are strict civil and criminal penalties for the breach of EPBC Act. Depending on the kind of breach, civil penalty (maximum) may go up to $550,000 for an individual and $5.5 million for a body corporate, or for criminal penalty (maximum) of seven years imprisonment and/ or penalty of $46,200.

The State and Territory Level

Australian Capital Territory (ACT): EIA provisions within Ministerial Authorities in the ACT are found in the Chapters 7 and 8 of the *Planning and Development Act 2007* (ACT). EIA in ACT was previously administered with the help of Part 4 of the Land (Planning and Environment) Act 1991 (Land Act) and Territory Plan (plan for land-use). Note that some EIA may occur in the ACT on Commonwealth land under the EPBC Act (Cth). Further provisions of the *Australian Capital Territory (Planning and Land Management) Act 1988* (Cth) may also be applicable particularly to national land and "designated areas".

New South Wales (NSW)

In New South Wales, the Environment Planning Assessment Act 1979 (EPA) establishes three pathways for EIA. The first is under Part 5.1 of the EPAA, which provides for EIA of 'State Significant Infrastructure' projects. (From June 2011, this Part replaced Part 3A, which previously covered EIA of major projects). The second is under Part 4 of the Act dealing with development control. If a project does not require approval under Part 3A or Part 4 it is then potentially captured by the third pathway, Part 5 dealing with environment impact assessment.

Northern Territory (NT)

The EIA process in Northern Territory is chiefly administered under the Environmental Assessment Act (EAA). Although EAA is the primary tool for EIA in Northern Territory, there are further provisions for proposals in the Inquiries Act 1985 (NT).

Queensland (QLD)

There are four main EIA processes in Queensland. Firstly, under the Integrated Planning Act 1997 (IPA) for development projects other than mining. Secondly, under the Environmental Protection Act 1994 (EP Act) for some mining and petroleum activities. Thirdly, under the State Development and Public Works Organisation Act 1971 (State Development Act) for 'significant projects'. Finally, Environment Protection and Biodiversity Conservation Act 1999 (Cth) for 'controlled actions'.

South Australia (SA)

The local governing tool for EIA in South Australia is the Development Act 1993. There are three levels of assessment possible under the Act in the form of an environment impact statement (EIS), a public environmental report (PER) or a Development Report (DR).

Tasmania (TAS)

In Tasmania, an integrated system of legislation is used to govern development and approval process, this system is a mixture of the Environmental Management and Pollution Control Act 1994 (EMPCA), Land Use Planning and Approvals Act 1993 (LUPAA), State Policies and Projects Act 1993 (SPPA), and Resource Management and Planning Appeals Tribunal Act 1993.

Victoria (VIC)

The EIA process in Victoria is intertwined with the Environment Effects Act 1978 and the Ministerial Guidelines for Assessment of Environmental Effects (made under the s. 10 of the EE Act).

Western Australia (WA)

The Environmental Protection Act 1986 (Part 4) provides the legislative framework for the EIA process in Western Australia. The EPA Act oversees the planning and development proposals and assesses their likely impacts on the environment.

Canada

In *Friends of the Oldman River Society v. Canada (Minister of Transportation)*,(SCC 1992) La Forest J of the Supreme Court of Canada described environmental impact assessment in terms of the proper scope of federal jurisdiction with respect to environments matters,

"Environmental impact assessment is, in its simplest form, a planning tool that is now generally regarded as an integral component of sound decision-making."

Supreme Court Justice La Forest cited (Cotton, Emond & 1981 245), "The basic concepts behind environmental assessment are simply stated: (1) early identification and evaluation of all potential environmental consequences of a proposed undertaking; (2) decision making that both guarantees the adequacy of this process and reconciles, to the greatest extent possible, the proponent's development desires with environmental protection and preservation."

La Forest referred to (Jeffrey 1989, 1.2,1.4) and (Emond 1978, p. 5) who described "...environmental assessments as a planning tool with both an information-gathering and a decision-making component" that provide "...an objective basis for granting or denying approval for a proposed development."

Justice La Forest addressed his concerns about the implications of Bill C-45 regarding public navigation rights on lakes and rivers that would contradict previous cases.(La Forest & 1973 178-80)

The Canadian Environmental Assessment Act 2012 (CEAA 2012) "and its regulations establish the legislative basis for the federal practice of environmental assessment in most regions of Canada." CEAA 2012 came into force July 6, 2012 and replaces the former *Canadian Environmental Assessment Act* (1995). EA is defined as a planning tool to identify, understand, assess and mitigate, where possible, the environmental effects of a project.

"The purposes of this Act are: (a) to protect the components of the environment that are within the legislative authority of Parliament from significant adverse environmental effects caused by a designated project; (b) to ensure that designated projects that require the exercise of a power or performance of a duty or function by a federal authority under any Act of Parliament other than this Act to be carried out, are considered in a careful and precautionary manner to avoid significant adverse environmental effects; (c) to promote cooperation and coordinated action between federal and provincial governments with respect to environmental assessments; (d) to promote communication and cooperation with aboriginal peoples with respect to environmental assessments; (e) to ensure that opportunities are provided for meaningful public participation during an environmental assessment; (f) to ensure that an environmental assessment is completed in a timely manner; (g) to ensure that projects, as defined in section 66, that are to be carried out on federal lands, or those that are outside Canada and that are to be carried out or financially supported by a federal authority, are considered in a careful and precautionary manner to avoid significant adverse environmental effects; (h) to encourage federal authorities to take actions that promote sustainable development in order to achieve or maintain a healthy environment and a healthy economy; and (i) to encourage the study of the cumulative effects of physical activities in a region and the consideration of those study results in environmental assessments."

Canadian Environmental Assessment Act

Opposition

Environmental Lawyer Dianne Saxe argued that the CEAA 2012 "allows the federal government to create mandatory timelines for assessments of even the largest and most important projects, regardless of public opposition." (Saxe 2012)

"Now that federal environmental assessments are gone, the federal government will only assess very large, very important projects. But it's going to do them in a hurry."

Dianne Saxe

On 3 August 2012 the Canadian Environmental Assessment Agency nine "designated projects" with their timelines: Enbridge Northern Gateway Pipeline Joint Review Panel (JRP) 18 months; Marathon Platinum Group Metals and Copper Mine Project (JRP): 13 months; Site C Clean Energy Project (JRP) 8.5 months; Deep Geologic Repository Project (JRP) 17 months; Enbridge Northern Gateway Project (JRP) 18 months; Jackpine Mine Expansion Project (JRP) 11.5 months; Pierre River Mine Project: 8 months; New Prosperity Gold-Copper Mine Project (JRP) 7.5 months; Frontier Oil Sands Mine Project (JRP)8.5 months; EnCana/Cenovus Shallow Gas Infill Project (JRP) 5 months.

Saxe compares these timelines with environmental assessments for the Mackenzie Valley Pipeline. Thomas R. Berger, Royal Commissioner of the Mackenzie Valley Pipeline Inquiry (9 May 1977), worked extremely hard to ensure that industrial development on Aboriginal people's land resulted in benefits to those indigenous people.

On 22 April 2013, Official Opposition Environment critic Megan Leslie issued a statement claiming that the federal government's recent changes to "fish habitat protection, the Navigable Waters Protection Act and the Canadian Environmental Assessment Act", along with gutting existing laws and making cuts to science and research, "will be disastrous, not only for the environment, but also for Canadians' health and economic prosperity." On 26 September 2012, Leslie argued that with the changes to the Canadian Environmental Assessment Act that came into effect 6 July 2012, "seismic testing, dams, wind farms and power plants" no longer required any federal environmental assessment. She also claimed that because the CEAA 2012—which she claimed was rushed through Parliament—dismantled the CEAA 1995, the Oshawa ethanol plant project would no longer have a full federal environmental assessment. Mr. Peter Kent (Minister of the Environment) explained that the CEAA 2012 "provides for the Government of Canada and the Environmental Assessment Agency to focus on the large and most significant projects that are being proposed across the country." The 2,000 to 3,000-plus smaller screenings that were in effect under CEAA 1995 became the "responsibility of lower levels of government but are still subject to the same strict federal environmental laws." Anne Minh-Thu Quach, MP for Beauharnois—Salaberry, QC, argued that the mammoth budget bill dismantled 50 years of environmental protection without consulting Canadians about the "colossal changes they are making to environmental assessments." She claimed that the federal government is entering into "limited consultations, by invitation only, months after the damage was done."

China

The Environmental Impact Assessment Law (EIA Law) requires that an environmental impact assessment be completed prior to project construction. However, if a developer completely ignores this requirement and builds a project without submitting an environmental impact statement, the only penalty is that the environmental protection bureau (EPB) may require the developer to do a make-up environmental assessment. If the developer does not complete this make-up assessment within the designated time, only then is the EPB authorized to fine the developer. Even so, the possible fine is capped at a maximum of about US$25,000, a fraction of the overall cost of most major projects. The lack of more stringent enforcement mechanisms has resulted in a significant percentage of projects not completing legally required environmental impact assessments prior to construction.

China's State Environmental Protection Administration (SEPA) used the legislation to halt 30 projects in 2004, including three hydropower plants under the Three Gorges Project Company. Although one month later (Note as a point of reference, that the typical EIA for a major project in the USA takes one to two years.), most of the 30 halted projects resumed their construction, reportedly having passed the environmental assessment, the fact that these key projects' construction was ever suspended was notable.

A joint investigation by SEPA and the Ministry of Land and Resources in 2004 showed that 30-40% of the mining construction projects went through the procedure of environment impact assessment as required, while in some areas only 6-7% did so. This partly explains why China has witnessed so many mining accidents in recent years.

SEPA alone cannot guarantee the full enforcement of environmental laws and regulations, observed Professor Wang Canfa, director of the centre to help environmental victims at China University of Political Science and Law. In fact, according to Wang, the rate of China's environmental laws and regulations that are actually enforced is estimated at barely 10%.

Egypt

Environmental Impact Assessment (EIA) EIA is implemented in Egypt under the umbrella of the Ministry of state for environmental affairs. The Egyptian Environmental Affairs Agency (EEAA) is responsible for the EIA services.

In June 1997, the responsibility of Egypt's first full-time Minister of State for Environmental Affairs was assigned as stated in the Presidential Decree no.275/1997. From thereon, the new ministry has focused, in close collaboration with the national and international development partners, on defining environmental policies, setting priorities and implementing initiatives within a context of sustainable development.

According to the Law 4/1994 for the Protection of the Environment, the Egyptian Environmental Affairs Agency (EEAA) was restructured with the new mandate to substitute the institution initially established in 1982. At the central level, EEAA represents the executive arm of the Ministry.

The purpose of EIA is to ensure the protection and conservation of the environment and natural resources including human health aspects against uncontrolled development. The long-term objective is to ensure a sustainable economic development that meets present needs without compromising future generations ability to meet their own needs. EIA is an important tool in the integrated environmental management approach.

EIA must be performed for new establishments or projects and for expansions or renovations of existing establishments according to the Law for the Environment.

EU

There is a wide range of instruments in the Environmental policy of the European Union. Among them the European Union has established a mix of mandatory and discretionary procedures to assess environmental impacts. European Union Directive (85/337/EEC) on Environmental Impact Assessments (known as the *EIA Directive*) was first introduced in 1985 and was amended in 1997. The directive was amended again in 2003, following EU signature of the 1998 Aarhus Convention, and once more in 2009. The initial Directive of 1985 and its three amendments have been codified in Directive 2011/92/EU of 13 December 2011. In 2001, the issue was enlarged to the assessment of plans and programmes by the so-called *Strategic Environmental Assessment (SEA) Directive* (2001/42/EC), which is now in force. Under the EU directive, an EIA must provide certain information to comply. There are seven key areas that are required:

1. Description of the project
   - o Description of actual project and site description
   - o Break the project down into its key components, i.e. construction, operations, decommissioning
   - o For each component list all of the sources of environmental disturbance
   - o For each component all the inputs and outputs must be listed, e.g., air pollution, noise, hydrology
2. Alternatives that have been considered
   - o Examine alternatives that have been considered
   - o Example: in a biomass power station, will the fuel be sourced locally or nationally?
3. Description of the environment
   - o List of all aspects of the environment that may be affected by the development
   - o Example: populations, fauna, flora, air, soil, water, humans, landscape, cultural heritage
   - o This section is best carried out with the help of local experts, e.g. the RSPB in the UK
4. Description of the significant effects on the environment
   - o The word significant is crucial here as the definition can vary
   - o 'Significant' must be defined
   - o The most frequent method used here is use of the Leopold matrix
   - o The matrix is a tool used in the systematic examination of potential interactions
   - o Example: in a windfarm development a significant impact may be collisions with birds
5. Mitigation
   - o This is where EIA is most useful
   - o Once section 4 is complete, it is obvious where impacts are greatest
   - o Using this information ways to avoid negative impacts should be developed

   - o Best working with the developer with this section as they know the project best
   - o Using the windfarm example again construction could be out of bird nesting seasons
6. Non-technical summary (EIS)
   - o The EIA is in the public domain and be used in the decision making process
   - o It is important that the information is available to the public
   - o This section is a summary that does not include jargon or complicated diagrams
   - o It should be understood by the informed lay-person
7. Lack of know-how/technical difficulties
   - o This section is to advise any areas of weakness in knowledge
   - o It can be used to focus areas of future research
   - o Some developers see the EIA as a starting block for poor environmental management

Annexed Projects

All projects are either classified as Annex 1 or Annex 2 projects. Those lying in Annex 1 are large scale developments such as motorways, chemical works, bridges, powerstations etc. These always require an EIA under the Environmental Impact Assessment Directive (85,337,EEC as amended). Annex 2 projects are smaller in scale than those referred to in Annex 1. Member States must determine whether these project shall be made subject to an assessment subject to a set of criteria set out in Annex 3 of codified Directive 2011/95/EU.

The Netherlands

EIA was implemented in Dutch legislation on September 1, 1987. The categories of projects that require an EIA are summarised in Dutch legislation, the Wet milieubeheer. The use of thresholds for activities makes sure that EIA is obligatory for those activities that may have considerable impacts on the environment.

For projects and plans that fit these criteria, an EIA report is required. The EIA report defines a.o. the proposed initiative, it makes clear the impact of that initiative on the environment and compares this with the impact of possible alternatives with less a negative impact.

Hong Kong

EIA in Hong Kong, since 1998, is regulated by the *Environmental Impact Assessment Ordinance 1997.*

The original proposal to construct the Lok Ma Chau Spur Line overground across the Long Valley failed to get through EIA, and the Kowloon–Canton Railway Corporation had to change its plan and build the railway underground. In April 2011, the EIA of the Hong Kong section of the Hong Kong-Zhuhai-Macau Bridge was found to have breached the ordinance, and was declared unlawful. The appeal by the government was allowed in September 2011. However, it was estimated that this EIA court case had increased the construction cost of the Hong Kong section of the bridge by HK$6.5 billion in money-of-the-day prices.

India

The Ministry of Environment and Forests (MoEF) of India has been in a great effort in Environmental Impact Assessment in India. The main laws in action are the Water Act(1974), the Indian Wildlife (Protection) Act (1972), the Air (Prevention and Control of Pollution) Act (1981) and the Environment (Protection) Act (1986), Biological Diversity Act(2002). The responsible body for this is the Central Pollution Control Board. Environmental Impact Assessment (EIA) studies need a significant amount of primary and secondary environmental data. Primary data are those collected in the field to define the status of the environment (like air quality data, water quality data etc.). Secondary data are those collected over the years that can be used to understand the existing environmental scenario of the study area. The environmental impact assessment (EIA) studies are conducted over a short period of time and therefore the understanding of the environmental trends, based on a few months of primary data, has limitations. Ideally, the primary data must be considered along with the secondary data for complete understanding of the existing environmental status of the area. In many EIA studies, the secondary data needs could be as high as 80% of the total data requirement. EIC is the repository of one stop secondary data source for environmental impact assessment in India.

The Environmental Impact Assessment (EIA) experience in India indicates that the lack of timely availability of reliable and authentic environmental data has been a major bottle neck in achieving the full benefits of EIA. The environment being a multi-disciplinary subject, a multitude of agencies are involved in collection of environmental data. However, no single organisation in India tracks available data from these agencies and makes it available in one place in a form required by environmental impact assessment practitioners. Further, environmental data is not available in enhanced forms that improve the quality of the EIA. This makes it harder and more time-consuming to generate environmental impact assessments and receive timely environmental clearances from regulators. With this background, the Environmental Information Centre (EIC) has been set up to serve as a professionally managed clearing house of environmental information that can be used by MoEF, project proponents, consultants, NGOs and other stakeholders involved in the process of environmental impact assessment in India. EIC caters to the need of creating and disseminating of organised environmental data for various developmental initiatives all over the country.

EIC stores data in GIS format and makes it available to all environmental impact assessment studies and to EIA stakeholders in a cost effective and timely manner. So that we can manage that in different proportions such as remedy measures etc., Aion 34A, Environmental Quality Act, 1974 requires developments that have significant impact to the environment are required to conduct the Environmental impact assessment.

Nepal

In Nepal, EIA has been integrated in major development projects since the early 1980s. In the planning history of Nepal, the sixth plan (1980–85), for the first time, recognised the need for EIA with the establishment of Environmental Impact Study Project (EISP) under the Department of Soil Conservation in 1982 to develop necessary instruments for integration of EIA in infrastructure development projects. However, the government of Nepal enunciated environment conservation related policies in the seventh plan (NPC, 1985–1990). To enforce this policy and make necessary arrangements, a series of guidelines were developed, thereby incorporating the elements of environmental factors right from the project formulation stage of the development plans and projects and to avoid or minimize adverse effects on the ecological system. In addition, it has also emphasized that EIAs of industry, tourism, water resources, transportation, urbanization, agriculture, forest and other developmental projects be conducted.

In Nepal, the government's Environmental Impact Assessment Guideline of 1993 inspired the enactment of the Environment Protection Act (EPA) of 1997 and the Environment Protection Rules (EPR) of 1997 (EPA and EPR have been enforced since 24 and 26 June 1997 respectively in Nepal) to internalizing the environmental assessment system. The process institutionalized the EIA process in development proposals and enactment, which makes the integration of IEE and EIA legally binding to the prescribed projects. The projects, requiring EIA or IEE, are included in Schedules 1 and 2 of the EPR, 1997 (GoN/MoLJPA 1997). Progresses were made in the Environmental protection issue during the 8th five year plan (1992–1997). The following development in Environmental protection were achieved during that time:

- Formulation of Environmental Protection Act 1997
- Establishment of Ministry of Environment
- Development of National Environmental Policies and Action Plan, EIA guidelines developed
- Consideration of environmental concerns in hydropower projects
- Development of industrial, irrigation and agricultural policies that undertook environmental concerns

Source: Bhatta R. and Khanal S. 2010.African Journal of Environmental Science and Technology Vol. 4(9), pp. 586–594

New Zealand

In New Zealand, EIA is usually referred to as *Assessment of Environmental Effects* (AEE). The first use of EIA's dates back to a Cabinet minute passed in 1974 called Environmental Protection and Enhancement Procedures. This had no legal force and only related to the activities of government departments. When the Resource Management Act was passed in 1991, an EIA was required as part of a resource consent application. Section 88 of the Act specifies that the AEE must include "such detail as corresponds with the scale and significance of the effects that the activity may have on the environment". While there is no duty to consult any person when making a resource consent application (Sections 36A and Schedule 4), proof of consultation is almost certain required by local councils when they decide whether or not to publicly notify the consent application under Section 93.

Russian Federation

As of 2004, the state authority responsible for conducting the State EIA in Russia has been split between two Federal bodies: 1) Federal service for monitoring the use of natural resources – a part of the Russian Ministry for Natural Resources and Environment and 2) Federal Service for Ecological, Technological and Nuclear Control. The two main pieces of environmental legislation in Russia are: The Federal Law 'On Ecological Expertise, 1995 and the 'Regulations on Assessment of Impact from Intended Business and Other Activity on Environment in the Russian Federation, 2000.

Federal Service for Monitoring the Use of Natural Resources

In 2006, the parliament committee on ecology in conjunction with the Ministry for Natural Resources and Environment, created a working group to prepare a number of amendments to existing legislation to cover such topics as stringent project documentation for building of potentially environmentally damaging objects as well as building of projects on the territory of protected areas. There has been some success in this area, as evidenced from abandonment of plans to construct a gas pipe-line through the only remaining habitat of the critically endangered Amur leopard in the Russian Far East.

Federal Service for Ecological, Technological and Nuclear Control

The government's decision to hand over control over several important procedures, including state EIA in the field of all types of energy projects, to the Federal Service for Ecological, Technological and Nuclear Control had caused a major controversy and criticism from environmental groups that blamed the government for giving nuclear power industry control over the state EIA.

Not surprisingly the main problem concerning State EIA in Russia is the clear differentiation of jurisdiction between the two above-mentioned Federal bodies.

Sri Lanka

Environmental Impact Assessments: One popular approach to assist in smart growth in democratic countries is for law-makers to require prospective developers to prepare environmental impact assessments of their plans as a condition for state and/or local governments to go for Environmental Impact Assessments.

These reports often indicate how significant impacts the development generates can be mitigated, usually at developer expense. These assessments are frequently controversial. Conservationists, neighbourhood advocacy groups and NIMBYs are often skeptical about such impact reports, even when prepared by independent agencies and approved by decision makers rather than promoters. Conversely, developers sometimes strongly resist requirements to implement the mitigation measures required by the local government, as they may be quite costly.

The importance of the Environmental Impact Assessment as an effective tool for the purpose of integrating environmental considerations with development planning is highly recognised in Sri Lanka. The application of this technique is considered as a means of ensuring that the likely effects of new development projects on the environment are fully understood and taken into account before development is allowed to proceed. The importance of this management tool to foresee potential environmental impacts and problems caused by proposed projects and its use as a mean to make project more suitable to the environment are highly appreciated.

United States

The National Environmental Policy Act of 1969 (NEPA), enacted in 1970, established a policy of environmental impact assessment for federal agency actions, federally funded activities or federally permitted/licensed activities that in the U. S. is termed "environmental review" or simply "the NEPA process." The law also created the Council on Environmental Quality, which promulgated regulations to codify the law's requirements. Under United States environmental law an Environmental Assessment (EA) is compiled to determine the need for an *Environmental Impact Statement* (EIS). Federal or federalized actions expected to subject or be subject to significant environmental impacts will publish a Notice of Intent to Prepare an EIS as soon as significance is known. Certain actions of federal agencies must be preceded by the NEPA process. Contrary to a widespread misconception, NEPA does not prohibit the federal government or its licensees/permittees from harming the environment, nor does it specify any penalty if an environmental impact assessment turns out to be inaccurate, intentionally or otherwise. NEPA requires that plausible statements as to the prospective impacts be disclosed in advance. The purpose of NEPA process is to ensure that the decision maker is fully informed of the environmental aspects and consequences prior to making the final decision.

Environmental Assessment

An environmental assessment (EA) is an environmental analysis prepared pursuant to the National Environmental Policy Act to determine whether a federal action would significantly affect the environment and thus require a more detailed *Environmental Impact Statement (EIS).* The certified release of an Environmental Assessment results in either a *Finding of No Significant Impact (FONSI)* or an EIS.

The Council on Environmental Quality (CEQ), which oversees the administration of NEPA, issued regulations for implementing the NEPA in 1979. Eccleston reports that the NEPA regulations barely mention preparation of EAs. This is because the EA was originally intended to be a simple document used in relatively rare instances where an agency was not sure if the potential significance of an action would be sufficient to trigger preparation of an EIS. But today, because EISs are so much longer and complicated to prepare, federal agencies are going to great effort to avoid preparing EISs by using EAs, even in cases where the use of EAs may be inappropriate. The ratio of EAs that are being issued compared to EISs is about 100 to 1.

Likewise, even the preparation of an accurate EA is viewed today as an onerous burden by many entities responsible for the environmental review of a proposal. Federal agencies have responded by streamlining their regulations that implement NEPA environmental review, by defining categories of projects that by their well understood nature may be safely excluded from review under NEPA, and by drawing up lists of project types that have negligible material impact upon the environment and can thus be exempted.

Content

The Environmental Assessment is a concise public document prepared by the federal action agency that serves to:

1. briefly provide sufficient evidence and analysis for determining whether to prepare an EIS or a Finding of No Significant Impact (FONSI)
2. Demonstrate compliance with the act when no EIS is required
3. facilitate the preparation of an EIS when a FONSI cannot be demonstrated

The Environmental Assessment includes a brief discussion of the purpose and need of the proposal and of its alternatives as required by NEPA 102(2)(E), and of the human environmental impacts resulting from and occurring to the proposed actions and alternatives considered practicable, plus a listing of studies conducted and agencies and stakeholders consulted to reach these conclusions. The action agency must approve an EA before it is made available to the public. The EA is made public through notices of availability by local, state, or regional clearing houses, often triggered by the purchase of a public notice advertisement in a newspaper of general circulation in the proposed activity area.

Structure

The structure of a generic Environmental Assessment is as follows:

1. Summary
2. Introduction
    - Background
    - Purpose and Need for Action

- o Proposed Action
- o Decision Framework
- o Public Involvement
- o Issues

3. Alternatives, including the Proposed Action
   - o Alternatives
   - o Mitigation Common to All Alternatives
   - o Comparison of Alternatives
4. Environmental Consequences
5. Consultation and Coordination

Procedure

The EA becomes a draft public document when notice of it is published, usually in a newspaper of general circulation in the area affected by the proposal. There is a 15 day review period required for an Environmental Assessment (30 days if exceptional circumstances) while the document is made available for public commentary, and a similar time for any objection to improper process. Commenting on the Draft EA is typically done in writing or email, submitted to the lead action agency as published in the notice of availability. An EA does not require a public hearing for verbal comments. Following the mandated public comment period, the lead action agency responds to any comments, and certifies either a FONSI or a Notice of Intent (NOI) to prepare an EIS in its public environmental review record. The preparation of an EIS then generates a similar but more lengthy, involved and expensive process.

Environmental Impact Statement

The adequacy of an environmental impact statement (EIS) can be challenged in federal court. Major proposed projects have been blocked because of an agency's failure to prepare an acceptable EIS. One prominent example was the Westway landfill and highway development in and along the Hudson River in New York City. Another prominent case involved the Sierra Club suing the Nevada Department of Transportation over its denial of the club's request to issue a supplemental EIS addressing air emissions of particulate matter and hazardous air pollutants in the case of widening U.S. Route 95 through Las Vegas. The case reached the United States Court of Appeals for the Ninth Circuit, which led to construction on the highway being halted until the court's final decision. The case was settled prior to the court's final decision.

Several state governments that have adopted "little NEPAs," state laws imposing EIS requirements for particular state actions. Some those state laws such as the California Environmental Quality Act refer to the required environmental impact study as an environmental impact report.

These variety of state requirements are yielding voluminous data not just upon impacts of individual projects, but also to elucidate scientific areas that had not been sufficiently researched. For example, in a seemingly routine *Environmental Impact Report* for the city of Monterey, California, information came to light that led to the official federal endangered species listing of Hickman's potentilla, a rare coastal wildflower.

Transboundary Application

Environmental threats do not respect national borders. International pollution can have detrimental effects on the atmosphere, oceans, rivers, aquifers, farmland, the weather and biodiversity. Global climate change is transnational. Specific pollution threats include acid rain, radioactive contamination, debris in outer space, stratospheric ozone depletion and toxic oil spills. The Chernobyl disaster, precipitated by a nuclear accident on April 26, 1986, is a stark reminder of the devastating effects of transboundary nuclear pollution.

Environmental protection is inherently a cross-border issue and has led to the creation of transnational regulation via multilateral and bilateral treaties. The United Nations Conference on the Human Environment (UNCHE or Stockholm Conference) held in Stockholm in 1972 and the United Nations Conference on the Environment and Development (UNCED or Rio Summit, Rio Conference, or Earth Summit) held in Rio de Janeiro in 1992 were key in the creation of about 1,000 international instruments that include at least some provisions related to the environment and its protection.

The United Nations Economic Commission for Europe's Convention on Environmental Impact Assessment in a Transboundary Context was negotiated to provide an international legal framework for transboundary EIA.

However, as there is no universal legislature or administration with a comprehensive mandate, most international treaties exist parallel to one another and are further developed without the benefit of consideration being given to potential conflicts with other agreements. There is also the issue of international enforcement. This has led to duplications and failures, in part due to an inability to enforce agreements. An example is the failure of many international fisheries regimes to restrict harvesting practises.

Criticism

As per Jay *et al.*, EIA is used as a decision aiding tool rather than decision making tool. There is growing dissent about them as their influence on decisions is limited. Improved training for practitioners, guidance on best practice and continuing research have all been proposed.

EIAs have been criticized for excessively limiting their scope in space and time. No accepted procedure exists for determining such boundaries. The boundary refers to 'the spatial and temporal boundary of the proposal's effects'. This boundary is determined by the applicant and the lead assessor, but in practice, almost all EIAs address only direct and immediate on-site effects.

Development causes both direct and indirect effects. Consumption of goods and services, production, use and disposal of building materials and machinery, additional land use for activities of manufacturing and services, mining and refining, etc., all have environmental impacts. The indirect effects of development can be much higher than the direct effects examined by an EIA. Proposals such as airports or shipyards cause wide-ranging national and international effects, which should be covered in EIAs.

Broadening the scope of EIA can benefit the conservation of threatened species. Instead of concentrating on the project site, some EIAs employed a habitat-based approach that focused on much broader relationships among humans and the environment. As a result, alternatives that reduce the negative effects to the population of whole species, rather than local subpopulations, can be assessed.

Environmental Impact Design

The theory and practice of Environmental impact assessment developed from the appreciation that development projects can have *negative* impacts - externalities which harm the environment. This led to the enactment of the US National Environmental Policy Act of 1969.

Environmental impact design is concerned with modifications to the design of development projects to achieve *positive* impacts - externalities which benefit the environment and raise the stock of public goods. Examples of positive impacts include:

- Habitat creation as a result of afforestation projects
- Coastal management projects which contribute to ecological and recreational objectives
- flood defence projects which create greenways

- public open space projects which contribute to surface water management objectives
- bridge designs which enhance the landscape and contribute to non-transportation objectives

Life-Cycle Assessment

Life-cycle assessment (LCA, also known as life-cycle analysis, ecobalance, and cradle-to-grave analysis) is a technique to assess environmental impacts associated with all the stages of a product's life from cradle to grave (i.e., from raw material extraction through materials processing, manufacture, distribution, use, repair and maintenance, and disposal or recycling). LCAs can help avoid a narrow outlook on environmental concerns by:

- Compiling an inventory of relevant energy and material inputs and environmental releases;
- Evaluating the potential impacts associated with identified inputs and releases;
- Interpreting the results to help make a more informed decision.

Goals and Purpose

The goal of LCA is to compare the full range of environmental effects assignable to products and services by quantifying all inputs and outputs of material flows and assessing how these material flows impact the environment. This information is used to improve processes, support policy and provide a sound basis for informed decisions.

The term *life cycle* refers to the notion that a fair, holistic assessment requires the assessment of raw-material production, manufacture, distribution, use and disposal including all intervening transportation steps necessary or caused by the product's existence.

There are two main types of LCA. Attributional LCAs seek to establish the burdens associated with the production and use of a product, or with a specific service or process, at a point in time (typically the recent past). Consequential LCAs seek to identify the environmental consequences of a decision or a proposed change in a system under study (oriented to the future), which means that market and economic implications of a decision may have to be taken into account. Social LCA is under development as a different approach to life cycle thinking intended to assess social implications or potential impacts. Social LCA should be considered as an approach that is complementary to environmental LCA.

The procedures of life cycle assessment (LCA) are part of the ISO 14000 environmental management standards: in ISO 14040:2006 and 14044:2006. (ISO 14044 replaced earlier versions of ISO 14041 to ISO 14043.) GHG product life cycle assessments can also comply with standards such as PAS 2050 and the GHG Protocol Life Cycle Accounting and Reporting Standard.

Four Main Phases

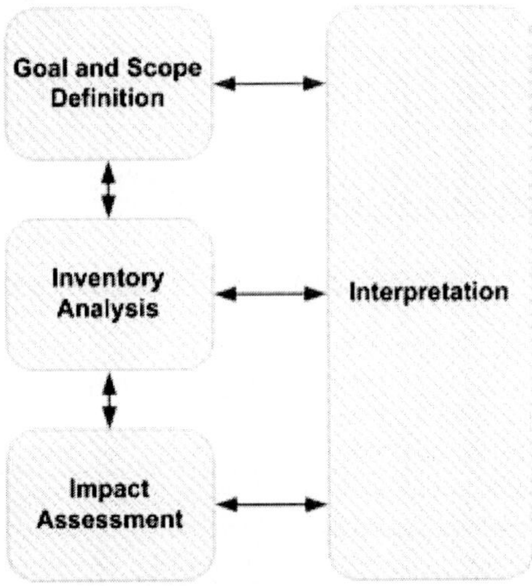

Figure: *Illustration of LCA phases.*

According to the ISO 14040 and 14044 standards, a Life Cycle Assessment is carried out in four distinct phases as illustrated in the figure shown to the right. The phases are often interdependent in that the results of one phase will inform how other phases are completed.

Goal and Scope

An LCA starts with an explicit statement of the goal and scope of the study, which sets out the context of the study and explains how and to whom the results are to be communicated. This is a key step and the ISO standards require that the goal and scope of an LCA be clearly defined and consistent with the intended application. The goal and scope document therefore includes technical details that guide subsequent work:

- the functional unit, which defines what precisely is being studied and quantifies the service delivered by the product system, providing a reference to which the inputs and outputs can be related. Further, the functional unit is an important basis that enables alternative goods, or services, to be compared and analyzed.

- the system boundaries;
- any assumptions and limitations;
- the allocation methods used to partition the environmental load of a process when several products or functions share the same process; and
- the impact categories chosen.

Life Cycle Inventory

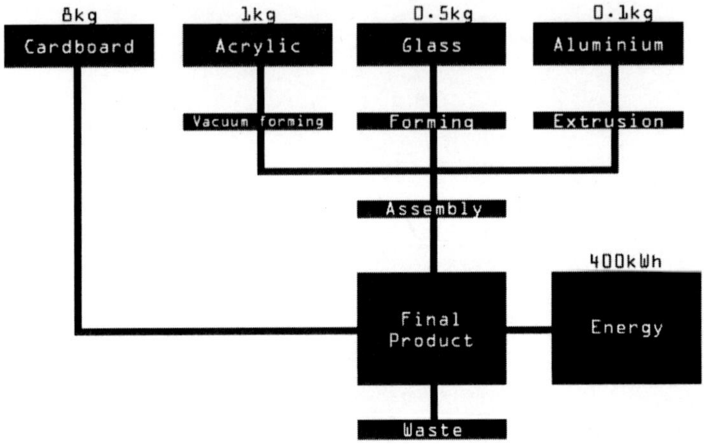

Figure: *This is an example of a Life-cycle inventory (LCI) diagram.*

Life Cycle Inventory (LCI) analysis involves creating an inventory of flows from and to nature for a product system. Inventory flows include inputs of water, energy, and raw materials, and releases to air, land, and water. To develop the inventory, a flow model of the technical system is constructed using data on inputs and outputs. The flow model is typically illustrated with a flow chart that includes the activities that are going to be assessed in the relevant supply chain and gives a clear picture of the technical system boundaries. The input and output data needed for the construction of the model are collected for all activities within the system boundary, including from the supply chain (referred to as inputs from the techno-sphere).

The data must be related to the functional unit defined in the goal and scope definition. Data can be presented in tables and some interpretations can be made already at this stage. The results of the inventory is an LCI which provides information about all inputs and outputs in the form of elementary flow to and from the environment from all the unit processes involved in the study.

Inventory flows can number in the hundreds depending on the system boundary. For product LCAs at either the generic (i.e., representative industry averages) or brand-specific level, that data is typically collected through survey questionnaires. At an industry level, care has to be taken to ensure that questionnaires are completed by a representative sample of producers, leaning toward neither the best nor the worst, and fully representing any regional differences due to energy use, material sourcing or other factors. The questionnaires cover the full range of inputs and outputs, typically aiming to account for 99% of the mass of a product, 99% of the energy used in its production and any environmentally sensitive flows, even if they fall within the 1% level of inputs.

One area where data access is likely to be difficult is flows from the techno-sphere. The technosphere is more simply defined as the man-made world. Considered by geologists as secondary resources, these resources are in theory 100% recyclable; however, in a practical sense the primary goal is salvage. For an LCI, these technosphere products (supply chain products) are those that have been produced by man and unfortunately those completing a questionnaire about a process which uses man-made product as a means to an end will be unable to specify how much of a given input they use. Typically, they will not have access to data concerning inputs and outputs for previous production processes of the product. The entity undertaking the LCA must then turn to secondary sources if it does not already have that data from its own previous studies. National databases or data sets that come with LCA-practitioner tools, or that can be readily accessed, are the usual sources for that information. Care must then be taken to ensure that the secondary data source properly reflects regional or national conditions.

Life Cycle Impact Assessment

Inventory analysis is followed by impact assessment. This phase of LCA is aimed at evaluating the significance of potential environmental impacts based on the LCI flow results. Classical life cycle impact assessment (LCIA) consists of the following mandatory elements:

- selection of impact categories, category indicators, and characterization models;
- the classification stage, where the inventory parameters are sorted and assigned to specific impact categories; and

- impact measurement, where the categorized LCI flows are characterized, using one of many possible LCIA methodologies, into common equivalence units that are then summed to provide an overall impact category total.

In many LCAs, characterization concludes the LCIA analysis; this is also the last compulsory stage according to ISO 14044:2006. However, in addition to the above mandatory LCIA steps, other optional LCIA elements – normalization, grouping, and weighting – may be conducted depending on the goal and scope of the LCA study. In normalization, the results of the impact categories from the study are usually compared with the total impacts in the region of interest, the U.S. for example. Grouping consists of sorting and possibly ranking the impact categories. During weighting, the different environmental impacts are weighted relative to each other so that they can then be summed to get a single number for the total environmental impact. ISO 14044:2006 generally advises against weighting, stating that "weighting, shall not be used in LCA studies intended to be used in comparative assertions intended to be disclosed to the public". This advice is often ignored, resulting in comparisons that can reflect a high degree of subjectivity as a result of weighting.

Interpretation

Life Cycle Interpretation is a systematic technique to identify, quantify, check, and evaluate information from the results of the life cycle inventory and/or the life cycle impact assessment. The results from the inventory analysis and impact assessment are summarized during the interpretation phase. The outcome of the interpretation phase is a set of conclusions and recommendations for the study. According to ISO 14040:2006, the interpretation should include:

- identification of significant issues based on the results of the LCI and LCIA phases of an LCA;
- evaluation of the study considering completeness, sensitivity and consistency checks; and
- conclusions, limitations and recommendations.

A key purpose of performing life cycle interpretation is to determine the level of confidence in the final results and communicate them in a fair, complete, and accurate manner. Interpreting the results of an LCA is not as simple as "3 is better than 2, therefore Alternative A is the best choice"! Interpreting the results of an LCA starts with understanding the accuracy of the results, and ensuring they meet the goal of the study. This is accomplished by identifying the data elements that contribute significantly to each impact category, evaluating the sensitivity of these significant data elements, assessing the completeness and consistency of the study, and drawing conclusions and recommendations based on a clear understanding of how the LCA was conducted and the results were developed.

Reference Test

More specifically, the best alternative is the one that the LCA shows to have the least cradle-to-grave environmental negative impact on land, sea, and air resources.

LCA Uses

Based on a survey of LCA practitioners carried out in 2006 LCA is mostly used to support business strategy (18%) and R&D (18%), as input to product or process design (15%), in education (13%) and for labelling or product declarations (11%). LCA will be continuously integrated into the built environment as tools such as the European ENSLIC Building project guidelines for buildings or developed and implemented, which provide practitioners guidance on methods to implement LCI data into the planning and design process.

Major corporations all over the world are either undertaking LCA in house or commissioning studies, while governments support the development of national databases to support LCA. Of particular note is the growing use of LCA for ISO Type III labels called Environmental Product Declarations, defined as "quantified environmental data for a product with pre-set categories of parameters based on the ISO 14040 series of standards, but not excluding additional environmental information". These third-party certified LCA-based labels provide an increasingly important basis for assessing the relative environmental merits of competing products. Third-party certification plays a major role in today's industry. Independent certification can show a company's dedication to safer and environmental friendlier products to customers and NGOs.

LCA also has major roles in environmental impact assessment, integrated waste management and pollution studies.

Data Analysis

A life cycle analysis is only as valid as its data; therefore, it is crucial that data used for the completion of a life cycle analysis are accurate and current. When comparing different life cycle analyses with one another, it is crucial that equivalent data are available for both products or processes in question. If one product has a much higher availability of data, it cannot be justly compared to another product which has less detailed data.

There are two basic types of LCA data – unit process data and environmental input-output data (EIO), where the latter is based on national economic input-output data. Unit process data are derived from direct surveys of companies or plants producing the product of interest, carried out at a unit process level defined by the system boundaries for the study.

Data validity is an ongoing concern for life cycle analyses. Due to globalization and the rapid pace of research and development, new materials and manufacturing methods are continually being introduced to the market. This makes it both very important and very difficult to use up-to-date information when performing an LCA. If an LCA's conclusions are to be valid, the data must be recent; however, the data-gathering process takes time. If a product and its related processes have not undergone significant revisions since the last LCA data was collected, data validity is not a problem. However, consumer electronics such as cell phones can be redesigned as often as every 9 to 12 months, creating a need for ongoing data collection.

The life cycle considered usually consists of a number of stages including: materials extraction, processing and manufacturing, product use, and product disposal. If the most environmentally harmful of these stages can be determined, then impact on the environment can be efficiently reduced by focusing on making changes for that particular phase. For example, the most energy-intensive life phase of an airplane or car is during use due to fuel consumption. One of the most effective ways to increase fuel efficiency is to decrease vehicle weight, and thus, car and airplane manufacturers can decrease environmental impact in a significant way by replacing aluminum with lighter materials such as carbon fibre reinforced fibres. The reduction during the use phase should be more than enough to balance additional raw material or manufacturing cost.

Variants

Cradle-to-Grave: Cradle-to-grave is the full Life Cycle Assessment from resource extraction ('cradle') to use phase and disposal phase ('grave'). For example, trees produce paper, which can be recycled into low-energy production cellulose (fibreised paper) insulation, then used as an energy-saving device in the ceiling of a home for 40 years, saving 2,000 times the fossil-fuel energy used in its production. After 40 years the cellulose fibres are replaced and the old fibres are disposed of, possibly incinerated. All inputs and outputs are considered for all the phases of the life cycle.

Cradle-to-Gate

Cradle-to-gate is an assessment of a *partial* product life cycle from resource extraction (*cradle*) to the factory gate (i.e., before it is transported to the consumer). The use phase and disposal phase of the product are omitted in this case. Cradle-to-gate assessments are sometimes the basis for environmental product declarations (EPD) termed business-to-business EDPs. One of the significant uses of the cradle-to-gate approach compiles the life cycle inventory (LCI) using cradle-to-gate. This allows the LCA to collect all of the impacts leading up to resources being purchased by the facility. They can then add the steps involved in their transport to plant and manufacture process to more easily produce their own cradle-to-gate values for their products.

Cradle-to-Cradle or Closed Loop Production

Cradle-to-cradle is a specific kind of cradle-to-grave assessment, where the end-of-life disposal step for the product is a recycling process. It is a method used to minimize the environmental impact of products by employing sustainable production, operation, and disposal practices and aims to incorporate social responsibility into product development. From the recycling process originate new, identical products (e.g., asphalt pavement from discarded asphalt pavement, glass bottles from collected glass bottles), or different products (e.g., glass wool insulation from collected glass bottles).

Allocation of burden for products in open loop production systems presents considerable challenges for LCA. Various methods, such as the avoided burden approach have been proposed to deal with the issues involved.

Gate-to-Gate

Gate-to-gate is a partial LCA looking at only one value-added process in the entire production chain. Gate-to-gate modules may also later be linked in their appropriate production chain to form a complete cradle-to-gate evaluation.

Well-to-Wheel

Well-to-wheel is the specific LCA used for transport fuels and vehicles. The analysis is often broken down into stages entitled "well-to-station", or "well-to-tank", and "station-to-wheel" or "tank-to-wheel", or "plug-to-wheel". The first stage, which incorporates the feedstock or fuel production and processing and fuel delivery or energy transmission, and is called the "upstream" stage, while the stage that deals with vehicle operation itself is sometimes called the "downstream" stage. The well-to-wheel analysis is commonly used to assess total energy consumption, or the energy conversion efficiency and emissions impact of marine vessels, aircraft and motor vehicles, including their carbon footprint, and the fuels used in each of these transport modes.

The well-to-wheel variant has a significant input on a model developed by the Argonne National Laboratory. The Greenhouse gases, Regulated Emissions, and Energy use in Transportation (GREET) model was developed to evaluate the impacts of new fuels and vehicle technologies. The model evaluates the impacts of fuel use using a well-to-wheel evaluation while a traditional cradle-to-grave approach is used to determine the impacts from the vehicle itself. The model reports energy use, greenhouse gas emissions, and six additional pollutants: volatile organic compounds (VOCs), carbon monoxide (CO), nitrogen oxide (NOx), particulate matter with size smaller than 10 micrometre (PM10), particulate matter with size smaller than 2.5 micrometre (PM2.5), and sulfur oxides (SOx).

Economic Input–Output Life Cycle Assessment

Economic input–output LCA (EIOLCA) involves use of aggregate sector-level data on how much environmental impact can be attributed to each sector of the economy and how much each sector purchases from other sectors. Such analysis can account for long chains (for example, building an automobile requires energy, but producing energy requires vehicles, and building those vehicles requires energy, etc.), which somewhat alleviates the scoping problem of process LCA; however, EIOLCA relies on sector-level averages that may or may not be representative of the specific subset of the sector relevant to a particular product and therefore is not suitable for evaluating the environmental impacts of products. Additionally the translation of economic quantities into environmental impacts is not validated.

Ecologically based LCA

While a conventional LCA uses many of the same approaches and strategies as an Eco-LCA, the latter considers a much broader range of ecological impacts. It was designed to provide a guide to wise management of human activities by understanding the direct and indirect impacts on ecological resources and surrounding ecosystems. Developed by Ohio State University Centre for resilience, Eco-LCA is a methodology that quantitatively takes into account regulating and supporting services during the life cycle of economic goods and products. In this approach services are categorized in four main groups: supporting, regulating, provisioning and cultural services.

Life Cycle Energy Analysis

Life cycle energy analysis (LCEA) is an approach in which all energy inputs to a product are accounted for, not only direct energy inputs during manufacture, but also all energy inputs needed to produce components, materials and services needed for the manufacturing process. An earlier term for the approach was *energy analysis*. With LCEA, the *total life cycle energy input* is established.

Energy Production

It is recognised that much energy is lost in the production of energy commodities themselves, such as nuclear energy, photovoltaic electricity or high-quality petroleum products. *Net energy content* is the energy content of the product minus energy input used during extraction and conversion, directly or indirectly. A controversial early result of LCEA claimed that manufacturing solar cells requires more energy than can be recovered in using the solar cell. The result was refuted. Another new concept that flows from life cycle assessments is Energy Cannibalism. Energy Cannibalism refers to an effect where rapid growth of an entire energy-intensive industry creates a need for energy that uses (or cannibalizes) the energy of existing power plants. Thus during rapid growth the industry as a whole produces no energy because new energy is used to fuel the embodied energy of future power plants. Work has been undertaken in the UK to determine the life cycle energy (alongside full LCA) impacts of a number of renewable technologies.

Energy Recovery

If materials are incinerated during the disposal process, the energy released during burning can be harnessed and used for electricity production. This provides a low-impact energy source, especially when compared with coal and natural gas. While incineration produces more greenhouse gas emissions than landfilling, the waste plants are well-fitted with filters to minimize this negative impact. A recent study comparing energy consumption and greenhouse gas emissions from landfilling (without energy recovery) against incineration (with energy recovery) found incineration to be superior in all cases except for when landfill gas is recovered for electricity production.

Criticism

A criticism of LCEA is that it attempts to eliminate monetary cost analysis, that is replace the currency by which economic decisions are made with an energy currency. It has also been argued that energy efficiency is only one consideration in deciding which alternative process to employ, and that it should not be elevated to the only criterion for determining environmental acceptability; for example, simple energy analysis does not take into account the renewability of energy flows or the toxicity of waste products; however the life cycle assessment does help companies become more familiar with environmental properties and improve their environmental system. Incorporating Dynamic LCAs of renewable energy technologies (using sensitivity analyses to project future improvements in renewable systems and their share of the power grid) may help mitigate this criticism.

In recent years, the literature on life cycle assessment of energy technology has begun to reflect the interactions between the current electrical grid and future energy technology. Some papers have focused on energy life cycle, while others have focused on carbon dioxide and other greenhouse gases. The essential critique given by these sources is that when considering energy technology, the growing nature of the power grid must be taken into consideration. If this is not done, a given class of energy technology may emit more carbon dioxide over its lifetime than it mitigates.

A problem the energy analysis method cannot resolve is that different energy forms (heat, electricity, chemical energy etc.) have different quality and value even in natural sciences, as a consequence of the two main laws of thermodynamics. A thermodynamic measure of the quality of energy is exergy. According to the first law of thermodynamics, all energy inputs should be accounted with equal weight, whereas by the second law diverse energy forms should be accounted by different values.

The Conflict is Resolved in One of These Ways

- value difference between energy inputs is ignored,
- a value ratio is arbitrarily assigned (e.g., a joule of electricity is 2.6 times more valuable than a joule of heat or fuel input),
- the analysis is supplemented by economic (monetary) cost analysis,
- exergy instead of energy can be the metric used for the life cycle analysis.

Critiques

Life cycle assessment is a powerful tool for analyzing commensurable aspects of quantifiable systems. Not every factor, however, can be reduced to a number and inserted into a model. Rigid system boundaries make accounting for changes in the system difficult. This is sometimes referred to as the boundary critique to systems thinking. The accuracy and availability of data can also contribute to inaccuracy. For instance, data from generic processes may be based on averages, unrepresentative sampling, or outdated results. Additionally, social implications of products are generally lacking in LCAs. Comparative life-cycle analysis is often used to determine a better process or product to use. However, because of aspects like differing system boundaries, different statistical information, different product uses, etc., these studies can easily be swayed in favour of one product or process over another in one study and the opposite in another study based on varying parameters and different available data. There are guidelines to help reduce such conflicts in results but the method still provides a lot of room for the researcher to decide what is important, how the product is typically manufactured, and how it is typically used.

An in-depth review of 13 LCA studies of wood and paper products found a lack of consistency in the methods and assumptions used to track carbon during the product life cycle. A wide variety of methods and assumptions were used, leading to different and potentially contrary conclusions – particularly with regard to carbon sequestration and methane generation in landfills and with carbon accounting during forest growth and product use.

Streamline LCA

This process includes three steps. First, a proper method should be selected to combine adequate accuracy with acceptable cost burden in order to guide decision making. Actually, in LCA process, besides streamline LCA, Eco-screening and complete LCA are usually considered as well. However, the former one only could provide limited details and the latter one with more detailed information is more expensive. Second, single measure of stress should be selected. Typical LCA output includes resource consumption, energy consumption, water consumption, emission of CO2, toxic residues and so on. One of these output is used as the main factor to measure in streamline LCA. Energy consumption and CO2 emission are often regarded as "practical indicators". Last, stress selected in step 2 is used as standard to assess phase of life separately and identify the most damaging phase. For instance, for a family car, energy consumption could be used as the single stress factor to assess each phase of life. The result shows that the most energy intensive phase for a family car is usage stage.

- global warming
- toxic waste
- species extinction and biodiversity

- business and the environment
- organisations and the natural environment
- restorative economy
- energy efficiency
- natural capitalism
- greening business
- sustainable enterprise
- environmental policy

Design for the Environment

Design for the Environment Program (DfE) is a United States Environmental Protection Agency (EPA) program, created in 1992, that works to prevent pollution, and the risk pollution presents to humans and the environment. The DfE program provides information regarding safer electronics, safer flame retardants, safer chemical formulations, and best environmental practices. DfE employs design approaches to reduce the overall human health and environmental impact of a product, process or service, where impacts are considered across its life cycle. Different software tools have been developed to assist designers in finding optimized products or processes/services. The three main goals of DfE are:

- Promoting green cleaning and recognising safer consumer and industrial and institutional products through safer product labelling.
- Defining Best Practices in areas ranging from auto refinishing to nail salon safety.
- Identifying safer chemicals, including life cycle considerations, through alternatives assessment.

Introduction

Design for the Environment is a global movement targeting design initiatives and incorporating environmental motives to improve product design in order to minimize health and environmental impacts. The Design for the Environment (DfE) strategy aims to improve technology and design tactics to expand the scope of products. By incorporating eco-efficiency into design tactics, DfE takes into consideration the entire life-cycle of the product, while still making products usable but minimizing resource use. The key focus of DfE is to minimize the environmental-economic cost to consumers while still focusing on the life-cycle framework of the product. By balancing both customer needs as well as environmental and social impacts DfE aims to "improve the product use experience both for consumers and producers, while minimally impacting the environment".

In the US, Design for the Environment is an EPA program works to "notify the public" of less harmful substitutes to certain products. They do so by labelling environmentally safe products with a DfE label to provide information on safer or alternative products to those which use harmful chemicals.

Design for Environment Practices

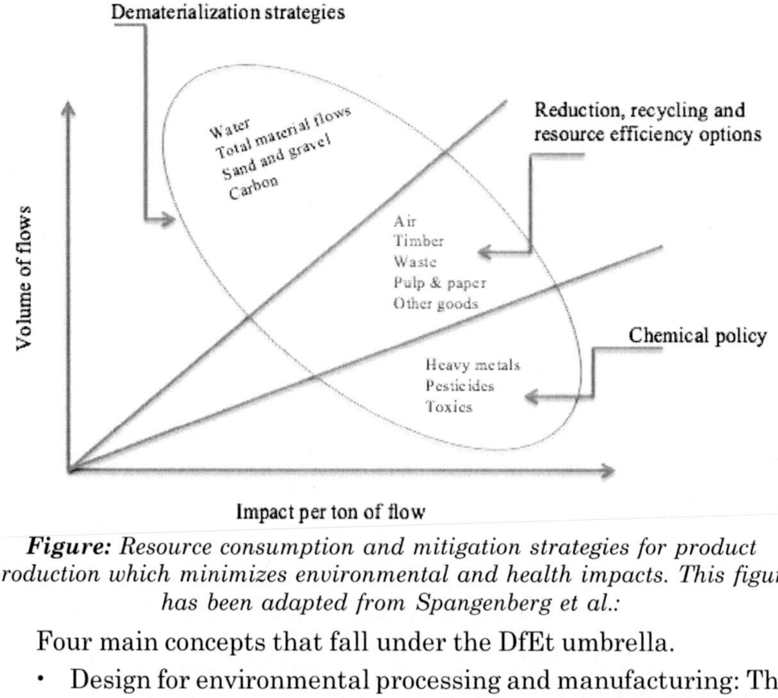

Figure: *Resource consumption and mitigation strategies for product production which minimizes environmental and health impacts. This figure has been adapted from Spangenberg et al.:*

Four main concepts that fall under the DfEt umbrella.

- Design for environmental processing and manufacturing: This ensures that raw material extraction (mining, drilling, etc.), processing (processing reusable materials, metal melting, etc.) and manufacturing are done using materials and processes which are not dangerous to the environment or the employees working on said processes. This includes the minimization of waste and hazardous by-products, air pollution, energy expenditure and other factors.
- Design for environmental packaging: This ensures that the materials used in packaging are environmentally friendly, which can be achieved through the reuse of shipping products,

elimination of unnecessary paper and packaging products, efficient use of materials and space, use of recycled and/or recyclable materials.

- Design for disposal or reuse: The end-of-life of a product is very important, because some products emit dangerous chemicals into the air, ground and water after they are disposed of in a landfill. Planning for the reuse or refurbishing of a product will change the types of materials that would be used, how they could later be disassembled and reused, and the environmental impacts such materials have.
- Design for energy efficiency: The design of products to reduce overall energy consumption throughout the product's life.

Life cycle assessment (LCA) is employed to forecast the impacts of different (production) alternatives of the product in question, thus being able to choose the most environmentally friendly. A life cycle analysis can serve as a tool when determining the environmental impact of a product or process. Proper LCAs can help a designer compare several different products according to several categories, such as energy use, toxicity, acidification, CO2 emissions, ozone depletion, resource depletion and many others. By comparing different products, designers can make decisions about which environmental hazard to focus on in order to make the product more environmentally friendly.

Why do Firms Want to Design for the Environment?

Modern day businesses all aim to produce goods at a low cost while maintaining quality, staying competitive in the global marketplace, and meeting consumer preferences for more environmentally friendly products. To help businesses meet these challenges, EPA encourages businesses to incorporate environmental considerations into the design process. The benefits of incorporating DfE include: cost savings, reduced business and environmental risks, expanded business and market opportunities, and to meet environmental regulations.

Companies and Products

- Starbucks: Starbucks is decreasing its carbon footprint by building more energy efficient stores and facilities, conserving energy and water, and purchasing renewable energy credits. Starbucks has achieved LEED certificates in 116 stores in 12 countries. Starbucks has even created a portable, LEED certified store in Denver. It is Starbucks' goal to reduce energy consumption by 25% and to cover 100% of its electricity with renewable energy by 2015.

- Hewlett Packard: HP is working towards reducing energy used in manufacturing, developing materials that have less environmental impact, and designing easily recyclable equipment.
- IBM: Their goal is to extend product life beyond just production, and to use reusable and recyclable products. This means that IBM is currently working on creating products that can be safely disposed of at the end of its product life. They are also reducing consumption of energy to minimize their carbon footprint.
- Philips: For almost 20 years now, sustainable development has been a crucial part of Philips decision making and manufacturing process. Philips' goal is to produce products with their environmental responsibility in mind. Not only are they working on reducing energy during the manufacturing process, Phillips is also participating in a unique project, philanthropy through design. Since 2005, Philips has been working on and developing philanthropy through design. They collaborate with other organisations to use their expertise and innovation to help the more fragile parts of our society.

Besides these large brand names there are several other consumer product companies in the DfE program this including:

- Atlantic Chemical & Equipment Co.
- American Cleaning Solutions
- BCD Supply
- Beta Technology
- Brighton USA

How does a Business Design for the Environment?

A business can design for the environment by:

- Evaluating the human health and environmental impacts of its processes and products.
- Identifying what information is needed to make human health and environment decisions
- Conducting an assessment of alternatives
- Considering cross-media impacts and the benefits of substituting chemicals
- Reducing the use and release of toxic chemicals through the innovation of cleaner technologies that use safer chemicals.
- Implementing pollution prevention, energy efficiency, and other resource conservation measures.

- Making products that can be reused and recycled
- Monitoring the environmental impacts and costs associated with each product or process
- Recognising that although change can be rapid, in many cases a cycle of evaluation and continuous improvement is needed

Safer Product Labelling Program

The design for the environment safer product labelling program aims to protect human health and the environment. DfE works alongside consumers and producers to enhance the safety of a wide assortment of products. The program is important because it only labels products as "DfE" when they have met an environmental standard set by the EPA. According to the EPA website currently over 2,700 products carry the DfE label making it easier for consumers to identify products which utilise safer chemicals in products such as household cleaning supplies. However, cleaning products are only one of many products that are eligible for the label. Other products include septic system treatments and wastewater inoculants, car care products, carpet cleaners, several types of degreasing products, laundry-care products and several others. Furthermore the DfE program works alongside producers to assist them in finding safer substitutes to current chemicals used, and thus helping to minimize the companies environmental impact and human health effects. The procedure for safer product labelling consists of several steps which include selecting materials which will have the lowest environmental and health impacts, reducing the amount of material used, incorporating the "cradle-to-grave" concept of minimizing the impact of production/disposal as well as the impact during use of the product and enhancing the disposal process by using materials which can be recycled, disassembled or that will have a minimum landfill impact.

For Consumers

EPA certified safe products are recognisable by the DfE label. The label helps the consumer identify and choose products that are safer for human health and protect the environment. The DfE logo on a product symbolizes that the DfE scientific review team has screened each ingredient contained in the product for potential human health and environmental effects and have recognised the product as being the safest option for consumers.

For Product Manufacturers

Manufacturers who are partners for the Design for the Environment program have the right to display the DfE logo on recognised products.

These manufacturers invest in research, development and reformulation, to ensure the ingredients contained in the finished product are safe to humans and protect the environment while maintaining or improving product performance.

For Industrial and Institutional Purchasers

Design for the Environment is an EPA program that distinguishes safer chemical products. EPA uses rigorous criteria to ensure that Design for the Environment-labelled products are safe for human health and the environment. The Design for the Environment label makes it easy for purchasers and users to quickly identify safer chemical products that do not sacrifice quality or performance. Design for the Environment has approved more than 2,000 industrial and institutional products.

Current Laws and Regulations Encouraging DfE in the Electronics Industry

The National Ambient Air Quality Standards (NAAQS): The EPA has imposed the National Ambient Air Quality Standards (NAAQS) to establish an air quality standard across the U.S. The NAAQS sets standards on six main sources of pollutants, which include emissions of: ozone (0.12 ppm per 1 hour), carbon monoxide (35 ppm per 1 hour), pollutant (primary standards), particulate matter (50g/m^3 at an annual arithmetic mean), sulfur dioxide (80g/m^3 at an annual arithmetic mean), nitrogen dioxide (100g/m^3 at an annual arithmetic mean), and lead emissions (1.5g/m^3 at an annual arithmetic mean).

Stratospheric Ozone Protection

The Stratospheric Ozone Protection is under section 602 of the Clean Air Act of 1990. This regulation aims to decrease emission of chlorofluorocarbons (CFCs) and other chemicals that are destroying the stratospheric ozone layer. The protection initiative categorizes ozone-depleting substances into two classes: Class I, and Class II.

Class I substances include 20 different kinds of chemicals and have all been phased-out of production processes since 2000. Class II substances consist of the 33 different HCFCs. The EPA has already begun plans to decrease emissions in HCFCs and plan to completely phase out the class II substances by 2030.

Reporting Requirements for Releases of Toxic Substances

A firm operating in the electronics industry in SIC Codes 20-39 that has more than 10 full-time employees and consumes more than 10,000 lbs per year of any toxic chemical lists in 40 CFR 372.65 must file a toxic release inventory.

Other Regulations

- Hazardous Air Pollutants and Maximum Achievable Control Technology (MACT) Standards
- EPA National Pollutant Discharge Elimination System
- Underground Injection Control Program
- Hazardous Waste Management
- Underground Storage Tank Management

Alternatives Assessment Program

In order to help industries choose safer chemicals for applications, DfE conducts Alternatives Assessments. This program brings together environmental organisations, industry leaders, academia, and others to evaluate the environmental and health impacts of potential alternatives to problematic chemicals. The program uses a variety of approaches to investigate safer chemistries. Life-cycle assessment can be conducted to understand the phases (e.g., production, use, and disposal) where industry can make changes to realise environmental and health benefits. DfE Hazard-based Alternatives Analyses evaluate the hazards posed by chemicals during relevant phases in the product life cycle. These approaches can be applied to identifying safer alternative chemicals for applications that now use priority chemicals of concern. The outcome of an Alternatives Assessments Partnership provides industry with the information they need to choose safer chemicals, as well as avoid unintended consequences of switching to a poorly understood substitute.

Best Practices Approach

DfE's Best Practices approach is designed to enhance the awareness of health and environmental concerns, minimize pollution, and protect workers and communities by promoting the use of safer alternative chemical products and cleaner, more efficient practices. After a chemical ingredient has been reviewed by a DfE Alternatives Assessment and no clear alternative is available, the industry is encouraged to use the Best Practices approach as formulated by DfE. Currently, there is a Best Practices approach for both the Automotive Refinishing industry and Spray Polyurethane Foam.

Design Impact Measures

Design impact measures are used to qualify projects for various rating systems and to guide both design and regulatory decisions from beginning to end. Some like the greenhouse gas inventory may also be required globally for all business decisions. Some like the LEED point rating system are used only for its own ratings, and the qualification for 'points' may include some physical measures to qualify, but the points do not represent measurements. Others like the Athena life-cycle impact assessment tool attempt to add up all the kinds of measurable impacts of all parts of a building throughout its life and are quite rigorous and complex.

The general field also includes environmental impact assessment and environmental accounting, and to tie them together, systems ecology, cost estimation models and cost–benefit analysis.

For sustainable design the number and types of methods and resources that have become available in 2008 is suddenly much larger than before. Because they help you with it, all these tools also require beginning to think about real complex processes. The reason for the sudden appearance of so many new methods appears to be the natural rapidly increasing complexity of the physical design problem we confront as our interactions with the earth become larger, more complex and more critical to account for.

Simple Online Calculators

The Energy Star building energy calculator & targeting tool based on the US IEA and CBECS data from long term US nationwide energy use surveys. This is the estimator that projects use to qualify for a Green Globes rating. It is solid and simple but tells you less about your particular choices – Easy carbon footprint tools, the UK "Footprinter" and "Build Carbon Neutral" These are the simplest of the tools that estimate the total by adding up the easily visible parts.

Advanced Impact and Energy Analysis Tools

US DOE list of "building energy tools" This is a huge list and is probably quite incomplete, but has good concise software reviews. All the design and engineering software packages are also starting to build in energy impact tools and climate modelling, etc. Many of them rely on the move to BIM whole building design data models that allow many consultants to work on the same building or urban design scheme at once.

The "Greenhouse gas protocol" is an intergovernmental data service used by the major international bodies for organising the greenhouse gas data and reporting requirements. It's organised primarily by industry. – "Athena Eco-Calculator" is an advanced and thorough Life-Cycle impact assessment tool for buildings. This can be read at the US DOE list above.

"EcoFootprinting" provides a way to measure your total use of productive land, or 'ecological footprint'. Its figures are based on studies showing that our burden on renewable resources is significantly greater than the Earth's regenerative capacities, and still increasing. The results may not measured uncertainty, but would probably be comparable to each other.

Cradle-to-Cradle Design

Cradle to Cradle design (also referred to as Cradle to Cradle, C2C, cradle 2 cradle, or regenerative design) is a biomimetic approach to the design of products and systems. It models human industry on nature's processes viewing materials as nutrients circulating in healthy, safe metabolisms. It suggests that industry must protect and enrich ecosystems and nature's biological metabolism while also maintaining a safe, productive technical metabolism for the high-quality use and circulation of organic and technical nutrients. Put simply, it is a holistic economic, industrial and social framework that seeks to create systems that are not only efficient but also essentially waste free. The model in its broadest sense is not limited to industrial design and manufacturing; it can be applied to many aspects of human civilization such as urban environments, buildings, economics and social systems.

The term Cradle to Cradle is a registered trademark of McDonough Braungart Design Chemistry (MBDC) consultants. Cradle to Cradle product certification began as a proprietary system; however, in 2012 MBDC turned the certification over to an independent non-profit called the Cradle to Cradle Products Innovation Institute. Independence, openness, and transparency are the Institute's first objectives for the certification protocols. The phrase "cradle to cradle" itself was coined by Walter R. Stahel in the 1970s. The current model is based on a system of "lifecycle development" initiated by Michael Braungart and colleagues at the *Environmental Protection Encouragement Agency* (EPEA) in the 1990s and explored through the publication *A Technical Framework for Life-Cycle Assessment.*

In 2002, Braungart and William McDonough published a book called *Cradle to Cradle: Remaking the Way We Make Things*, a manifesto for cradle to cradle design that gives specific details of how to achieve the model. The model has been implemented by a number of companies, organisations and governments around the world, predominantly in the European Union, China and the United States. Cradle to cradle has also been the subject of many documentary films, including the critically acclaimed *Waste=Food.*

Introduction

In the cradle to cradle model, all materials used in industrial or commercial processes—such as metals, fibres, dyes—fall into one of two categories: "technical" or "biological" nutrients. *Technical nutrients* are strictly limited to non-toxic, non-harmful synthetic materials that have no negative effects on the natural environment; they can be used in continuous cycles as the same product without losing their integrity or quality. In this manner these materials can be used over and over again instead of being "downcycled" into lesser products, ultimately becoming waste.

Biological Nutrients are organic materials that, once used, can be disposed of in any natural environment and decompose into the soil, providing food for small life forms without affecting the natural environment. This is dependent on the ecology of the region; for example, organic material from one country or landmass may be harmful to the ecology of another country or landmass.

The two types of materials each follow their own cycle in the regenerative economy envisioned by Keunen and Huizing.

Structure

Initially defined by McDonough and Braungart, the Cradle to Cradle Products Innovation Institute's five certification criteria are:

- Material health, which involves identifying the chemical composition of the materials that make up the product. Particularly hazardous materials (e.g. heavy metals, pigments, halogen compounds etc.) have to be reported whatever the concentration, and other materials reported where they exceed 100 ppm. For wood, the forest source is required. The risk for each material is assessed against criteria and eventually ranked on a scale with green being materials of low risk, yellow being those with moderate risk but are acceptable to continue to use, and red for materials that have high risk and need to be phased out. Grey for materials with incomplete data. The method uses the term 'risk' in the sense of hazard (as opposed to consequence and likelihood).
- Material reutilisation, which is about recovery and recycling at the end of product life.
- Assessment of energy required for production, which for the highest level of certification needs to be based on at least 50% renewable energy for all parts and subassemblies.

- Water, particularly usage and discharge quality.
- Social responsibility, which assesses fair labour practices.

The certification is available at several levels: basic, silver, gold, platinum, with more stringent requirements at each. Prior to 2012, MBDC controlled the certification protocol.

Health

Currently, many human beings come into contact or consume, directly or indirectly, many harmful materials and chemicals daily. In addition, countless other forms of plant and animal life are also exposed. C2C seeks to remove dangerous *technical nutrients* (synthetic materials such as mutagenic materials, heavy metals and other dangerous chemicals) from current life cycles. If the materials we come into contact with and are exposed to on a daily basis are not toxic and do not have long term health effects, then the health of the overall system can be better maintained. For example, a fabric factory can eliminate all harmful *technical nutrients* by carefully reconsidering what chemicals they use in their dyes to achieve the colours they need and attempt to do so with fewer base chemicals.

Economics

The use of a C2C model often lowers the financial cost of systems. For example, in the redesign of the Ford River Rouge Complex, the planting of Sedum (stonecrop) vegetation on assembly plant roofs retains and cleanses rain water. It also moderates the internal temperature of the building in order to save energy. The roof is part of an $18 million rainwater treatment system designed to clean 20 billion US gallons (76,000,000 m^3) of rainwater annually. This saved Ford $50 million that would otherwise have been spent on mechanical treatment facilities. If products are designed according to C2C design principles, they can be manufactured and sold for less than alternative designs. They eliminate the need for waste disposal such as landfills.

Definitions

- Cradle to cradle a play on the phrase "Cradle to Grave", implying that the C2C model is sustainable and considerate of life and future generations.
- Technical nutrients are basically inorganic or synthetic materials manufactured by humans—such as plastics and metals—that can be used many times over without any loss in quality, staying in a continuous cycle.

- Biological nutrients and materials are organic materials that can decompose into the natural environment, soil, water, etc. without affecting it in a negative way, providing food for bacteria and microbiological life.
- Materials are usually referred to as the building blocks of other materials, such as the dyes used in colouring fibres or rubbers used in the sole of a shoe.
- Downcycling is the reuse of materials into lesser products. For example, a plastic computer case could be downcycled into a plastic cup, which then becomes a park bench, etc.; this may eventually lead to waste. In conventional understanding, this is no different from recycling that produces a supply of the same product or material.
- Waste = Food is a basic concept of organic waste materials becoming food for bugs, insects and other small forms of life who can feed on it, decompose it and return it to the natural environment which we then indirectly use for food ourselves.

Existing Synthetic Materials

The question of how to deal with the countless existing *technical nutrients* (synthetic materials) that cannot be recycled or reintroduced to the natural environment is dealt with in C2C design. The materials that can be reused and retain their quality can be used within the technical nutrient cycles while other materials are far more difficult to deal with, such as plastics in the Pacific Ocean.

Hypothetical Examples

One effective example is a shoe that is designed and mass-produced using the C2C model. The sole might be made of "biological nutrients" while the upper parts might be made of "technical nutrients." The shoe is mass-produced at a manufacturing plant that utilises its waste material by putting it back into the cycle; an example of this is using off-cuts from the rubber soles to make more soles instead of merely disposing of them (this is dependent on the technical materials not losing their quality as they are reused). Once the shoes have been manufactured, they are distributed to retail outlets where the customer buys the shoe at a fraction of the price they would normally pay for a shoe of comparable aspects; the customer is only paying for the use of the materials in the shoe for the period of time that they will be using the shoe. When they outgrow the shoe or it is damaged, they return it to the manufacturer. When the manufacturer separates the sole from the upper parts (separating the technical and biological nutrients), the biological nutrients are returned to the natural environment while the technical nutrients are used to create the sole of another shoe.

Another example of C2C design is a disposable cup, bottle, or wrapper made entirely out of biological materials. When the user is finished with the item, it can be disposed of and returned to the natural environment; the cost of disposal of waste such as landfill and recycling is eliminated. The user could also potentially return the item for a refund so it can be used again.

Ford Model U is a design concept of a car, made completely from cradle-to-cradle materials. It also uses hydrogen propulsion.

Finished Products

- Cradle-to-cradle shoes have been made through the Nike Considered project.
- The Edag light car
- Rohner Textile AG Climatex-textile
- Biofoam; a cradle-to-cradle alternative to expanded polystyrene
- Sewage sludge processing plants are facilities that create fertiliser from sewage sludge. This approach is green retrofit for the current (inefficient) system of organic waste disposal; as composting toilets are a better approach in the long run.

Implementation

The C2C model can be applied to almost any system in modern society: urban environments, buildings, manufacturing, social systems. 5 steps are outlined in *Cradle to Cradle – Remaking the way we make things*:

- Get "free of" known culprits
- Follow informed personal preferences
- Create "passive positive" lists – lists of materials used categorised according to their safety level

The X List – substances that must be phased out, such as teratogenic, mutagenic, carcinogenic.

The Gray List – problematic substances that are not so urgently in need of phasing out

The P List – the "positive" list, substances actively defined as safe for use

- Activate the positive list
- Reinvent – the redesign of the former system

Products that adhere to all steps can generally be granted a certification. Two certifications used for cradle-to-cradle products include Leadership in Energy and Environmental Design (LEED) and BRE Environmental Assessment Method (BREEAM).

C2C principles were first applied to systems in the early 1990s by Braungart's Hamburger Umweltinstitut (HUI) and The Environmental Institute in Brazil for biomass nutrient recycling of effluent to produce agricultural products and clean water as a byproduct.

In 2007, MBDC and the EPEA formed a strategic partnership with global materials consultancy Material ConneXion to help promote and disseminate C2C design principles by providing greater global access to C2C material information, certification and product development.

As of January 2008, Material ConneXion's Materials Libraries in New York, Milan, Cologne, Bangkok and Daegu, Korea started to feature C2C assessed and certified materials and, in collaboration with MBDC and EPEA, the company now offers C2C Certification, and C2C product development.

While the C2C model has influenced the construction or redevelopment of many smaller buildings, several large companies, organisations and governments have also implemented the C2C model and its ideas and concepts:

Major Implementations

- The Lyle Centre for Regenerative Studies incorporates cradle to cradle systems throughout the centre. The use of the term C2C is replaced with Regenerative.
- The Chinese Government is constructing many cities like Huangbaiyu based on C2C principles, utilising the rooftops for agriculture.
- The Ford River Rouge Complex redevelopment. Cleaning 20 billion US gallons (76,000,000 m^3) of rainwater annually.
- The Netherlands Institute of Ecology (NIOO-KNAW) will make its laboratory and office complex completely cradle to cradle compliant
- Several private houses and communal buildings in the Netherlands
- Fashion Positive, an initiative to assist the fashion world in implementing the cradle-to-cradle model in five areas: material health, material reuse, renewable energy, water stewardship and social fairness.

Coordination with Other Models

The Cradle to Cradle model can be viewed as a framework that considers systems as a whole or holistically. It can be applied to many aspects of human society, and is related to Life cycle assessment. The Cradle to Cradle model in some implementations is closely linked with the Car-free movement, such as in the case of large-scale building projects or the construction or redevelopment of urban environments. It is closely linked with passive solar design in the building industry and with permaculture in agriculture within or near urban environments. An earthship is a perfect example where different re-use models are used, cradle to cradle and permaculture.

Constraints

A major constraint in the optimal recycling of materials is that at civic amenity sites, products are not disassembled by hand and have each individual part sorted into a bin, but instead have the entire product sorted into a certain bin.

This makes that extracting of rare earths and other materials is uneconomical (at recycling sites, products typically get crushed after which the materials are extracted by means of magnets, chemicals, special sorting methods, ...) and optimal recycling of for example metals is impossible (an optimal recycling method for metals would require to sort all similar alloys together rather than mixing plain iron with alloys).

Obviously, disassembling products is not feasible at civic amenity sites, and a better method would be to sent back the broken products to the manufacturer, so that the manufacturer can disassemble the product, for example for making new products or at least to have the components sent separately to recycling sites (for proper recycling, by the exact type of material). At present though, no laws are put in place in any country to oblige manufacturers of taking back their products for disassembly, nor are there even such obligations for manufacturers of cradle-to-cradle products.

Criticism and Response

Criticism has been advanced on the fact that McDonough and Braungart previously kept C2C consultancy and certification in their inner circle. Critics argued that this lack of competition prevented the model from fulfilling its potential. Many critics pled for a public-private partnership overseeing the C2C concept, thus enabling competition and growth of practical applications and services.

McDonough and Braungart responded to this criticism by giving control of the certification protocol to a non-profit, independent Institute called the Cradle to Cradle Products Innovation Institute. McDonough said the new institute "will enable our protocol to become a public certification program and global standard." The new Institute announced the creation of a Certification Standards Board in June 2012. The new board, under the auspices of the Institute, will oversee the certification moving forward.

Experts in the field of environment protection have questioned the practicability of the concept. Friedrich Schmidt-Bleek, head of the German Wuppertal Institute called his assertion, that the "old" environmental movement had hindered innovation with its pessimist approach "pseudo-psychological humbug".

I can feel very nice on Michael's seat covers in the airplane. Nevertheless I am still waiting for a detailed proposal for a design of the other 99.99 percent of the Airbus 380 after his principles.

In 2009 Schmidt-Bleek stated that it is out of the question that the concept can be realised on a bigger scale.

Some claim that C2C certification may not be entirely sufficient in all eco-design approaches. Quantitative methodologies (LCAs) and more adapted tools (regarding the product type which is considered) could be used in tandem. The C2C concept ignores the use phase of a product. According to the Variants of Life Cycle Assessment the entire life cycle of a product or service has to be evaluated, not only the material itself. For many goods e.g. in transport, the use phase has the most influence on the environmental footprint. E.g. the more lightweight a car or a plane the less fuel it consumes and consequently the less impact it has. Braungart fully ignores the use phase.

It is safe to say that every production step or resource-transformation step needs a certain amount of energy.

The C2C concept foresees an own certification of its analysis and therefore is in contradiction to international ISO standards 14040 and 14044 for Life Cycle Assessment whereas an independent and critical review is needed in order to obtain comparative and resilient results. Independent external review.

Eco-Industrial Park

An eco-industrial park (EIP) is an industrial park in which businesses cooperate with each other and with the local community in an attempt to reduce waste and pollution, efficiently share resources (such as information, materials, water, energy, infrastructure, and natural resources), and help achieve sustainable development, with the intention of increasing economic gains and improving environmental quality. An EIP may also be planned, designed, and built in such a way that it makes it easier for businesses to co-operate, and that results in a more financially sound, environmentally friendly project for the developer.

The Eco-industrial Park Handbook states that "An Eco-Industrial Park is a community of manufacturing and service businesses located together on a common property. Members seek enhanced environmental, economic, and social performance through collaboration in managing environmental and resource issues."

Based on the concepts of industrial ecology, collaborative strategies not only include by-product synergy ("waste-to-feed" exchanges), but can also take the form of wastewater cascading, shared logistics and shipping & receiving facilities, shared parking, green technology purchasing blocks, multi-partner green building retrofit, district energy systems, and local education & resource centres. This is an application of a systems approach, in which designs and processes/activities are integrated to address multiple objectives.

EIPs can be developed as greenfield land projects, where the eco-industrial intent is present throughout the planning, design and site construction phases, or developed through retrofits and new strategies in existing industrial developments.

Examples

"Industrial symbiosis" is a related but more limited concept in which companies in a region collaborate to utilise each other's by-products and otherwise share resources. In Kalundborg, Denmark a symbiosis network links a 1500MW coal-fired power plant with the community and other companies. Surplus heat from this power plant is used to heat 3500 local homes in addition to a nearby fish farm, whose sludge is then sold as a fertilizer. Steam from the power plant is sold to Novo Nordisk, a pharmaceutical and enzyme manufacturer, in addition to a Statoil plant. This reuse of heat reduces the amount thermal pollution discharged to a nearby fjord. Additionally, a by-product from the power plant's sulfur dioxide scrubber contains gypsum, which is sold to a wallboard manufacturer. Almost all of the manufacturer's gypsum needs are met this way, which reduces the amount of open-pit mining needed. Furthermore, fly ash and clinker from the power plant is utilised for road building and cement production.

The industrial symbiosis at Kalundborg was not created as a top-down initiative, but instead evolved gradually. As environmental regulations became stricter, firms were motivated reduce the cost of compliance, and turn their by-products into economic products.

In Canada, eco-industrial parks exist across the country and have enjoyed some success. The best known example is Burnside Park, in Halifax, Nova Scotia. With support from Dalhousie University's Eco-Efficiency Centre, the more than 1,500 businesses have been improving their environmental performance and developing profitable partnerships. Subsequently, two greenfield industrial developments have been started in Alberta: TaigaNova Eco-Industrial Park is in the heart of the Athabasca oil sands, while Innovista Eco-Industrial Park is a gateway to the Rocky Mountains ~300km west of Edmonton.

Other Usage

EIPs also refer to industrial parks where a "green" approach has been taken towards the infrastructure and development of the site. This can include green infrastructure related to Renewable Energy Systems; stormwater, groundwater and wastewater management; road surfaces; and transportation demand management. Green building practices can also be encouraged or mandated

EIPs are often used as a stimulus for economic diversification in the community or region where they are located. Anchor tenants, such as bio-based product manufacturers or waste-to-energy facilities, etc., can attract complementary businesses as suppliers, scavengers/recyclers, service providers, downstream users and other businesses that could benefit from eco-industrial strategies.

Suggested Usage

It is suggested that EIPs be used as a means of growing the renewable energy sector. In the case of a Solar Photovoltaic (PV) Manufacturing plant, an EIP can increase the manufacturing efficiency to make it more economical, while reducing the environmental impact of producing the solar cells. In essence, this assists the growth of the renewable energy industry and the environmental benefits that come with replacing fossil-fuels.

Eco-Industrial Development

Eco-industrial development (EID) is a framework for industry to develop while reducing its impact on the environment. It uses a closed loop production cycle to tackle a broad set of environmental challenges such as soil and water pollution, desertification, species preservation, energy management, by-product synergy, resource efficiency, air quality, etc.

Mutually beneficial connections among industry, natural systems, energy, material and local communities become central factors in designing industrial production processes.

The approach itself is largely voluntary and market-driven but often pressed ahead by favourable government treatment or efforts of development co-operation.

History

Since the early 1990s the idea of EID evolved from biological symbiosis. This concept was adapted by industrial ecologists in the search for innovative approaches to solve problems of waste, energy shortage and degradation of the environment. A continuous approach towards improving both environmental and economic outcomes is used.

In 1992, the international community officially connected development co-operation to sustainable environmental protection for the first time. At the United Nations Conference on Environment and Development (UNCED) in Rio de Janeiro, Brazil nearly 180 states signed the conference's Rio Declaration. Although non-binding, the Rio Declaration on Environment and Development laid out 27 principles that shall guide the increasing inter-connectedness of development cooperation and sustainability. Moreover, the documents drafting was accompanied by a presentation describing the idea of eco-industrial development for the first time.

In the following years, EID became popular throughout the United States. The recently elected Clinton administration installed a summit of business, labour, government and environmental protection representatives to further develop the approach. This summit established the idea of eco-industrial parks but soon realised that at first a more efficient management of raw materials, energy and waste has to be achieved.

Since then, the broad goals and application principles of EID have hardly changed and only became adapted to the rapid technological progress.

In 2012 the IGEP Foundation, for the promotion of trade, published a report called *Pathway to Eco Industrial Development in India – Concepts and Cases.*

The field is researched by the Nation Centre for Eco-Industrial Development, a joint project by the University of Southern California and Cornell University.

Goals and Concepts

The primary goal of eco-industrial development is a significant and continuous improvement in both business and environmental performance. Herein, the notion of industry not only relates to private-sector manufacturing but also covers state-owned enterprise, the service sector as well as transportation. EID's twin guideline is reflected specifically in the "eco" of eco-industrial as it resembles ecology (decrease in pollution and waste) and economy (increase in commercial success) at the same time. In order to build a framework of defining an enterprise's sustainable performance at the micro level, resource use optimization, minimization of waste, cleaner technologies and pollution limits are used in achieving a broad range of goals in EID:

- Resource efficiency minimizes the use of energy, materials, water and transportation. This, in turn, lowers production costs due to savings in virtually all areas of business.
- Cleaner production is a predominantly environmental measure, which aims at the reduction or even substitution of toxics, emissions-control or the re-use of residual material.
- Renewables in both energy and material use shall eliminate all pollution through fossil fuels.
- Greening of buildings or production sites installs high energy and environmental standards by relying on innovation in green architecture or engineering. Moreover, new facility and infrastructure design may also enhance the quality of life in neighbouring communities significantly.
- Environmental management systems such as the ISO 14000 ensure a continuous improvement through regular audits and the progressing establishment of environmental targets.
- Ecological site planning can then combine each of these aspects by developing a clear understanding of air, water and ground system capacities throughout the surrounding eco-system.

Eco-industrial development hence explores the possibility of improvement at the local level. In unique case-to-case analyses, particular geography, human potential or business climate are investigated. In contrast to the widespread race for top-down governmental support such as tax cuts, EID emphasizes locally achievable success and rooms for improvement. As a result, purposeful enforcements of action plans can make a large difference by optimizing the interaction of business, community and ecological systems.

Instruments

Eco-industrial development includes and employs four major conceptual instruments. Each of the approaches intends to combine the seemingly antithetic processes of industrial development and bolstering sustainability.

- Industrial Ecology focuses on both industrial as well as consumer behaviour. By assessing flows of energy and material, the approach determines the flows influences on the environment. In turn, it explores ways and means of optimizing the whole production chain from flow and use of resources to their final transformation. During these analyses, influences of economic, political, regulatory and social factors are key.
- The concept of Industrial Symbiosis is based on mainly voluntary cooperation of different industries. By conglomerating complementary enterprises and by then adapting their respective production chains, the presence of each may increase viability and profitability of the others. Therefore, symbiosis consider resource scarcity and environmental protection as crucial factors in developing sustainable industries and profits. Industrial Symbiosis often becomes manifest in Eco-industrial parks.
- Environmental Management Systems include a wide range of different environmental management approaches in order to ensure continual improvement in sustainability. In early stages, monitoring companies facilitates the identification of hazardous environmental aspects. Further on, objectives and targets are set under consideration of legal requirements. Finally, the establishment of regular audits and other reporting systems combined with continuous follow-up targets shall ensure a constant improvement towards greener industrial production.
- The Design for the Environment concept originated in engineering disciplines as well as from the product life-cycle analysis. It is a simple but all-encompassing assessment of a product's potential environmental impact – ranging from energy and materials used for packaging, transportation, consumer use and disposal.

Industrial Symbiosis

Industrial symbiosis is the sharing of services, utility, and by-product resources among industries in order to add value, reduce costs and improve the environment. Industrial symbiosis is a subset of industrial ecology, with a particular focus on material and energy exchange. Industrial ecology is a relatively new field that is based on a natural paradigm, claiming that an industrial ecosystem may behave in a similar way to the natural ecosystem wherein everything gets recycled.

Eco-industrial development is one of the ways in which industrial ecology contributes to the integration of economic growth and environmental protection. Some of the examples of eco-industrial development are:

- Circular economy (single material and/or energy exchange)
- Greenfield eco-industrial development (geographically confined space)
- Brownfield eco-industrial development (geographically confined space)
- Eco-industrial network (no strict requirement of geographical proximity)
- Virtual eco-industrial network (networks spread in large areas e.g. regional network)
- Networked Eco-industrial System (macro level developments with links across regions)

"*This classification omits any industrial sector-wide approaches and appreciates the diversity of the industrial system which is a key feature of industrial symbiosis. It is aimed to include initiatives that focus on achieving utility sharing and symbiosis among diverse sectors of industry*". It is the diversity and the openness of industrial symbiosis that makes it a unique approach to eco-industrial development.

Industrial symbiosis engages traditionally separate industries in a collective approach to competitive advantage involving physical exchange of materials, energy, water, and/or by-products. The keys to industrial symbiosis are collaboration and the synergistic possibilities offered by geographic proximity". The sharing of information is even more critical with the emergence of virtual globes such as Google Earth. These tools can greatly simplify the geographical analysis involved in determining potential IS opportunities.

Industrial symbiosis systems collectively optimize material and energy use at efficiencies beyond those achievable by any individual process alone. IS systems such as the web of materials and energy exchanges among companies in Kalundborg, Denmark have spontaneously evolved from a series of micro innovations over a long time scale; however, the engineered design and implementation of such systems from a macro planner's perspective, on a relatively short time scale, proves challenging. Nevertheless there are examples of industrial symbiosis being approached as national / regional initiatives with some significant success particularly in Europe.

Often, access to information on available by-products is non-existent. These by-products are considered waste and typically not traded or listed on any type of exchange.

Example

Recent work reviewed government policies necessary to construct a multi-gigaWatt photovoltaic factory and complementary policies to protect existing solar companies are outlined and the technical requirements for a symbiotic industrial system are explored to increase the manufacturing efficiency while improving the environmental impact of solar photovoltaic cells. The results of the analysis show that an eight-factory industrial symbiotic system can be viewed as a medium-term investment by any government, which will not only obtain direct financial return, but also an improved global environment. This is because synergies have been identified for co-locating glass manufacturing and photovoltaic manufacturing. The waste heat from glass manufacturing can be used in industrial-sized greenhouses for food production. Even within the PV plant itself a secondary chemical recycling plant can reduce environmental impact while improving economic performance for the group of manufacturing facilities.

Extended Producer Responsibility

In the field of waste management, extended producer responsibility (EPR) is a strategy designed to promote the integration of environmental costs associated with goods throughout their life cycles into the market price of the products.

The concept was first formally introduced in Sweden by Thomas Lindhqvist in a 1990 report to the Swedish Ministry of the Environment. In subsequent reports prepared for the Ministry, the following definition emerged: "[EPR] is an environmental protection strategy to reach an environmental objective of a decreased total environmental impact of a product, by making the manufacturer of the product responsible for the entire life-cycle of the product and especially for the take-back, recycling and final disposal.

Definition

EPR uses financial incentives to encourage manufacturers to design environmentally friendly products by holding producers responsible for the costs of managing their products at end of life. This policy approach, which differs from product stewardship, which shares responsibility across the chain of custody of a product, attempts to relieve local governments of the costs of managing certain priority products by requiring manufacturers internalize the cost of recycling within the product price. EPR is based upon the principle that because producers (usually brand owners) have the greatest control over product design and marketing and these same companies have the greatest ability and responsibility to reduce toxicity and waste.

EPR may take the form of a reuse, buy-back, or recycling program. The producer may also choose to delegate this responsibility to a third party, a so-called *producer responsibility organisation* (PRO), which is paid by the producer for used-product management. In this way, EPR shifts the responsibility for waste management from government to private industry, obliging producers, importers and/or sellers to internalise waste management costs in their product prices and ensuring the safe handling of their products.

A good example for producer responsibility organisations are the member organisations of PRO EUROPE. PRO EUROPE s.p.r.l. (Packaging Recovery Organisation Europe), founded in 1995, is the umbrella organisation for European packaging and packaging waste recovery and recycling schemes. Product stewardship organisations like PRO EUROPE are intended to relieve industrial companies and commercial enterprises of their individual obligation to take back used products through the operation of an organisation which fulfills these obligations on a nation-wide basis on behalf of their member companies. The aim is to ensure the recovery and recycling of packaging waste in the most economically efficient and ecologically sound manner. In many countries, this is done through the Green Dot (symbol) trademark of which PRO EUROPE is the general licensor. The "Green Dot" has evolved into a proven concept in many countries as implementation of Producer Responsibility. In twenty-five nations companies are now using the "Green Dot" as the financing symbol for the organisation of recovery, sorting and recycling of sales packaging.

Take-back

In response to the growing problem of excessive waste, several countries adopted waste management policies in which manufacturers are responsible for taking back their products from end users at the end of the products' useful life, or partially financing a collection and recycling infrastructure. These policies were adopted due to the lack of collection infrastructure for certain products that contain hazardous materials, or due to the high costs to local governments of providing such collection services. The primary goals of these take-back laws therefore are to partner with the private sector to ensure that all wastes are managed in a way that protects public health and the environment. The goals of take-back laws are to

1. encourage companies to design products for reuse, recyclability, and materials reduction;
2. correcting market signals to the consumer by incorporating waste management costs into the product's price;
3. promoting innovation in recycling technology.

Take-back programs help promote these goals by creating incentives for companies to redesign their products to minimize waste management costs, by designing their products to contain safer materials (so they do not need to be managed separately) or designing products that are easier to recycle and reuse (so recycling becomes more profitable). The earliest take-back activity began in Europe, where government-sponsored take-back initiatives arose from concerns about scarce landfill space and potentially hazardous substances in component parts. The European Union adopted a directive on Waste Electrical and Electronic Equipment (WEEE). The purpose of this directive is to prevent the production of waste electronics and also to encourage reuse and recycling of such waste. The directive requires the Member States to encourage design and production methods that take into account the future dismantling and recovery of their products. These take-back programs have been now adopted in nearly every OECD country. In the United States, most of these policies have been implemented at the state level, due to the political impasse at the federal level.

Electronics

Many governments and companies have adopted Extended Producer Responsibility to help address the growing problem of e-waste—used electronics contain materials that cannot be safely thrown away with regular household trash. Many governments have partnered with corporations in creating the necessary collection and recycling infrastructure. Some argue that local and manufacturer-supported Extended Producer Responsibility laws give manufacturers greater responsibility for the reuse, recycling, and disposal of their own products.

In the United States, most producer responsibility laws in effect have been passed at the state level, due to unique political circumstances at the federal level. Twenty-five states have already passed laws requiring producer responsibility and many others are currently working towards passing producer responsibility laws.

Advantages

When producers either face a financial or physical burden of recycling their electronics after use, they may be incentivized to design more sustainable, less toxic, and easily recyclable electronics. Using fewer materials and designing products to last longer can directly reduce producers' end-of-life costs. Thus, Extended Producer Responsibility is often cited as one way to fight planned obsolescence, because it financially encourages manufacturers to design for recycling and make products last longer.

Disadvantages

Some people have concerns about extended producer responsibility programs for complex electronics that can be difficult to safely recycle, such as Lithium-ion polymer batteries. Others worry such laws could increase the cost of electronics because producers would be adding recycling costs into the initial price tag. When companies are required to transport their products to a recycling facility, it can be expensive if the product contains hazardous materials and does not have a scrap value, such as with CRT televisions, which can contain up to 5 pounds of lead. Organisations and researchers against EPR claim that the mandate would slow technical innovation and impede technological process. Other critics are concerned that manufacturers may use takeback programs to take secondhand electronics off the reuse market, by shredding rather than reusing or repairing goods that come in for recycling.

Implementation

EPR has been implemented in many forms, which may be classified into three major approaches:

- Mandatory
- Negotiated
- Voluntary

It is perhaps because of the tendency of economic policy in market-driven economies not to interfere with consumers' preferences that the producer-centric representation is the dominant form of viewing the environmental impacts of industrial production: in statistics on energy, emissions, water, etc., impacts are almost always presented as attributes of industries ('on-site' or 'direct' allocation) rather than as attributes of the supply chains of products for consumers. On a smaller scale, most existing schemes for corporate sustainability reporting include only impacts that arise out of operations controlled by the reporting company, and not supply-chain impacts. According to this world view, "upstream and downstream [environmental] impacts are [...] allocated to their immediate producers. The institutional setting and the different actors' spheres of influence are not reflected.".

On the other hand, a number of studies have highlighted that final consumption and affluence, especially in the industrialised world, are the main drivers for the level and growth of environmental pressure. Even though these studies provide a clear incentive for complementing producer-focused environmental policy with some consideration for consumption-related aspects, demand-side measures to environmental problems are rarely exploited.

The nexus created by the different views on impacts caused by industrial production is exemplified by several contributions to the discussion about producer or consumer responsibility for greenhouse gas emissions. Emissions data are reported to the IPCC as contributions of producing industries located in a particular country rather than as embodiments in products consumed by a particular population, irrespective of productive origin. However, especially for open economies, taking into account the greenhouse gases embodied in internationally traded commodities can have a considerable influence on national greenhouse gas balance sheets. Assuming consumer responsibility, exports have to be subtracted from, and imports added to national greenhouse gas inventories. In Denmark for example, Munksgaard and Pedersen (2001) report that a significant amount of power and other energy-intensive commodities are traded across Danish borders, and that between 1966 and 1994 the Danish foreign trade balance in terms of CO_2 developed from a 7 Mt deficit to a 7 Mt surplus, compared to total emissions of approximately 60 Mt. In particular, electricity traded between Norway, Sweden and Denmark is subject to large annual fluctuations due to varying rainfall in Norway and Sweden. In wet years Denmark imports hydro-electricity whereas electricity from coal-fired power plants is exported in dry years. The official Danish emissions inventory includes a correction for electricity trade and thus applies the consumer responsibility principle.

Similarly, at the company level, "when adopting the concept of eco-efficiency and the scope of an environmental management system stated in for example ISO 14001, it is insufficient to merely report on the carbon dioxide emissions limited to the judicial borders of the company". 7 "Companies must recognise their wider responsibility and manage the entire life-cycle of their products ... Insisting on high environmental standards from suppliers and ensuring that raw materials are extracted or produced in an environmentally conscious way provides a start". A life-cycle perspective is also taken in Extended Producer Responsibility (EPR) frameworks: "Producers of products should bear a significant degree of responsibility (physical and/or financial) not only for the environmental impacts of their products downstream from the treatment and disposal of their product, but also for their upstream activities inherent in the selection of materials and in the design of products". "The major impetus for EPR came from northern European countries in the late 1980s and early 1990s, as they were facing severe landfill shortages. [... As a result,] EPR is generally applied to post-consumer wastes which place increasing physical and financial demands on municipal waste management."

EPR has rarely been consistently quantified. Moreover, applying conventional life cycle assessment, and assigning environmental impacts to producers and consumers can lead to double-counting. Using input-output analysis, researchers have attempted for decades to account for both producers and consumers in an economy in a consistent way. Gallego and Lenzen demonstrate and discuss a method of consistently delineating producers' supply chains, into mutually exclusive and collectively exhaustive responsibilities to be shared by all agents in an economy. Their method is an approach to allocating responsibility across agents in a fully inter-connected circular system. Upstream and downstream environmental impacts are shared between all agents of a supply chain - producers and consumers.

Examples

Auto Recycling Nederland (ARN) is a Producer Responsibility Organisation (PRO) that organises vehicle recycling in the Netherlands. An advanced recycling fee is charged to those who purchase a new vehicle and is used to fund the recycling of it at the end of its useful life. The PRO was set up to satisfy the European Union End of Life Vehicles Directive.

The Swiss Association for Information, Communication and Organisational Technology (SWICO), an ICT industry organisation, became a PRO to address the problem of electronic waste.

Eco-Efficiency

Over the years, as countries and regions around the world began to develop, it slowly became evident that industrialization and economic growth come hand in hand with environmental degradation. Eco-Efficiency has been proposed as one of the main tools to promote a transformation from unsustainable development to one of sustainable development. It is based on the concept of creating more goods and services while using fewer resources and creating less waste and pollution. "It is measured as the ratio between the (added) value of what has been produced (eg. GDP) and the (added) environment impacts of the product or service (eg. S02 emissions)." The term was coined by the World Business Council for Sustainable Development (WBCSD) in its 1992 publication "Changing Course," and at the 1992 Earth Summit, eco-efficiency was endorsed as a new business concept and means for companies to implement Agenda 21 in the private sector. Ergo the term has become synonymous with a management philosophy geared towards sustainability, combing ecological and economic efficiency.

History

Although eco-efficiency is a rather new method, the idea is not. In the early 1970s Paul R. Ehrlich and John Holdren developed the lettering formula I = PAT to describe the impact of human activity on the environment. Furthermore the concept of eco-efficiency was first described by Schaltegger and Sturm in 1989, but it wasn't until 1992, when the term was formally coined and widely publicized by Schmidheiny in "Changing Course". Stephan Schhmidheiny set out "to change the perception of industry as being part of the problem of environmental degradation to the reality of its becoming part—a key part—of the solution for sustainability and global development." The major drivers in the early phase of eco-efficiency's development were the "forward-looking managers and thinkers in 3M and Dow." It was their involvement which catapulted eco-efficiency from a brilliant idea to a workable concept. The results of the WBCSD's work creating the "linkage between environmental performance and the bottom line was published in 1997 in its report Environmental Performance and Shareholder Value."

Methods

According to the WBCSD definition, eco-efficiency is achieved through the delivery of "competitively priced goods and services that satisfy human needs and bring quality of life while progressively reducing environmental impacts of goods and resource intensity throughout the entire life-cycle to a level at least in line with the Earth's estimated carrying capacity." It works by implementing 4 main types of ratios.

"The first two are environmental productivity and its inverse, environmental intensity of production, referring to the realm of production. The second pair, environmental improvement cost and its inverse, environmental cost-effectiveness, are defined from an environmental improvements measures point-of-view."

The ratios may be applied to any unit comprising economic activities because such activities always relate to cost and value, “and having some physical substrate, always influence the environment.” Furthermore, there are two different levels upon which to orchestrate the ratios: ”micro” and ”macro”. There are three different methods to determine eco-efficiency at the micro-level. First, ”incremental eco-efficiency”, which “specifies the effects of the total value of a product system or sector and its total concomitant environmental effects.” Second, an analysis method nicknamed ”win-win”, which “gives a comparison between a historical reference situation and potentially new situations based on the use of new technologies.” It should be noted that the win-win micro-method is limited because it cannot give a concrete answer on the question of whether it improves overall environmental performance. And the third is ”difference eco-efficiency”, which is similar to the win-win variant, but removes all irrelevant alternatives to heighten potential for optimal technologies while comparing two alternatives. Now the macro-level is much less defined and has shown less accurate results. However, “the ultimate aim of eco-efficiency analysis is to help move micro-level decision making into macro-level optimality.” The main goal in years to come is to create headline indicators to carry out macro-level analysis at a country/world scale.

There are two LCA-based calculation systems on eco-efficiency: the Analysis Method of BASF, and the method of the Eco-costs value ratio of the Delft University of Technology.

Uses

The reduction in ecological impacts translates into an increase in resource productivity, which in turn can create a competitive advantage. According to the WBCSD, critical aspects of eco-efficiency are:

- A reduction in the material intensity of goods or services;
- A reduction in the energy intensity of goods or services;
- Reduced dispersion of toxic materials;
- Improved recyclability;
- Maximum use of renewable resources;
- Greater durability of products;
- Increased service intensity of goods and services.

Strategies that have been linked to eco-efficiency include “Factor 4” and “Factor 10”, which call for specific reductions in resource use, “natural capitalism”, which incorporates eco-efficiency as part of a broader strategy, and the “cradle-to-cradle” movement, which claims to go beyond eco-efficiency in abolishing the very idea of waste. According to Boulanger, all versions of eco-efficiency share four key characteristics:

- Confidence in technological innovation as the main solution to un-sustainability;
- Reliance on business as the principal actor of transformation. The emphasis is on firms designing new products, shifting to new production processes, and investing in R&D, etc., more than on the retailer or the consumer, let alone the citizen.
- Trust in markets (if they are functioning well);
- "Growthphilia": there is nothing wrong with growth as such.

The view that improvements in eco-efficiency are sufficient for achieving sustainability has been challenged by Huesemann and Huesemann who demonstrate, using extensive historical evidence, that increases in technological efficiency have not reduced overall resource use and pollution. Moreover, with "cradle-to-cradle", growth is conducive to sustainability per se. This broader concept is called "Sustainable Production and Consumption" (SPC). "This concept involves changes in production and consumption patterns that lead to sustainable use of natural resources;" business has taken a key role in accelerating the use of this concept because businesses both consume and produce. Eco-efficiency is routinely a concept used because it combines performance along two of the three axes of sustainable development, making it easier for academics and leading thinkers to tease out the associated social issues.

Examples

Furthermore, eco-efficiency is also a very useful tool because it can adapt and flex to be fit different sizes of companies, while also maintaining relevance with the larger scale of government and national policies. For example, larger national players such as the Organisation for Economic Co-operation and Development (OECD 2002), European Commission (EU 2005), European Environment Agency (EEA) and the National Round Table on the Environment and the Economy (NRTEE) have all recognised that eco-efficiency is a practical approach that businesses should adopt in setting and achieving their environmental performance objectives. It has be proven to heighten market values for firms, serve as an effective management tool for governments, benefit civil society, and increase quality of life. "It does this by changing industrial processes, creating new products and changing and influencing markets with new ideas and with new rules." More people aim to get more value for their money in the market, while also enjoying a better environment.

Recently, there has also been use of eco-efficiency in more non-traditional ways, such as a use in banks to integrate environmental criteria into their credit-approval process; looking at "eco-integrated economic risks of a customer." And is also being implemented as marketing advantages where, "eco-efficient choices are always preferred," especially in service sectors such as tourism.

Eco-Costs Value Ratio

The EVR model is a Life Cycle Assessment based method to analyse consumption patterns, business strategies and design options in terms of eco-efficient value creation. Next to this it is used to compare products and service systems (e.g. benchmarking).

The eco-costs/value ratio (EVR) is an indicator to reveal sustainable and unsustainable consumption patterns of people. The eco-costs is an indicator for the environmental pollution of the products people buy, the value is the price they pay for it in our free market economy. Example: When somebody spends 1000 euro per month on housing (in Europe: EVR approx. 0,3) it is less harmful for the environment than when 1000 euro is spend on diesel (in Europe: EVR approx. 1,0).

The EVR is also relevant for business strategies, because companies are facing the slow but inevitable internalization of environmental costs. At the moment the costs of products don't take into account the environmental damage caused by these products. This "pollution is for free" mentality is less and less accepted by communities.

The EVR makes companies aware of the relative importance of the environmental pollution of their products, and the relative risk they run that future production costs will increase because of this internalization of environmental costs. By using the EVR, companies can make decisions for their product portfolio: abandon products with low value and high environmental costs and stimulate products with high value and low environmental costs.

Background Information

The EVR model has been introduced in 1998 and published in 2000-2004 in the International Journal of LCA, and in the Journal of Cleaner Production. In 2007, and in 2012, the system was updated. The concept of EVR is based on eco-costs. General databases of eco-costs (the so-called eco-costs 2012) are provided (open source) at www.ecocostsvalue.com of Delft University of Technology (the

Netherlands). In 2010 a book named "LCA-based assessment of sustainability: the Eco-costs/Value Ratio (EVR)" was published containing the most important articles about the EVR.

Working Principle

The Model: EVR = Eco-costs/value. The basic idea of the EVR model is to link the 'value chain' to the ecological product chain. In the value chain, the added value (in terms of money) and the added costs are determined for each step of the product 'from cradle to grave'. Similarly, the ecological impact of each step in the product chain is expressed in terms of money, the so-called 'eco-costs'. In this way the Porter chain becomes circular.

Eco-Costs

Eco-costs express the amount of environmental burden of a product on basis of prevention of that burden. They are the marginal prevention costs (money) which should be made to reduce the environmental pollution and materials depletion in our world to a level which is in line with the carrying capacity of our earth.

As such, the eco-costs are virtual costs, since they are not yet integrated in the real life costs of current production chains (Life Cycle Costs). The eco-costs should be regarded as hidden obligations.

For example: for each 1000 kg CO2 emission, one should invest € 135,- in offshore windmill parks (or other CO2 reduction systems at that price or less). When this is done consequently, the total CO2 emissions in the world will be reduced by 65% compared to the emissions in 2008. As a result global warming will stabilise. In short: "the eco-costs of 1000kg CO2 are € 135,-". Similar calculations can be made on the environmental burden of acidification, eutrification, summer smog, fine dust, eco-toxicity, and the use of metals, fossil fuels and land (nature). Eco-costs are used in Life Cycle Assessment, LCA, to assess the environmental performance of different materials, processes and End of Life methods.

EVR of Products

The EVR combines eco-cost and value to see whether a product will be successful. The product should have low environmental impact in its lifecycle (low eco-costs) and an attractive value for consumers. The value here is the market value (perceived customer value, also called fair price).

It is a trend in society that heavy pollution of industry is not accepted anymore by the inhabitants of a country. This results in stricter regulations by countries (e.g. tradable emission rights, enforcement of best available technologies, eco-taxes, etc.). Eco-costs will then become part of the internal production costs. This internalizing of eco-costs might be a threat to a company, but it might also be an opportunity: "When my product has less eco-burden than that of my competitor, my product can withstand stricter regulations of the government. So this characteristic of low eco-costs of my product is a competitive edge."

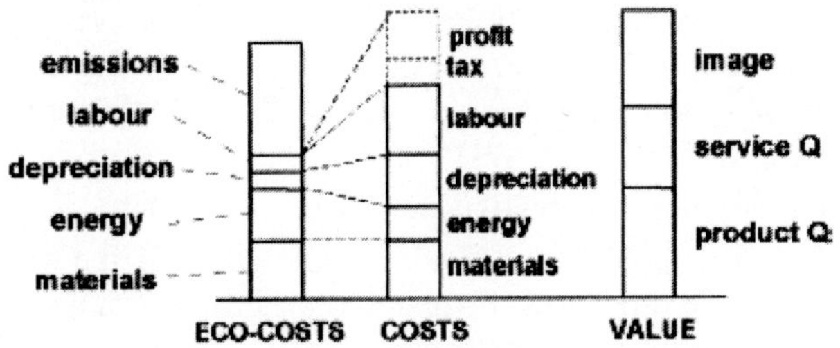

Figure: *The decomposition of 'virtual eco-costs', costs and value of a product.*

To analyse the short term and the long term market prospects of a product or a product service combination (Product Service System, PSS). The basic idea of the product portfolio matrix is the notion that a product, service or PSS is characterized by:

- its short term market potential: high value/costs ratio
- its long term market requirement: low eco-costs.

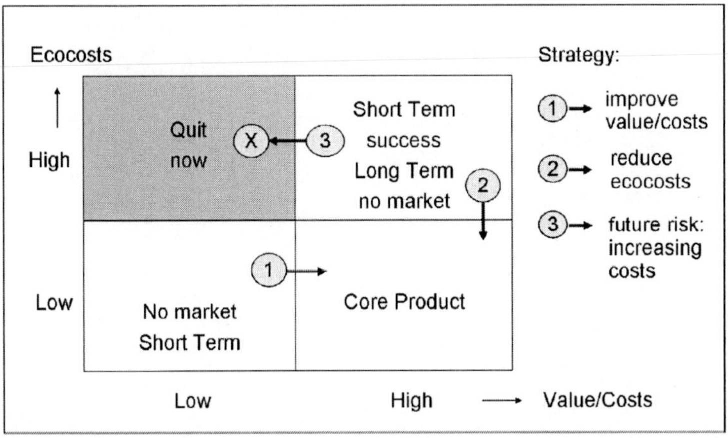

Figure: *Product portfolio matrix for EVR product strategy of companies.*

In terms of product strategy, the matrix results in 3 strategic directions:

1. enhance the value/costs ratio of a green design to create a bigger market
2. lower the eco-costs of current successful products to make it fit for future markets
3. abandon products with a low value/ costs ratio (not much profit, small market) and high eco-costs

For many 'green designs', the usual problem is that they have a low current value/costs ratio. In most of the cases the production costs are higher than the production costs of the classic solution, in some cases even the (perceived) quality is poor. There are two ways to do something about it:

a. enhance the (perceived) quality of the product
b. attach to the product a service (create a PSS) in a way that the value of the bundle of the product and the service is more than the value of its components.

For a product which has a good present value/costs ratio, but high eco-costs, the product and the production process have to be redesigned to lower the eco-costs. This road towards sustainability is often far more promising than the strategy of enhancing the value/costs ratio of a green design.

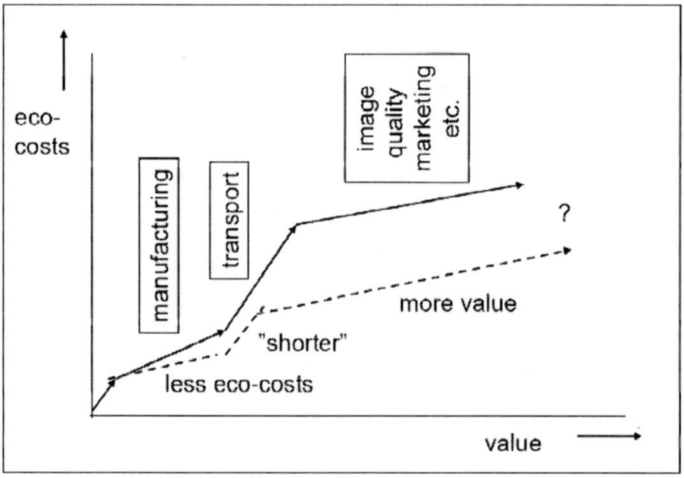

Figure: *Design strategies to enhance the EVR of a product.*

The reason is that the economies of scale for production and distribution are available and that the new product is marketed to an existing client base which is used to the brand name, the quality standards, the service system, etc.

Note: The most common fear of business managers is that their new green products end up with a deteriorated value/costs ratio, and hence will have a cumbersome position in the market. The stability of the governmental policy plays an important role here. When governmental regulations which level the playing field are postponed or even abandoned, proactive companies with sound product strategies are harmed. This can cause severe damage to the transition process and may lead to reluctance of players to move proactively in the future.

The most successful design options are depicted in Figure. The best design strategy is:

- to increase value where value is high
- to decrease the eco-costs where the eco-costs are high

Use

EVR & De-linking: In economics, de-linking (also known as decoupling) is often used in the context of economic production and environmental quality. In this context, it refers to the ability of an economy to grow without corresponding increases in environmental pressure. In many economies increasing production (GDP) would involve increased pressure on the environment. An economy that is able to sustain GDP growth, without also experiencing a worsening of environmental conditions, is said to be de-linked.

There is a consumer's side of the de-linking of economy and ecology. Under the assumption that most of the households spend in their life what they earn in their life, the total EVR of the spending of households is the key towards sustainability. Only when this total EVR of the spending gets lower, the eco-costs related to the total spending can be reduced even at a higher level of spending. There are two ways of achieving this:

- At the production side: the improvement of eco-efficiency ('lowering EVR') of products and services by the industry
- At the consumer's side: the change of lifestyle of customers in the direction of 'low EVR' products.

At the production side, our society is heading in the right direction: gradually, industrial production is achieving higher levels of the value/ costs ratio and is at the same time becoming cleaner. At the consumer's side, however, our society is suffering from the fact that the consumers preferences are heading in the wrong direction: towards products and services with an unfavourable EVR (like driving in SUVs, more kilometres, intercontinental flights for holidays).

Figure shows that people in the Netherlands (and probably in the other EC countries as well) spend relatively more money on cars and holidays when they have more money available. Other studies show that people tend to have intercontinental holidays at the moment they can afford it. This shift in consumer spending will become a big problem in the near future, since the EVR of e.g. housing and health care is much lower than the EVR of transport and (inter)continental holidays by plane. Figure depicted earlier, shows the EVR (= ecocosts/price) on the Y/axis as a function of the cumulative expenditures of all products and services of all citizens in the EU 25 on the X-axis. The data is from the EIPRO study of the European Commission (EIPRO = environmental impact of products).

The area underneath the curve is proportional to the total eco-costs of the EU25. Basically there are two strategies to reduce the area under the curve: - ask industry to reduce the eco-costs of their products (this will shift the curve downward) - try to reduce expenditures of consumers in high end of the curve, and let them spend this money at the low end of the curve (this will shift the middle part of the curve to the right). The question is now how designers and engineers can contribute to this required shift towards sustainability and what this means to product portfolio strategies of companies. The solution is Eco-efficient Value Creation.

Eco-Efficient Value Creation

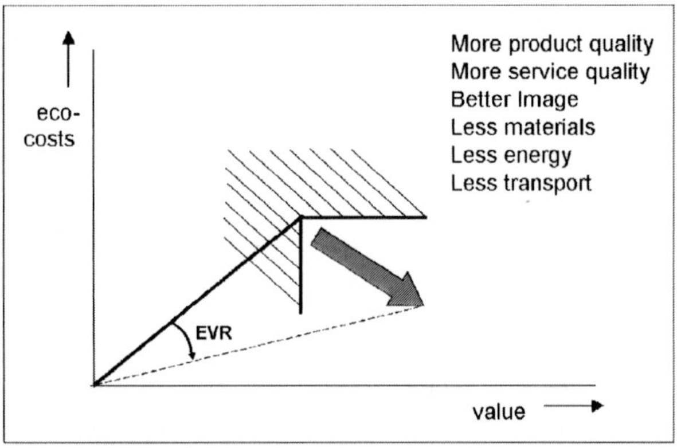

Figure: *The double objective for design & engineering: less eco-costs, more value.*

The way towards sustainability requires a double aim in product innovation:

- lower eco-costs, and at the same time
- higher value (a higher market price).

We call this: Eco-efficient Value Creation. The reason we need value creation for eco-efficient products is threefold:

1. the higher price in the market is required to cover the higher production cost of green products (note that a higher price is only accepted by the consumer when the perceived value is higher, otherwise the consumer will not buy the product)
2. the higher price prevents the rebound effect
3. lowering the EVR appears the key to a sustainable development at the level of countries

Below, an example of eco-efficient value creation is given, which is the introduction of the Lexus RX 400h in the USA:

- the customer value has increased, by emphasising its combined power and comfort (from the advertisement in the US: "......While it may have a V6 engine under the hood, the extra boost from the electric-drive motor gives the vehicle the acceleration power of a V8....... and the noise levels in Lexus hybrid vehicles have been reduced even more")
- the eco-costs of driving are lower, since its excellent overall fuel economy

Note that the acceleration of a car is an interesting issue in terms of value. High acceleration is associated with expensive sports cars (Porsche, Ferrari). But people who buy these fast cars hardly use it. For these people acceleration is more part of the image of the product than it is part of the product qualities they use on a daily basis. So reducing the acceleration is the wrong strategy: it eliminates the extra value, and it hardly reduces the overall eco-costs in practice.

Environmental Benchmarking in LCA

Life Cycle Assessment (LCA) is the generally accepted method to compare two (or more) alternative products or services. A prerequisite for such a comparison is that the functionality ('functional unit') and the quality of the alternatives are the same (you cannot compare apples and oranges in the classical LCA). In cases of product design and architecture, however, this prerequisite seems to be a fundamental flaw in the application of LCA: the designer or architect is aiming at a better quality (in the broad sense of the word: including intangible aspects like beauty and image), so the new design never has the same quality. In some cases the functionality of the design is not the same, since the design solution is limited by a maximum budget, in some cases the functionality is the same, but the higher quality results in a higher price. In all these cases a single indicator in LCA (like the eco-costs) is not suitable for environmental benchmarking. In these cases however, it does make sense to compare the design alternatives on the basis of the eco-costs/value ratio (EVR), where the value is the perceived customer value (the fair price).

Example 1. Different types of armchairs differ in terms of comfort, aesthetics, etc. rather than in terms of functionality. A classical LCA (with a single indicator like eco-costs, carbon footprint, etc.) does not make sense here. Selection on the basis of EVR, however, is the key to a sustainable consumption pattern. The chair with the lowest EVR is the best solution in terms of sustainability.

Example 2. In LCA, the comparison of a new building and a renovated building is in the majority of cases not possible, since, in practice, both solutions differ in almost all quality aspects (tangible as well as intangible). However, the solution with lowest EVR is the best in terms of sustainable consumption.

Note that the renovated building is the best solution in most of the cases, because it has the lowest EVR in the production phase. However, in some cases the renovated building is not the best solution, because of unfavourable energy consumption (high EVR) in the use phase.

Sustainable Value

Sustainable value is a way of managing and measuring sustainability performance. The concept was developed by researchers who are working today for Euromed Management School (Marseille/ France) and the IZT - Institute for Futures Studies and Technology Assessment (Berlin/Germany). To date Sustainable Value is primarily used to assess corporate sustainability performance.

Sustainable value differs from existing approaches by the fact that it is value-based while all other existing approaches to sustainability assessment (such as environmental impact assessments) are burden-based, i.e. they are assessing environmental and social resource use based on the burden that is created. Using the sustainable value approach, economic, environmental and social resources are assessed and aggregated based on their relative value contribution and can be expressed in a monetary unit like euros, dollars or pounds.

The Concept

Sustainable value is based on the notion of opportunity costs. Opportunity costs are used in financial markets to calculate the cost of capital. In financial markets, the cost of using € 100 over the course of one year is determined by the return that could have been generated through an alternative investment of the capital. Sustainable Value is the first concept to extend this logic to environmental and social resources.

Sustainable value is calculated in five steps:

1. Calculate the environmental, social and economic efficiencies of the entity using the resources. Efficiency is calculated by relating the return to resource use.
2. Calculate the environmental, social and economic efficiencies of the benchmark (= calculate opportunity costs).
3. Calculate the value spreads by subtracting the efficiency of the benchmark (Step 2) from the efficiency of the entity (Step 1).
4. Calculate the value contributions by multiplying the amount of environmental, social and economic resources used with the corresponding value spread (Step 3), respectively.
5. Calculate sustainable value by adding up the value contributions (Step 4) and dividing by the number of resources considered. This avoids double counting.

Sample Application

The sustainable value approach can be demonstrated using the example of British Petroleum (BP): "The Cost of Sustainability Capital and the Creation of Sustainable Value by Companies", Journal of Industrial Ecology, 9(4), 47-58.).

In 2001, BP created the following return and employed the following economic, environmental and social resources:

Table: *Performance data of BP in 2001*

BP (2001)	Amount
Net Value Added [£ million]	15,563
Nonfinancial Assets [£ million]	69,885
CO_2 [t]	73,420,000
CH_4 [t]	367,201
SO_2 [t]	224,541
NO_x [t]	266,133
CO [t]	124,584
Work accidents [number]	83
PM_{10} [t]	16,666

Note: t = metric tonne = megagram (Mg) = 1000 kilograms (kg, SI) H" 1.102 short tons

Source: Figge & Hahn 2005

In this example the return of BP is measured as Net Value Added and the UK economy is used as a benchmark. The macroeconomic equivalent of Net Value Added is the Net Domestic Product (NDP).

Table: *Performance data of the United Kingdom in 2001*

UK Economy (2001)	***Amount***
Net Domestic Product [£ million]	884,718
Total Net Wealth [£ million]	4,375,200
CO_2 [t]	572,500,000
CH_4 [t]	2,195,238
SO_2 [t]	1,125,000
NO_x [t]	1,680,000
CO [t]	3,966,500
Work accidents [number]	132,696
PM_{10} [t]	178,000

Source: Figge & Hahn (2005)

The next table shows how Sustainable Value is calculated.

As described above, in the first step the return on resources of BP is calculated. BP generated about £ 212 Net value Added per ton of CO_2 in 2001. In a second step the return on resources of the UK economy (benchmark) is calculated. The UK economy generated about £ 1,545 Net Domestic Product per ton of CO_2 in 2001. In a third step the value spread is calculated. In 2001, BP generated £ 1,333 less return than the UK economy per ton of CO_2.

In a fourth step the value contribution is calculated. In 2001, the use of 73,420,000 t of CO_2 generated about £98bn less return than if CO_2 had been given to the UK economy on average. This step is repeated for all resources employed by the company.

In a fifth step all value contribution are added up and divided by the number of resources considered. The result is called Sustainable Value.

BP's Sustainable Value amounts to about £72bn. Put differently, had BP's set of financial, environmental and social resources been used by the UK economy on average rather than by BP an additional £72bn Net Domestic Product could have been created.

Projects

The Sustainable value approach has been applied in several projects and case studies.

The EU-funded project ADVANCE (Application and Dissemination of Value-based Eco-ratings financial markets) used the Sustainable Value approach to assess the environmental performance of 65 European companies in monetary terms.

In a project that is funded by the German Federal Ministry of Education and Research (NeW – Nachhaltig erfolgreich Wirtschaften) the Sustainable Value approach is used to assess the triple bottom line performance of 28 German companies.

In a new EU-funded project SVAPPAS (Sustainable Value Analysis of Policy and Performance in the Agricultural Sector) a European consortium of research organisations uses the Sustainable Value approach to measure the sustainability performance of the agricultural sector in Europe.

Source Reduction

Source reduction is activities designed to reduce the volume or toxicity of waste generated, including the design and manufacture of products with minimum toxic content, minimum volume of material, and/or a longer useful life. An example of source reduction is bringing a reusable bag to the grocery store.

Synonyms

Pollution Prevention (or P2) and Toxics use reduction are also called source reduction because they address the use of hazardous substances at the source.

Procedures

Source Reduction is achieved through improvements in production and product design, or through Environmentally Preferable Purchasing (EPP).

Source Reduction in the United States

In the United States, the Federal Trade Commission offers guidance for labelling claims: "Source reduction" refers to reducing or lowering the weight, volume or toxicity of a product or package. To avoid being misleading, source reduction claims must qualify the amount of the source reduction and give the basis for any comparison that is made. These principles apply regardless of whether a term like "source reduced" is used.

The Massachusetts Toxics Use Reduction Program (TURA) offers 6 strategies to achieve source reduction:

1. Toxic chemical substitution
2. Production process modification
3. Finished product reformulation
4. Production modernisation
5. Improvements in operations and maintenance
6. In-process recycling of production material

Eco-Innovation

Eco-innovation is the development of products and processes that contribute to sustainable development, applying the commercial application of knowledge to elicit direct or indirect ecological improvements. This includes a range of related ideas, from environmentally friendly technological advances to socially acceptable innovative paths towards sustainability.

Origins of the Concept of Eco-Innovation

The idea of eco-innovation is fairly recent. One of the first appearances of the concept of eco-innovation in the literature is in the book by Claude Fussler and Peter James. In a subsequent article, Peter James defines eco-innovation as "new products and processes which provide customer and business value but significantly decrease environmental impacts".

Related Concepts

Eco-innovation is closely linked to a variety of related concepts. It is often used interchangeably with "environmental innovation", and is also often linked with environmental technology, eco-efficiency, eco-design, environmental design, sustainable design, or sustainable innovation. While the term "environmental innovation" is used in similar contexts to "eco-innovation", the other terms are mostly used when referring to product or process design, and therefore focus more on the technological aspects of eco-innovation rather than the societal or political aspects.

Eco-Innovation as a Technological Term

The most common usage of the term "eco-innovation" is to refer to innovative products and processes that reduce environmental impacts. This is often used in conjunction with eco-efficiency and eco-design. Leaders in many industries have been developing innovative technologies in order to work towards sustainability. However, these are not always practical, or enforced by policy and legislation.

Eco-Innovation as a Social Process

Another position held (for example, by the organisation Eco Innovation) is that this definition should be complemented: eco-innovations should also bring greater social and cultural acceptance. In this view, this "social pillar" added to James's definition is necessary because it determines learning and the effectiveness of eco-innovations.

This approach gives eco-innovations a social component, a status that is more than a new type of commodity, or a new sector, even though environmental technology and eco-innovation are associated with the emergence of new economic activities or even branches (e.g., waste treatment, recycling, etc.). This approach considers eco-innovation in terms of usage rather than merely in terms of product. The social pillar associated with eco-innovation introduces a governance component that makes eco-innovation a more integrated tool for sustainable development.

Ecovation is the process by which responsible capitalism aligns with ecological innovation to construct products which have a generative nature and are recyclable back into the environment for usage in other industries.

Shripad Vaidya's name figures in the 26th edition of the famous American publication 'Who's Who In The World' as the first record holder in the field of development of eco-innovation.

Chapter 5

Concepts in Corporate Ecology

Circular Economy

The circular economy is a generic term for an industrial economy that is, by design or intention, restorative and in which material flows are of two types, biological nutrients, designed to re-enter the biosphere safely, and technical nutrients, which are designed to circulate at high quality without entering the biosphere.

The term encompasses more than the production and consumption of goods and services, including a shift from fossil fuels to the use of renewable energy, and the role of diversity as a characteristic of resilient and productive systems. It includes discussion of the role of money and finance as part of the wider debate, and some of its pioneers have called for a revamp of economic performance measurement tools. The circular economy is grounded in the study of feedback rich (non-linear) systems, particularly living systems. A major outcome of this is the notion of optimising systems rather than components, or the notion of 'design for fit'. As a generic notion it draws from a number of more specific approaches including cradle to cradle, biomimicry, industrial ecology, and the 'blue economy'. Most frequently described as a framework for thinking, its supporters claim it is a coherent model that has value as part of a response to the end of the era of cheap oil and materials.

Moving away from the Linear Model

Linear "Take, Make, Dispose" industrial processes and the lifestyles that feed on them deplete finite reserves to create products that end up in landfills or in incinerators.

This realisation triggered the thought process of a few scientists and thinkers, including Walter R. Stahel, an architect, economist, and a founding father of industrial sustainability. Credited with having coined the expression "Cradle to Cradle" (in contrast with "Cradle to Grave", illustrating our "Resource to Waste" way of functioning) in the late 1970s, Stahel worked on developing a "closed loop" approach to production processes, co-founding the Product-Life Institute in Geneva more than 25 years ago.

Creating the Circular Framework

In their 1976 research report to the European Commission, "The Potential for Substituting Manpower for Energy", Walter Stahel and Genevieve Reday sketched the vision of an economy in loops (or circular economy) and its impact on job creation, economic competitiveness, resource savings, and waste prevention. The report was published in 1982 as the book *Jobs for Tomorrow: The Potential for Substituting Manpower for Energy*.

Considered as one of the first pragmatic and credible sustainability think tanks, the main goals of Stahel's institute are product-life extension, long-life goods, reconditioning activities, and waste prevention. It also insists on the importance of selling services rather than products, an idea referred to as the "functional service economy" and sometimes put under the wider notion of "performance economy" which also advocates "more localisation of economic activity".

In broader terms, the circular approach is a framework that takes insights from living systems. It considers that our systems should work like organisms, processing nutrients that can be fed back into the cycle—whether biological or technical—hence the "closed loop" or "regenerative" terms usually associated with it.

Emergence of the Idea

The generic Circular Economy label can be applied to, and claimed by, several different schools of thought, that all gravitate around the same basic principles which they have refined in different ways. The idea itself, which is centred on taking insights from living systems, is hardly a new one and hence cannot be traced back to one precise date or author, yet its practical applications to modern economic systems and industrial processes have gained momentum since the late 1970s, giving birth to four prominent movements, detailed below. The idea of circular material flows as a model for the economy was presented in 1966 by Kenneth E. Boulding in his paper, The Economics of the Coming Spaceship Earth. Promoting a circular economy was identified as national policy in China's 11th five-year plan starting in 2006. The Ellen MacArthur Foundation, an independent charity established in

2010, has more recently outlined the economic opportunity of a circular economy. As part of its educational mission, the Foundation has worked to bring together complementary schools of thought and create a coherent framework, thus giving the concept a wide exposure and appeal.

Founding Principles

Waste is Food

Waste does not exist... the biological and technical components (nutrients) of a product are designed by intention to fit within a materials cycle, designed for disassembly and re-purposing. The biological nutrients are non-toxic and can be simply composted. Technical nutrients – polymers, alloys and other man-made materials are designed to be used again with minimal energy.

Diversity is Strength

Modularity, versatility and adaptiveness are to be prioritised in an uncertain and fast evolving world. Diverse systems, with many connections and scales are more resilient in the face of external shocks, than systems built simply for efficiency.

Energy must Come from Renewable Sources

As in life, any system should ultimately aim to run on 'current sunshine' and generate energy through renewable sources.

Systems Thinking

The ability to understand how things influence one another within a whole. Elements are considered as 'fitting in' their infrastructure, environment and social context. Whilst a machine is also a system, systems thinking usually refers to non linear systems: systems where through feedback and imprecise starting conditions the outcome is not necessarily proportional to the input and where evolution of the system is possible : the system can display emergent properties. Examples of these systems are all living systems and any open system such as meteorological systems or ocean currents, even the orbits of the planets have non linear characteristics.

Understanding a system is crucial when trying to decide and plan (corrections) in a system. Missing or misinterpreting the trends, flows, functions of, and human influences on, our socio-ecological systems could result in disastrous results. In order to prevent errors in planning or design an understanding of the system should be applied to the whole and to the details of the plan or design. The Natural Step created a set of systems conditions (or sustainability principles) that can be applied when designing for (parts of) a circular economy to ensure alignment with functions of the socio-ecological system.

The Circular Economy Framework

The circular economy is a framework that draws upon and encompasses principles from:

Biomimicry

Janine Benyus, author of "Biomimicry: Innovation Inspired by Nature", defines her approach as "a new discipline that studies nature's best ideas and then imitates these designs and processes to solve human problems. Studying a leaf to invent a better solar cell is an example. I think of it as "innovation inspired by nature. Biomimicry relies on three key principles:

- Nature as model: Biomimicry studies nature's models and emulates these forms, processes, systems, and strategies to solve human problems.
- Nature as measure: Biomimicry uses an ecological standard to judge the sustainability of our innovations.
- Nature as mentor: Biomimicry is a way of viewing and valuing nature. It introduces an era based not on what we can extract from the natural world, but what we can learn from it.

Industrial Ecology

Industrial Ecology is the study of material and energy flows through industrial systems. Focusing on connections between operators within the "industrial ecosystem", this approach aims at creating closed loop processes in which waste is seen as input, thus eliminating the notion of undesirable by-product. Industrial ecology adopts a systemic - or holistic - point of view, designing production processes according to local ecological constraints whilst looking at their global impact from the outset, and attempting to shape them so they perform as close to living systems as possible. This framework is sometimes referred to as the "science of sustainability", given its interdisciplinary nature, and its principles can also be applied in the services sector. With an emphasis on natural capital restoration, Industrial Ecology also focuses on social wellbeing.

Cradle to Cradle

Created by German chemist Michael Braungart and American architect Bill McDonough, the Cradle to Cradle Design model considers that all material involved in industrial and commercial processes can be seen as nutrients, of which there are two main categories: technical and biological. Technical nutrients should include only materials that do not have a negative impact on the environment (so non-harmful synthetic ones are accepted), while Biological nutrients are organic and can be returned to the soil without specific treatment to decompose and eventually become food for the ecosystem. What we need are "completely healthy products that are either returned to the soil or flow back to industry forever", say McDonough and Braungart.

Blue Economy

Initiated by former Ecover CEO and Belgian businessman Gunter Pauli, the Blue Economy is an open-source movement bringing together concrete case studies, initially compiled in an eponymous report handed over to the Club of Rome. As the official manifesto states, "using the resources available in cascading systems, (...) the waste of one product becomes the input to create a new cash flow". Based on 21 founding principles, the Blue Economy insists on solutions being determined by their local environment and physical / ecological characteristics, putting the emphasis on gravity as the primary source of energy - a point that differentiates this school of thought from the others within the Circular Economy. The report - which doubles as the movement's manifesto - describes "100 innovations which can create 100 million jobs within the next 10 years", and provides many example of winning South-South collaborative projects, another original feature of this approach intent on promoting its hands-on focus.

Towards the Circular Economy

In January 2012, a report was released entitled *Towards the Circular Economy: Economic and business rationale for an accelerated transition*. The report, commissioned by the Ellen MacArthur Foundation and developed by McKinsey & Company, was the first of its kind to consider the economic and business opportunity for the transition to a restorative, circular model. Using product case studies and economy-wide analysis, the report details the potential for significant benefits across the EU. It argues that a subset of the EU manufacturing sector could realise net materials cost savings worth up to $630 billion p.a. towards 2025—stimulating economic activity in the areas of product development, remanufacturing and refurbishment. *Towards the Circular Economy* also identified the key building blocks in making the transition to a circular economy, namely in skills in circular design and production, new business models, skills in building cascades and reverse cycles, and cross-cycle/cross-sector collaboration.

Impact in Europe

On 17 December 2012, the European Commission published a document entitled *Manifesto for a Resource Efficient Europe*. This manifesto clearly stated that "In a world with growing pressures on resources and the environment, the EU has no choice but to go for the transition to a resource-efficient and ultimately regenerative circular economy." Furthermore, the document highlighted the importance of "a systemic change in the use and recovery of resources in the economy" in ensuring future jobs and competitiveness, and outlined potential pathways to a circular economy, in innovation and investment, regulation, tackling harmful subsidies, increasing opportunities for new business models, and setting clear targets.

Resource

In March 2014 the first large scale event for the circular economy was held with over 11,000 attendees from across the globe and all the major stakeholders in attendance. The launch of such an event signals the rise of the topic and it will act as an enabler for business to transition towards more circular business models. This annual large scale event is now growing to represent the uptake of circular economy principles.

Ecological Modernisation

Ecological modernisation is an optimistic school of thought in the social sciences that argues that the economy benefits from moves towards environmentalism. It has gained increasing attention among scholars and policymakers in the last several decades internationally. It is an analytical approach as well as a policy strategy and environmental discourse (Hajer, 1995).

Origins and Key Elements

Ecological modernisation emerged in the early 1980s within a group of scholars at Free University and the Social Science Research Centre in Berlin, among them Joseph Huber, Martin Jänicke and Udo E. Simonis. Various authors pursued similar ideas at the time, e.g. Arthur H. Rosenfeld, Amory Lovins, Donald Huisingh, René Kemp, or Ernst Ulrich von Weizsäcker. Further substantial contributions were made by Arthur P.J. Mol, Gert Spaargaren and David A Sonnenfeld (Mol and Sonnenfeld, 2000; Mol, 2001).

One basic assumption of ecological modernisation relates to environmental readaptation of economic growth and industrial development. On the basis of enlightened self-interest, economy and ecology can be favourably combined: Environmental productivity, i.e.

productive use of natural resources and environmental media (air, water, soil, ecosystems), can be a source of future growth and development in the same way as labour productivity and capital productivity. This includes increases in energy and resource efficiency as well as product and process innovations such as environmental management and sustainable supply chain management, clean technologies, benign substitution of hazardous substances, and product design for environment. Radical innovations in these fields can not only reduce quantities of resource turnover and emissions, but also change the quality or structure of the industrial metabolism. In the co-evolution of humans and nature, and in order to upgrade the environment's carrying capacity, ecological modernisation gives humans an active role to play, which may entail conflicts with nature conservation.

There are different understandings of the scope of ecological modernisation - whether it is just about techno-industrial progress and related aspects of polity and economy, and to what extent it also includes cultural aspects (ecological modernisation of mind, value orientiations, attitudes, behaviour and lifestyles). Similarly, there is some pluralism as to whether ecological modernisation would need to rely mainly on government, or markets and entrepreneurship, or civil society, or some sort of multi-level governance combining the three. Some scholars explicitly refer to general modernisation theory as well as non-Marxist world-system theory, others don't.

Ultimately, however, there is a common understanding that ecological modernisation will have to result in innovative structural change. So research is now still more focused on environmental innovations, or eco-innovations, and the interplay of various societal factors (scientific, economic, institutional, legal, political, cultural) which foster or hamper such innovations (Klemmer et al., 1999; Huber, 2004; Weber and Hemmelskamp, 2005; Olsthoorn and Wieczorek, 2006).

Ecological modernisation shares a number of features with neighbouring, overlapping approaches. Among the most important are

- the concept of sustainable development
- the approach of industrial metabolism (Ayres and Simonis, 1994)
- the concept of industrial ecology (Socolow, 1994).

Additional Elements

A special topic of ecological modernisation research during recent years was *sustainable household*, i.e. environment-oriented reshaping of lifestyles, consumption patterns, and demand-pull control of supply chains (Vergragt, 2000; OECD 2002). Some scholars of ecological modernisation share an interest in industrial symbiosis, i.e. inter-site recycling that helps to reduce the consumption of resources via increasing efficiency (i.e. pollution prevention, waste reduction), typically by taking externalities from one economic production process and using them as raw material inputs for another (Christoff, 1996). Ecological modernisation also relies on product life-cycle assessment and the analysis of materials and energy flows. In this context, ecological modernisation promotes 'cradle to cradle' manufacturing (Braungart and McDonough, 2002), contrasted against the usual 'cradle to grave' forms of manufacturing - where waste is not re-integrated back into the production process. Another special interest in the ecological modernisation literature has been the role of social movements and the emergence of civil society as a key agent of change (Fisher and Freudenburg, 2001).

As a strategy of change, some forms of ecological modernisation may be favoured by business interests because they seemingly meet the triple bottom line of economics, society and environment that is held underpin sustainability, yet do not challenge free market principles. This contrasts with many environmental movement perspectives, which regard free trade and its notion of business self-regulation as part of the problem, or even origin of environmental degradation. Under ecological modernisation, the state is seen in a variety of roles and capacities: as the enabler for markets that help produce the technological advances via competition; as the regulatory medium through which corporations are forced to 'take back' their various wastes and re-integrate them in some manner into the production of new goods and services (e.g. the way that car corporations in Germany are required to accept back cars they manufactured once those vehicles have reached the end of their product lifespan); and in some cases as an institution that is incapable of addressing critical local, national, and global environmental problems. In the latter case, ecological modernisation shares with Ulrich Beck (1999, 37-40) and others notions of the necessity of emergence of new forms of environmental governance, sometimes referred to as subpolitics or political modernisation, where the environmental movement, community groups, businesses, and other stakeholders increasingly take on direct and leadership roles in stimulating environmental transformation. Political modernisation of this sort requires certain supporting norms and institutions such as a free, independent, or at least critical press, basic human rights of expression, organisation, and assembly, etc. New media such as the Internet greatly facilitate this.

Criticisms

Critics argue that ecological modernisation will fail to protect the environment and does nothing to alter the impulses within the capitalist economic mode of production that inevitably lead to environmental degradation (Foster, 2002). As such, it is just a form of 'green-washing'. Critics question whether technological advances alone can achieve resource conservation and better environmental protection, particularly if left to business self-regulation practices (York and Rosa, 2003). For instance, many technological improvements are currently feasible but not widely utilised. The most environmentally friendly product or manufacturing process (which is often also the most economically efficient) is not always the one automatically chosen by self-regulating corporations (e.g. hydrogen or biofuel vs. peak oil). In addition, some critics have argued that ecological modernisation does not redress gross injustices that are produced within the capitalist system, such as environmental racism - where people of colour and low income earners bear a disproportionate burden of environmental harm such as pollution, and lack access to environmental benefits such as parks, and social justice issues such as eliminating unemployment (Bullard, 1993; Gleeson and Low, 1999; Harvey, 1996) - environmental racism is also referred to as issues of the asymmetric distribution of environmental resources and services (Everett & Neu, 2000). Moreover, the theory seems to have limited global efficacy, applying primarily to its countries of origin - Germany and the Netherlands, and having little to say about the developing world (Fisher and Freudenburg, 2001). Perhaps the harshest criticism though, is that ecological modernisation is predicated upon the notion of 'sustainable growth', and in reality this is not possible because growth entails the consumption of natural and human capital at great costs to ecosystems and societies.

Ecological modernisation, its effectiveness and applicability, strengths and limitations, remains a dynamic and contentious area of environmental social science research and policy discourse in the early 21st century.

Efficient Energy Use

Efficient energy use, sometimes simply called energy efficiency, is the goal to reduce the amount of energy required to provide products and services. For example, insulating a home allows a building to use less heating and cooling energy to achieve and maintain a comfortable temperature. Installing fluorescent lights or natural skylights reduces the amount of energy required to attain the same level of illumination compared with using traditional incandescent light bulbs. Compact fluorescent lights use one-third the energy of incandescent lights and may last 6 to 10 times longer. Improvements in energy efficiency are generally achieved by adopting a more efficient technology or production processes or by application of commonly accepted methods to reduce energy losses.

There are many motivations to improve energy efficiency. Reducing energy use reduces energy costs and may result in a financial cost saving to consumers if the energy savings offset any additional costs of implementing an energy efficient technology. Reducing energy use is also seen as a solution to the problem of reducing carbon dioxide emissions. According to the International Energy Agency, improved energy efficiency in buildings, industrial processes and transportation could reduce the world's energy needs in 2050 by one third, and help control global emissions of greenhouse gases.

Energy efficiency and renewable energy are said to be the *twin pillars* of sustainable energy policy and are high priorities in the sustainable energy hierarchy. In many countries energy efficiency is also seen to have a national security benefit because it can be used to reduce the level of energy imports from foreign countries and may slow down the rate at which domestic energy resources are depleted.

Overview

Energy efficiency has proved to be a cost-effective strategy for building economies without necessarily increasing energy consumption. For example, the state of California began implementing energy-efficiency measures in the mid-1970s, including building code and appliance standards with strict efficiency requirements. During the following years, California's energy consumption has remained approximately flat on a per capita basis while national U.S. consumption doubled. As part of its strategy, California implemented a "loading order" for new energy resources that puts energy efficiency first, renewable electricity supplies second, and new fossil-fired power plants last.

Lovins' Rocky Mountain Institute points out that in industrial settings, "there are abundant opportunities to save 70% to 90% of the energy and cost for lighting, fan, and pump systems; 50% for electric motors; and 60% in areas such as heating, cooling, office equipment, and appliances." In general, up to 75% of the electricity used in the U.S. today could be saved with efficiency measures that cost less than the electricity itself. The same holds true for home-owners, leaky ducts have remained an invisible energy culprit for years. In fact, researchers at the US Department of Energy and their consortium, Residential

Energy Efficient Distribution Systems (REEDS) have found that duct efficiency may be as low as 50-70%. The US Department of Energy has stated that there is potential for energy saving in the magnitude of 90 Billion kWh by increasing home energy efficiency.

Other studies have emphasized this. A report published in 2006 by the McKinsey Global Institute, asserted that "there are sufficient economically viable opportunities for energy-productivity improvements that could keep global energy-demand growth at less than 1 percent per annum"—less than half of the 2.2 percent average growth anticipated through 2020 in a business-as-usual scenario. Energy productivity, which measures the output and quality of goods and services per unit of energy input, can come from either reducing the amount of energy required to produce something, or from increasing the quantity or quality of goods and services from the same amount of energy.

The Vienna Climate Change Talks 2007 Report, under the auspices of the United Nations Framework Convention on Climate Change (UNFCCC), clearly shows "that energy efficiency can achieve real emission reductions at low cost."

Appliances

Modern appliances, such as, freezers, ovens, stoves, dishwashers, and clothes washers and dryers, use significantly less energy than older appliances. Installing a clothesline will significantly reduce your energy consumption as your dryer will be used less. Current energy efficient refrigerators, for example, use 40 percent less energy than conventional models did in 2001. Following this, if all households in Europe changed their more than ten-year-old appliances into new ones, 20 billion kWh of electricity would be saved annually, hence reducing CO_2 emissions by almost 18 billion kg. In the US, the corresponding figures would be 17 billion kWh of electricity and 27,000,000,000 lb (1.2×10^{10} kg) CO_2. According to a 2009 study from McKinsey & Company the replacement of old appliances is one of the most efficient global measures to reduce emissions of greenhouse gases. Modern power management systems also reduce energy usage by idle appliances by turning them off or putting them into a low-energy mode after a certain time. Many countries identify energy-efficient appliances using energy input labelling.

The impact of energy efficiency on peak demand depends on when the appliance is used. For example, an air conditioner uses more energy during the afternoon when it is hot. Therefore, an energy efficient air conditioner will have a larger impact on peak demand than off-peak demand. An energy efficient dishwasher, on the other hand, uses more energy during the late evening when people do their dishes. This appliance may have little to no impact on peak demand.

Building Design

A building's location and surroundings play a key role in regulating its temperature and illumination. For example, trees, landscaping, and hills can provide shade and block wind. In cooler climates, designing northern hemisphere buildings with south facing windows and southern hemisphere buildings with north facing windows increases the amount of sun (ultimately heat energy) entering the building, minimizing energy use, by maximizing passive solar heating. Tight building design, including energy-efficient windows, well-sealed doors, and additional thermal insulation of walls, basement slabs, and foundations can reduce heat loss by 25 to 50 percent.

Dark roofs may become up to 39 C° (70 F°) hotter than the most reflective white surfaces. They transmit some of this additional heat inside the building. US Studies have shown that lightly coloured roofs use 40 percent less energy for cooling than buildings with darker roofs. White roof systems save more energy in sunnier climates. Advanced electronic heating and cooling systems can moderate energy consumption and improve the comfort of people in the building.

Proper placement of windows and skylights as well as the use of architectural features that reflect light into a building can reduce the need for artificial lighting. Increased use of natural and task lighting has been shown by one study to increase productivity in schools and offices. Compact fluorescent lights use two-thirds less energy and may last 6 to 10 times longer than incandescent light bulbs. Newer fluorescent lights produce a natural light, and in most applications they are cost effective, despite their higher initial cost, with payback periods as low as a few months.

Effective energy-efficient building design can include the use of low cost Passive Infra Reds (PIRs) to switch-off lighting when areas are unnoccupied such as toilets, corridors or even office areas out-of-hours. In addition, lux levels can be monitored using daylight sensors linked to the building's lighting scheme to switch on/off or dim the lighting to pre-defined levels to take into account the natural light and thus reduce consumption. Building Management Systems (BMS) link all of this together in one centralised computer to control the whole building's lighting and power requirements.

The choice of which space heating or cooling technology to use in buildings can have a significant impact on energy use and efficiency. For example, replacing an older 50% efficient natural gas furnace with a new 95% efficient one will dramatically reduce energy use, carbon emissions, and winter natural gas bills. Ground source heat pumps can be even more energy efficient and cost effective. These systems use pumps and compressors to move refrigerant fluid around a thermodynamic cycle in order to "pump" heat against its natural flow from hot to cold, for the purpose of transferring heat into a building from the large thermal reservoir contained within the nearby ground. The end result is that heat pumps typically use four times less electrical energy to deliver an equivalent amount of heat than a direct electrical heater does. Another advantage of a ground source heat pump is that it can be reversed in summertime and operate to cool the air by transferring heat from the building to the ground. The disadvantage of ground source heat pumps is their high initial capital cost, but this is typically recouped within five to ten years as a result of lower energy use.

Smart metres are slowly being adopted by the commercial sector to highlight to staff and for internal monitoring purposes the building's energy usage in a dynamic presentable format. The use of Power Quality Analysers can be introduced into an existing building to assess usage, harmonic distortion, peaks, swells and interruptions amongst others to ultimately make the building more energy-efficient. Often such metres communicate by using wireless sensor networks.

Green Building XML (gbXML) is an emerging schema, a subset of the Building Information Modelling efforts, focused on green building design and operation. gbXML is used as input in several energy simulation engines. But with the development of modern computer technology, a large number of building energy simulation tools are available on the market. When choosing which simulation tool to use in a project, the user must consider the tool's accuracy and reliability, considering the building information they have at hand, which will serve as input for the tool. Yezioro, Dong and Leite developed an artificial intelligence approach towards assessing building performance simulation results and found that more detailed simulation tools have the best simulation performance in terms of heating and cooling electricity consumption within 3% of mean absolute error.

A deep energy retrofit is a whole-building analysis and construction process that uses to achieve much larger energy savings than conventional energy retrofits. Deep energy retrofits can be applied to both residential and non-residential ("commercial") buildings. A deep energy retrofit typically results in energy savings of 30 percent or more, perhaps spread over several years, and may significantly improve the building value. The Empire State Building has undergone a deep energy retrofit process that was completed in 2013. The project team, consisting of representatives from Johnson Controls, Rocky Mountain Institute, Clinton Climate Initiative, and Jones Lang LaSalle will have achieved an annual energy use reduction of 38% and $4.4 million. For example, the 6,500 windows were remanufactured onsite into superwindows which block heat but pass light. Air conditioning operating costs on hot days were reduced and this saved $17 million of the project's capital cost immediately, partly funding other retrofitting. Receiving a gold Leadership in Energy and Environmental Design (LEED) rating in September 2011, the Empire State Building is the tallest LEED certified building in the United States. The Indianapolis City-County Building recently underwent a deep energy retrofit process, which has achieved an annual energy reduction of 46% and $750,000 annual energy saving.

Energy retrofits, including deep, and other types undertaken in residential, commercial or industrial locations are generally supported through various forms of financing or incentives. Incentives include pre-packaged rebates where the buyer/user may not even be aware that the item being used has been rebated or "bought down". "Upstream" or "Midstream" buy downs are common for efficient lighting products. Other rebates are more explicit and transparent to the end user through the use of formal applications. In addition to rebates, which may be offered through government or utility programs, governments sometimes offer tax incentives for energy efficiency projects. Some entities offer rebate and payment guidance and facilitation services that enable energy end use customers tap into rebate and incentive programs.

Industry

Industry uses a large amount of energy to power a diverse range of manufacturing and resource extraction processes. Many industrial processes require large amounts of heat and mechanical power, most of which is delivered as natural gas, petroleum fuels and as electricity. In addition some industries generate fuel from waste products that can be used to provide additional energy.

Because industrial processes are so diverse it is impossible to describe the multitude of possible opportunities for energy efficiency in industry. Many depend on the specific technologies and processes in use at each industrial facility. There are, however, a number of processes and energy services that are widely used in many industries.

Various industries generate steam and electricity for subsequent use within their facilities. When electricity is generated, the heat that is produced as a by-product can be captured and used for process steam, heating or other industrial purposes. Conventional electricity generation is about 30% efficient, whereas combined heat and power (also called co-generation) converts up to 90 percent of the fuel into usable energy.

Advanced boilers and furnaces can operate at higher temperatures while burning less fuel. These technologies are more efficient and produce fewer pollutants.

Over 45 percent of the fuel used by US manufacturers is burnt to make steam. The typical industrial facility can reduce this energy usage 20 percent (according to the US Department of Energy) by insulating steam and condensate return lines, stopping steam leakage, and maintaining steam traps.

Electric motors usually run at a constant speed, but a variable speed drive allows the motor's energy output to match the required load. This achieves energy savings ranging from 3 to 60 percent, depending on how the motor is used. Motor coils made of superconducting materials can also reduce energy losses. Motors may also benefit from voltage optimisation.

Industry uses a large number of pumps and compressors of all shapes and sizes and in a wide variety of applications. The efficiency of pumps and compressors depends on many factors but often improvements can be made by implementing better process control and better maintenance practices. Compressors are commonly used to provide compressed air which is used for sand blasting, painting, and other power tools. According to the US Department of Energy, optimizing compressed air systems by installing variable speed drives, along with preventive maintenance to detect and fix air leaks, can improve energy efficiency 20 to 50 percent.

Vehicles

The estimated energy efficiency for an automobile is 280 Passenger-Mile/10^6 Btu. There are several ways to enhance a vehicle's energy efficiency. Using improved aerodynamics to minimize drag can increase vehicle fuel efficiency. Reducing vehicle weight can also improve fuel economy, which is why composite materials are widely used in car bodies.

More advanced tires, with decreased tire to road friction and rolling resistance, can save gasoline. Fuel economy can be improved by up to 3.3% by keeping tires inflated to the correct pressure. Replacing a clogged air filter can improve a cars fuel consumption by as much as 10 percent on older vehicles. On newer vehicles (1980s and up) with fuel-injected, computer-controlled engines, a clogged air filter has no effect on mpg but replacing it may improve acceleration by 6-11 percent.

Energy-efficient vehicles may reach twice the fuel efficiency of the average automobile. Cutting-edge designs, such as the diesel Mercedes-

Benz Bionic concept vehicle have achieved a fuel efficiency as high as 84 miles per US gallon (2.8 L/100 km; 101 mpg_{-imp}), four times the current conventional automotive average.

The mainstream trend in automotive efficiency is the rise of electric vehicles (all@electric or hybrid electric). Hybrids, like the Toyota Prius, use regenerative braking to recapture energy that would dissipate in normal cars; the effect is especially pronounced in city driving. Plug-in hybrids also have increased battery capacity, which makes it possible to drive for limited distances without burning any gasoline; in this case, energy efficiency is dictated by whatever process (such as coal-burning, hydroelectric, or renewable source) created the power. Plug-ins can typically drive for around 40 miles (64 km) purely on electricity without recharging; if the battery runs low, a gas engine kicks in allowing for extended range. Finally, all-electric cars are also growing in popularity; the Tesla Roadster sports car is the only high-performance all-electric car currently on the market, and others are in preproduction.

Alternative Fuels

Alternative fuels, known as non-conventional or advanced fuels, are any materials or substances that can be used as fuels, other than conventional fuels. Some well known alternative fuels include biodiesel, bioalcohol (methanol, ethanol, butanol), chemically stored electricity (batteries and fuel cells), hydrogen, non-fossil methane, non-fossil natural gas, vegetable oil, and other biomass sources.

Energy Conservation

Energy conservation is broader than energy efficiency in including active efforts to decrease energy consumption, for example through behaviour change, in addition to using energy more efficiently. Examples of conservation without efficiency improvements are heating a room less in winter, using the car less, air-drying your clothes instead of using the dryer, or enabling energy saving modes on a computer. As with other definitions, the boundary between efficient energy use and energy conservation can be fuzzy, but both are important in environmental and economic terms. This is especially the case when actions are directed at the saving of fossil fuels. Energy conservation is a challenge requiring policy programmes, technological development and behaviour change to go hand in hand. Many energy intermediary organisations, for example governmental or non-governmental organisations on local, regional, or national level, are working on often publicly funded programmes or projects to meet this challenge. Psychologists have also engaged with the issue of energy conservation and have provided guidelines for realising behaviour change to reduce energy consumption while taking technological and policy considerations into account.

The National Renewable Energy Laboratory maintains a comprehensive list of apps useful for energy efficiency.

Commercial property managers that plan and manage energy efficiency projects generally use a software platform to perform energy audits and to collaborate with contractors to understand their full range of options. The Department of Energy (DOE) Software Directory describes EnergyActio software, a cloud based platform designed for this purpose.

Sustainable Energy

Energy efficiency and renewable energy are said to be the "twin pillars" of a sustainable energy policy. Both strategies must be developed concurrently in order to stabilize and reduce carbon dioxide emissions. Efficient energy use is essential to slowing the energy demand growth so that rising clean energy supplies can make deep cuts in fossil fuel use. If energy use grows too rapidly, renewable energy development will chase a receding target. Likewise, unless clean energy supplies come online rapidly, slowing demand growth will only begin to reduce total carbon emissions; a reduction in the carbon content of energy sources is also needed. A sustainable energy economy thus requires major commitments to both efficiency and renewables.

Rebound Effect

If the demand for energy services remains constant, improving energy efficiency will reduce energy consumption and carbon emissions. However, many efficiency improvements do not reduce energy consumption by the amount predicted by simple engineering models. This is because they make energy services cheaper, and so consumption of those services increases. For example, since fuel efficient vehicles make travel cheaper, consumers may choose to drive farther, thereby offsetting some of the potential energy savings. Similarly, an extensive historical analysis of technological efficiency improvements has conclusively shown that energy efficiency improvements were almost always outpaced by economic growth, resulting in a net increase in resource use and associated pollution. These are examples of the direct rebound effect.

Estimates of the size of the rebound effect range from roughly 5% to 40%. The rebound effect is likely to be less than 30% at the household level and may be closer to 10% for transport. A rebound effect of 30%

implies that improvements in energy efficiency should achieve 70% of the reduction in energy consumption projected using engineering models. The rebound effect may be particularly large for lighting, because in contrast to tasks like transport there is effectively no upper limit on how much light could be considered useful. In fact, it appears that lighting has accounted for about 0.7% of GDP across many societies and hundreds of years, implying a rebound effect of 100%.

Rebound Effect (Conservation)

In conservation and energy economics, the rebound effect (or take-back effect) refers to the behavioural or other systemic responses to the introduction of new technologies that increase the efficiency of resource use. These responses tend to offset the beneficial effects of the new technology or other measures taken. While the literature on the rebound effect generally focuses on the effect of technological improvements on energy consumption, the theory can also be applied to the use of any natural resource or other input, such as labour. The rebound effect is generally expressed as a ratio of the lost benefit compared to the expected environmental benefit when holding consumption constant. For instance, if a 5% improvement in vehicle fuel efficiency results in only a 2% drop in fuel use, there is a 60% rebound effect (since $^{(5-2)}D_{5} = 60\%$). The 'missing' 3% might have been consumed by driving faster or further than before.

The existence of the rebound effect is uncontroversial. However, debate continues as to the size and importance of the effect in real world situations. There are three possible outcomes regarding the size of the rebound effect:

1. The actual resource savings are higher than expected – the rebound effect is negative. This will normally occur if the government mandates the use of more resource efficient technologies that are also more costly to use, but not if the increase in efficiency reduces costs
2. The actual savings are less than expected savings – the rebound effect is between 0% and 100%. This is sometimes known as 'take-back', and is the most common result of empirical studies on individual markets.
3. The actual resource savings are negative – the rebound effect is higher than 100%. This situation is commonly known as the Jevons paradox, and is sometimes referred to as 'back-fire'.

The full rebound effect can be distinguished into three different economic reactions to technological changes: The direct rebound effect refers to increases in consumption of a good because of the substitution effect from lower cost of use. Indirect rebound effects come about from the income effect as decreased costs enables increased household consumption of other goods and services. Economy wide effects occur because improved technology creates new production possibilities and increases economic growth.

In order to avoid the rebound effect, environmental economists have suggested that any cost savings from efficiency gains be taxed in order to keep the cost of use the same.

History

The rebound effect was first described by William Stanley Jevons in his 1865 book *The Coal Question*, where he observed that the invention in Britain of a more efficient steam engine meant that the use of coal became economically viable for many new uses. This ultimately led to increased coal demand and much increased coal consumption, even as the amount of coal required for any particular use fell. According to Jevons, "It is a confusion of ideas to suppose that the economical use of fuel is equivalent to diminished consumption. The very contrary is the truth."

However, most contemporary authors credit Daniel Khazzoom for the re-emergence of the rebound effect in the research literature. Although Khazzoom did not use the term, he raised the idea that there is a less than one-to-one correlation between gains in energy efficiency and reductions in energy use, because of a change in the 'price content' of energy in the provision of the final consumer product. His study was based on energy efficiency gains in home appliances, but the principle applies throughout the economy. A commonly studied example is that of a more fuel-efficient car. Since each kilometre of travel becomes cheaper, there will be an increase in driving speed and/or kilometres driven, as long as the price elasticity of demand for car travel is not zero. Other examples might include the growth in garden lighting after the introduction of energy-saving compact fluorescent lamps or the increasing size of houses driven partly by higher fuel efficiency in home heating technologies. If the rebound effect is larger than 100%, all gains from the increased fuel efficiency would be wiped out by increases in demand (the Jevons paradox).

Khazzoom's thesis was criticized heavily by Michael Grubb and Amory Lovins who dismissed any disconnection between energy efficiency improvements in an individual market, and an economy-wide reduction in energy consumption. Developing Khazzoom's idea further, and prompting heated debate in the Energy Policy journal at that time, Len Brookes wrote of the fallacies in the energy-efficiency solution to greenhouse gas emissions. His analysis showed that any economically justified improvements in energy efficiency would in fact stimulate economic growth and increase total energy use. For improvements in energy efficiency to contribute to a reduction in economy-wide energy consumption, the improvement must come at a greater economic cost. Commenting in regard to energy efficiency advocates, he concludes that, "the present high profile of the topic seems to owe more to the current tide of green fervor than to sober consideration of the facts, and the validity and cost of solutions."

Khazzoom-Brookes Postulate

In 1992, economist Harry Saunders coined the term "Khazzoom-Brookes postulate" to describe the idea that energy efficiency gains paradoxically result in increases in energy use (the modern day equivalent of the Jevons paradox). He modelled energy efficiency gains using a variety of neo-classical growth models, and showed that the postulate is true over a wide range of assumptions. In the conclusion of his paper, Saunders stated that:

In the absence of efficiency gains, energy use will grow in lock step with economic growth (energy intensity will stay fixed) when energy prices are fixed. ... Energy efficiency gains can increase energy consumption by two means: by making energy appear effectively cheaper than other inputs; and by increasing economic growth, which pulls up energy use. ... These results, while by no means proving the Khazzoom-Brookes postulate, call for prudent energy analysts and policy makers to pause a long moment before dismissing it.

This work provided a theoretical grounding for empirical studies and played an important role in framing the problem of the rebound effect. It also reinforced an emerging ideological divide between energy economists on the extent of the yet to be named effect. The two tightly held positions are:

- Technological improvements in energy efficiency enable economic growth that was otherwise impossible without the improvement; as such, energy efficiency improvements will usually back-fire in the long term.
- Technological improvements in energy efficiency may result in a small take-back. However, even in the long term, energy efficiency improvements usually result in large overall energy savings.

Even though many studies have been undertaken in this area, neither position has yet claimed a consensus view in the academic literature. Recent studies have demonstrated that direct rebound effects are significant (about 30% for energy), but that there is not enough information about indirect effects to know whether or how often back-fire occurs. Economists tend to the first position, but most governments, businesses, and environmental groups adhere to the second. Governments and environmental groups often advocate further research into fuel efficiency and radical increases in the efficient use of energy as the primary means for reducing energy use and reducing greenhouse gas emissions (to alleviate the impacts of climate change). However, if the first position more accurately reflects economic reality, current efforts to invent fuel-efficient technologies may not much reduce energy use, and may in fact paradoxically increase oil and coal consumption, and greenhouse gas emissions, over the long run.

Types of Effects

The full rebound effect can be distinguished into three different economic reactions:

1. Direct rebound effect: Increased fuel efficiency lowers the cost of consumption, and hence increases the consumption of that good because of the substitution effect.
2. Indirect rebound effect: Through the income effect, decreased cost of the good enables increased household consumption of other goods and services, increasing the consumption of the resource embodied in those goods and services.
3. Economy wide effects: New technology creates new production possibilities and increases economic growth.

In the example of improved vehicle fuel efficiency, the direct effect would be the increased fuel use from more driving as driving becomes cheaper. The indirect effect would incorporate the increased consumption of other goods enabled by household cost savings from increased fuel efficiency. Since consumption of other goods increase, the embodied fuel used in the production of those goods would increase as well. Finally, the economy wide effect would include the long term effect of the increase in vehicle fuel efficiency on production and consumption possibilities throughout the economy, including any effects on economic growth rates.

Direct and Indirect Effects

For cost reducing resource efficiency, distinguishing between direct and indirect effects is shown in Figure below. The horizontal axis shows units of consumption of the targets good (which could be for example clothes washing, and measured in terms of kilograms of clean clothes) with consumption of all other goods and services on the vertical axis. An economical technology change that enables each unit of washing to be produced with less electricity results in a reduction of the price per unit of washing. This shifts the household budget line rightwards. The result is a substitution effect because of the decreased relative price, but also an income effect due to the increased real income. The substitution effect increases consumption of washing from Q1 to QS, and the income effect from QS to Q2. The total increase in consumption of washing from Q1 to Q2 and the resulting increase in electricity consumption is the direct effect. The indirect effect comprises the increase in other consumption, from O1 to O2. The scale of each of these effects depends on the elasticity of demand for each of the goods, and the embodied resource or externality associated with each good. A parallel effect will happen for cost saving efficient technologies for producers, where output and substitution effects will occur.

The rebound effect can increase the difficulty of projecting the reduction in greenhouse emissions from an improvement in energy efficiency. Estimation of the scale of direct effects on residential electricity, heating and motor fuel consumption has been common motivation for research of rebound effects. Evaluation and econometric methods are the two approaches generally employed in estimating the size of this effect. Evaluation methods rely on quasi-experimental studies and measure the before and after changes to energy consumption from the implementation of energy efficient technology, while econometric methods utilise elasticity estimates to forecast the likely effects from changes in the effective price of energy services.

Research has found that in developed countries, the direct rebound effect is usually small to moderate, ranging from roughly 5% to 40%. However, the rebound effect may be more significant in the context of the undeveloped markets in developing economies.

Economy Wide Effects

Even if the direct and indirect rebound effects add up to less than 100%, technological improvements that increase efficiency may still result in economy wide effects that results in increased resource use for the economy as a whole. In particular, this would happen if resource efficiency enables an expansion of production in the economy, and an increase in the rate of economic growth. For example, for the case of energy use, more efficient technology is equivalent to a lower price for energy resources. It is well known that changes in energy costs have a large impact on economic growth rates. In the 1970s sharp increases in petroleum prices led to stagflation (recession and inflation) in the developed countries, whereas in the 1990s lower petroleum prices contributed to higher economic growth. An improvement in energy efficiency has the same effect as lower fuel prices, and leads to faster economic growth. Economists generally believe that especially for the case of energy use, more efficient technologies will lead to increased use, because of this growth effect.

To model the scale of this effect, economists use computational general equilibrium (CGE) models. While CGE methodology is by no means perfect, results indicate that economy wide rebound effects are likely to be very high, with estimates above 100% rather common. One simple CGE model has been made available online for use by economists.

Indirect Effects from Conservation

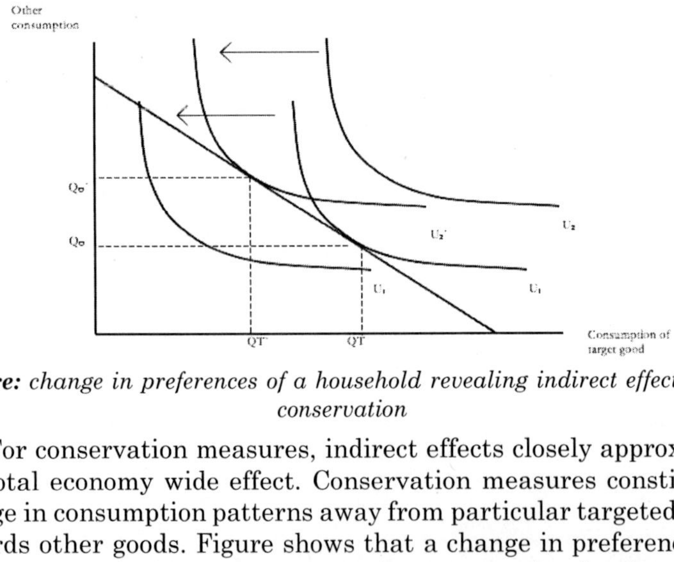

Figure: *change in preferences of a household revealing indirect effects from conservation*

For conservation measures, indirect effects closely approximate the total economy wide effect. Conservation measures constitute a change in consumption patterns away from particular targeted goods towards other goods. Figure shows that a change in preference of a household results in a new consumption pattern that has less of the target good (QT to QT'), and more of all other goods (QO to QO'). The resource consumption or externalities embodied in this other consumption is the indirect effect.

Although a persuasive view has prevailed that indirect effects with respect to energy and greenhouse emissions should be very small due to energy directly comprising only a small component of household expenditure, this view is gradually being eroded. Many recent studies based on life-cycle analysis show the energy consumed indirectly by households is often higher than consumed directly through electricity, gas, and motor fuel, and is a growing proportion. This is evident in the results of recent studies that indicate indirect effects from household conservation can range from 10% to 200% depending on the scenario, with higher indirect rebounds from diet changes aiming to reduce food miles.

Income Level Variation

Research has shown that the direct rebound effects for energy services is lower at high income levels, due to less price sensitivity. Studies have found that own-price elasticity of gas consumption by UK households was two times greater for households in the lowest income decile when compared to the highest decile. Studies have also observed higher rebounds in low-income houses for improvements in heating technology. Evaluation methods have also been used to assess the scale of rebound effects from efficient heating installations in lower income homes in the United Kingdom. This research found that direct effects are close to 100% in many cases. High income households in developed countries are likely to set the temperature at the optimum comfort level, regardless of the cost – therefore any cost reduction does not result in increased heating, for it was already optimal. But low-income households are more price sensitive, and have made thermal sacrifices due to the cost of heating. In this case, a high direct rebound is likely. This analogy can be extended to most household energy consumption.

The size of the rebound effect is likely to be higher in developing countries according to macro-level assessments and case studies. One case study was undertaken in rural India to evaluate the impact of an alternative energy scheme. Households were given solar powered lighting in an attempt to reduce the use of kerosene for lighting to zero except for seasons with insufficient sunshine. The scheme was also designed to encourage a future willingness to pay for efficient lighting. The results were surprising, with high direct rebounds between 50 and 80%, and total direct and indirect rebound above 100%. Because the new lighting source was essentially zero cost, operating hours for lighting went up from an average of 2 to 6 per day, with new lighting consisting of a combination of both the no-cost solar lamps and also kerosene lamps. Also, more cooking was undertaken which enabled an increased trade of food with neighbouring villages.

Rebounds with Respect to Time

The individual opportunity cost of time is not often considered. Hence, often overlooked in the rebound effect literature is the rebound effect with respect to savings in time. Faster modes of transport are a classic example. Since the time cost forms a major part of the total cost of commuter transport, faster modes will reduce real costs, but will also encourage longer commuting distances. While important, it is almost impossible to estimate empirically the scale of such effects due to the subjective nature of the value of time. Time saved can either be directed towards work or leisure. Labour time saved at work due to the increased labour productivity is likely to be spent on further labour time at higher productive rates. For leisure time saving, this may simply encourage people to diversify their leisure interests to fill their generally fixed period of leisure time.

Suggested Solution

In order to ensure that efficiency enhancing technological improvements actually reduce fuel use, the ecological economists Mathis Wackernagel and William Rees have suggested that any cost savings from efficiency gains be "taxed away or otherwise removed from further economic circulation. Preferably they should be captured for reinvestment in natural capital rehabilitation." This can be achieved through, for example, the imposition of a green tax, a cap and trade program, higher fuel taxes or the proposed "restore" approach.

Polluter Pays Principle

In environmental law, the polluter pays principle is enacted to make the party responsible for producing pollution responsible for paying for the damage done to the natural environment. It is regarded as a regional custom because of the strong support it has received in most Organisation for Economic Co-operation and Development (OECD) and European Community (EC) countries.

The polluter pays principle underpins environmental policy such as an ecotax, which, if enacted by government, deters and essentially reduces greenhouse gas emissions. Some eco-taxes underpinned by the polluter pays principle include: the Gas Guzzler Tax, in US, Corporate Average Fuel Economy (CAFE)- a "polluter pays" fine. The U.S. Superfund law requires polluters to pay for cleanup of hazardous waste sites, when the polluters can be identified.

Polluter pays is also known as extended producer responsibility (EPR). This is a concept that was probably first described by Thomas Lindhqvist for the Swedish government in 1990. EPR seeks to shift the responsibility dealing with waste from governments (and thus, taxpayers and society at large) to the entities producing it. In effect, it internalised the cost of waste disposal into the cost of the product, theoretically meaning that the producers will improve the waste profile of their products, thus decreasing waste and increasing possibilities for reuse and recycling.

OECD Defines EPR as: a concept where manufacturers and importers of products should bear a significant degree of responsibility for the environmental impacts of their products throughout the product life-cycle, including upstream impacts inherent in the selection of materials for the products, impacts from manufacturers' production process itself, and downstream impacts from the use and disposal of the products. Producers accept their responsibility when designing their products to minimise life-cycle environmental impacts, and when accepting legal, physical or socio-economic responsibility for environmental impacts that cannot be eliminated by design.

In International Environmental Law

In international environmental law it is mentioned in Principle 16 of the Rio Declaration on Environment and Development.

Inclusion in National Laws

The state of New South Wales in Australia has included the polluter pay principle with the other principles of ecologically sustainable development in the objectives of the Environment Protection Authority.

Limitations of Polluter Pays Principle

The U.S. Environmental Protection Agency (EPA) has observed that the polluter pays principle has typically not been fully implemented in U.S. laws and programs. For example, drinking water and sewage treatment services are subsidized and there are limited mechanisms in place to fully assess polluters for treatment costs.

Precautionary Principle

The precautionary principle or precautionary approach to risk management states that if an action or policy has a suspected risk of causing harm to the public or to the environment, in the absence of scientific consensus that the action or policy is not harmful, the burden of proof that it is *not* harmful falls on those taking an action.

The principle is used by policy makers to justify discretionary decisions in situations where there is the possibility of harm from making a certain decision (e.g. taking a particular course of action) when extensive scientific knowledge on the matter is lacking. The principle implies that there is a social responsibility to protect the public from exposure to harm, when scientific investigation has found a plausible risk. These protections can be relaxed only if further scientific findings emerge that provide sound evidence that no harm will result.

In some legal systems, as in the law of the European Union, the application of the precautionary principle has been made a statutory requirement in some areas of law. Regarding international conduct, the first endorsement of the principle was in 1982 when the World Charter for Nature was adopted by the United Nations General Assembly, while its first international implementation was in 1987 through the Montreal Protocol. Soon after, the principle integrated with many other legally binding international treaties such as the Rio Declaration and Kyoto Protocol.

Origins and Theory

The term "precautionary principle" is generally considered to have arisen in English from a translation of the German term *Vorsorgeprinzip* in the 1980s. The concepts underpinning the precautionary principle pre-date the term's inception. For example, the essence of the principle is captured in a number of cautionary aphorisms such as "an ounce of prevention is worth a pound of cure", "better safe than sorry", and "look before you leap". The precautionary principle may also be interpreted as the evolution of the ancient medical principle of "first, do no harm" to apply to institutions and institutional decision-making processes rather than individuals.

In economics, the precautionary principle has been analysed in terms of the effect on rational decision-making of the interaction of irreversibility and uncertainty. Authors such as Epstein (1980) and Arrow and Fischer (1974) show that irreversibility of possible future consequences creates a quasi-option effect which should induce a "risk-neutral" society to favour current decisions that allow for more flexibility in the future. Gollier et al. (2000) conclude that "more scientific uncertainty as to the distribution of a future risk – that is, a larger variability of beliefs – should induce Society to take stronger prevention measures today."

Formulations

Many definitions of the precautionary principle exist. Precaution may be defined as "*caution in advance*," "*caution practised in the context of uncertainty*," or *informed prudence*. Two ideas lie at the core of the principle:

1. an expression of a need by decision-makers to anticipate harm before it occurs. Within this element lies an implicit reversal of the onus of proof: under the precautionary principle it is the responsibility of an activity proponent to establish that the

proposed activity will not (or is very unlikely to) result in significant harm.

2. the concept of proportionality of the risk and the cost and feasibility of a proposed action

One of the primary foundations of the precautionary principle, and globally accepted definitions, results from the work of the Rio Conference, or "Earth Summit" in 1992. Principle #15 of the Rio Declaration notes: "In order to protect the environment, the precautionary approach shall be widely applied by States according to their capabilities. Where there are threats of serious or irreversible damage, lack of full scientific certainty shall not be used as a reason for postponing cost-effective measures to prevent environmental degradation."

The 1998 Wingspread Statement on the Precautionary Principle summarizes the principle this way: "When an activity raises threats of harm to human health or the environment, precautionary measures should be taken even if some cause and effect relationships are not fully established scientifically." The Wingspread Conference on the Precautionary Principle was convened by the Science and Environmental Health Network.

The February 2, 2000 Commission of the European Communities, Communication from the Commission on the Precautionary Principle, noted that, "The precautionary principle is not defined in the Treaty, which prescribes it only once - to protect the environment. But in practice, its scope is much wider, and specifically where preliminary objective scientific evaluation indicates that there are reasonable grounds for concern that the potentially dangerous effects on the environment, human, animal or plant health may be inconsistent with the high level of protection chosen for the Community."

The January 29, 2000 Cartagena Protocol on Biosafety says, in regard to controversies over GMOs: "Lack of scientific certainty due to insufficient relevant scientific information . . . shall not prevent the Party of import, in order to avoid or minimize such potential adverse effects, from taking a decision, as appropriate, with regard to the import of the living modified organism in question."

Application

The application of the precautionary principle is hampered by both lack of political will, as well as the wide range of interpretations placed on it. One study identified 14 different formulations of the principle in treaties and nontreaty declarations. R.B. Stewart (2002) reduced the precautionary principle to four basic versions:

1. Scientific uncertainty should not automatically preclude regulation of activities that pose a potential risk of significant harm (Non-Preclusion PP).
2. Regulatory controls should incorporate a margin of safety; activities should be limited below the level at which no adverse effect has been observed or predicted (Margin of Safety PP).
3. Activities that present an uncertain potential for significant harm should be subject to best technology available requirements to minimize the risk of harm unless the proponent of the activity shows that they present no appreciable risk of harm (BAT PP).
4. Activities that present an uncertain potential for significant harm should be prohibited unless the proponent of the activity shows that it presents no appreciable risk of harm (Prohibitory PP).

In deciding how to apply the principle, analysis may use a cost-benefit analysis that factors in both the opportunity cost of not acting, and the option value of waiting for further information before acting. One of the difficulties of the application of the principle in modern policy-making is that there is often an irreducible conflict between different interests, so that the debate necessarily involves politics.

Strong vs. Weak

Strong precaution holds that regulation is required whenever there is a possible risk to health, safety, or the environment, even if the supporting evidence is speculative and even if the economic costs of regulation are high. In 1982, the United Nations World Charter for Nature gave the first international recognition to the strong version of the principle, suggesting that when "potential adverse effects are not fully understood, the activities should not proceed." The widely publicized Wingspread Declaration, from a meeting of environmentalists in 1998, is another example of the strong version. 'Strong precaution' can also be termed as a "no-regrets" principle, where costs are not considered in preventative action.

Weak precaution holds that lack of scientific evidence does not preclude action if damage would otherwise be serious and irreversible. Humans practice weak precaution every day, and often incur costs, to avoid hazards that are far from certain: we do not walk in moderately dangerous areas at night, we exercise, we buy smoke detectors, we buckle our seatbelts.

According to a publication by the New Zealand Treasury Department,

The weak version [of the Precautionary Principle] is the least restrictive and allows preventive measures to be taken in the face of uncertainty, but does not require them (eg, Rio Declaration 1992; United Nations Framework Convention of Climate Change 1992). To satisfy the threshold of harm, there must be some evidence relating to both the likelihood of occurrence and the severity of consequences. Some, but not all, require consideration of the costs of precautionary measures. Weak formulations do not preclude weighing benefits against the costs. Factors other than scientific uncertainty, including economic considerations, may provide legitimate grounds for postponing action. Under weak formulations, the requirement to justify the need for action (the burden of proof) generally falls on those advocating precautionary action. No mention is made of assignment of liability for environmental harm.

Strong versions justify or require precautionary measures and some also establish liability for environmental harm, which is effectively a strong form of "polluter pays". For example, the Earth Charter states: "When knowledge is limited apply a precautionary approach ... Place the burden of proof on those who argue that a proposed activity will not cause significant harm, and make the responsible parties liable for environmental harm." Reversal of proof requires those proposing an activity to prove that the product, process or technology is sufficiently "safe" before approval is granted. Requiring proof of "no environmental harm" before any action proceeds implies the public is not prepared to accept any environmental risk, no matter what economic or social benefits may arise (Peterson, 2006). At the extreme, such a requirement could involve bans and prohibitions on entire classes of potentially threatening activities or substances (Cooney, 2005). Over time, there has been a gradual transformation of the precautionary principle from what appears in the Rio Declaration to a stronger form that arguably acts as restraint on development in the absence of firm evidence that it will do no harm.

International Agreements and Declarations

The World Charter for Nature, which was adopted by the UN General Assembly in 1982, was the first international endorsement of the precautionary principle. The principle was implemented in an international treaty as early as the 1987 Montreal Protocol, and among other international treaties and declarations [1] is reflected in the 1992 Rio Declaration on Environment and Development (signed at the United Nations Conference on Environment and Development).

"Principle" vs. "Approach"

No introduction to the precautionary principle would be complete without brief reference to the difference between the precautionary principle and the precautionary approach. Principle 15 of the Rio Declaration 1992 states that: "in order to protect the environment, the precautionary approach shall be widely applied by States according to their capabilities. Where there are threats of serious or irreversible damage, lack of full scientific certainty shall be not used as a reason for postponing cost-effective measures to prevent environmental degradation." As Garcia (1995) pointed out, "the wording, largely similar to that of the principle, is subtly different in that: (1) it recognises that there may be differences in local capabilities to apply the approach, and (2) it calls for cost-effectiveness in applying the approach, e.g., taking economic and social costs into account." The 'approach' is generally considered a softening of the 'principle'.

"As Recuerda has noted, the distinction between the ´precautionary principle` and a ´precautionary approach` is diffuse and, in some contexts, controversial. In the negotiations of international declarations, the United States has opposed the use of the term ´principle` because this term has special connotations in legal language, due to the fact that a ´principle of law` is a source of law. This means that it is compulsory, so a court can quash or confirm a decision through the application of the precautionary principle. In this sense, the precautionary principle is not a simple idea or a desideratum but a source of law. This is the legal status of the precautionary principle in the European Union. On the other hand, an ´approach` usually does not have the same meaning, although in some particular cases an approach could be binding. A precautionary approach is a particular ´lens` used to identify risk that every prudent person possesses (Recuerda, 2008)

European Commission

On 2 February 2000, the European Commission issued a Communication on the precautionary principle, in which it adopted a procedure for the application of this concept, but without giving a detailed definition of it. Paragraph 2 of article 191 of the Lisbon Treaty states that

> *"Union policy on the environment shall aim at a high level of protection taking into account the diversity of situations in the various regions of the Union. It shall be based on the precautionary principle and on the principles that preventive action should be taken, that*

environmental damage should as a priority be rectified at source and that the polluter should pay."

After the adoption of the European Commission's Communication on the precautionary principle, the principle has come to inform much EU policy, including areas beyond environmental policy. As of 2006 it had been integrated into EU laws "in matters such as general product safety, the use of additives for use in animal nutrition, the incineration of waste, and the regulation of genetically modified organisms." Through its application in case law, it has become a "general principle of EU law."

USA

On July 18, 2005, the City of San Francisco passed a Precautionary Principle Purchasing ordinance, which requires the city to weigh the environmental and health costs of its $600 million in annual purchases – for everything from cleaning supplies to computers. Members of the Bay Area Working Group on the Precautionary Principle including the Breast Cancer Fund, helped bring this to fruition.

Japan

In 1997, Japan tried to use the consideration of the precautionary principle in a WTO SPS Agreement on the Application of Sanitary and Phytosanitary Measures case, as Japan's requirement to test each variety of agricultural products (apples, cherries, peaches, walnuts, apricots, pears, plums and quinces) for the efficacy of treatment against codling moths was challenged.

This moth is a pest that does not occur in Japan, and whose introduction has the potential to cause serious damage. The United States claimed that it was not necessary to test each variety of a fruit for the efficacy of the treatment, and that this varietal testing requirement was unnecessarily burdensome.

Australia

The most important Australian court case so far, due to its exceptionally detailed consideration of the precautionary principle, is Telstra Corporation Limited v Hornsby Shire Council. The case was heard in the New South Wales Land and Environment Court under Justice CJ Preston (24 April 2006).

The Principle was summarised by reference to the NSW *Protection of the Environment Administration Act 1991*, which itself provides a good definition of the principle:

"If there are threats of serious or irreversible environmental damage, lack of full scientific certainty should not be used as a reasoning for postponing measures to prevent environmental degradation. In the application of the principle... decisions should be guided by: (i) careful evaluation to avoid, wherever practicable, serious or irreversible damage to the environment; and (ii) an assessment of risk-weighted consequence of various options".

The most significant points of Justice Preston's decision are the following findings:

1. The principle and accompanying need to take precautionary measures is "triggered" when two prior conditions exist: a threat of serious or irreversible damage, and scientific uncertainty as to the extent of possible damage.
2. Once both are satisfied, "a proportionate precautionary measure may be taken to avert the anticipated threat of environmental damage, but it should be proportionate."
3. The threat of serious or irreversible damage should invoke consideration of five factors: the scale of threat (local, regional etc.); the perceived value of the threatened environment; whether the possible impacts are manageable; the level of public concern, and whether there is a rational or scientific basis for the concern.
4. The consideration of the level of scientific uncertainty should involve factors which may include: what would constitute sufficient evidence; the level and kind of uncertainty; and the potential to reduce uncertainty.
5. The principle shifts the burden of proof. If the principle applies, the burden shifts: "a decision maker must assume the threat of serious or irreversible environmental damage is... a reality [and] the burden of showing this threat... is negligible reverts to the proponent..."
6. The precautionary principle invokes preventative action: "the principle permits the taking of preventative measures without having to wait until the reality and seriousness of the threat become fully known".
7. "The principle should not be used to try to avoid all risks."
8. The precautionary measures appropriate will depend on the combined effect of "the degree of seriousness and irreversibility of the threat and the degree of uncertainty... the more significant and uncertain the threat, the greater...the precaution required".

"...measures should be adopted... proportionate to the potential threats".

Corporate

The Body Shop International, a UK-based cosmetics company, recently included the Precautionary Principle in their 2006 Chemicals Strategy.

Environment and Health

Fields typically concerned by the precautionary principle are the possibility of:

- Global warming or abrupt climate change in general
- Extinction of species
- Introduction of new and potentially harmful products into the environment, threatening biodiversity (e.g., genetically modified organisms)
- Threats to public health, due to new diseases and techniques (e.g., AIDS transmitted through blood transfusion)
- Long term effects of new technologies (e.g. health concerns regarding radiation from cell phones and other electronics communications devices)
- Persistent or acute pollution (asbestos, endocrine disruptors...)
- Food safety (e.g., Creutzfeldt-Jakob disease)
- Other new biosafety issues (e.g., artificial life, new molecules)

The precautionary principle is often applied to biological fields because changes cannot be easily contained and have the potential of being global. The principle has less relevance to contained fields such as aeronautics, where the few people undergoing risk have given informed consent (e.g., a test pilot). In the case of technological innovation, containment of impact tends to be more difficult if that technology can self-replicate. Bill Joy emphasized the dangers of replicating genetic technology, nanotechnology, and robotic technology in his article in *Wired Magazine*, "Why the future doesn't need us", though he does not specifically cite the precautionary principle. The application of the principle can be seen in the public policy of requiring pharmaceutical companies to carry out clinical trials to show that new medications are safe.

Oxford based philosopher Nick Bostrom discusses the idea of a future powerful superintelligence, and the risks that we/it face should it attempt to gain atomic level control of matter.

Application of the principle modifies the status of innovation and risk assessment: it is not the risk that must be avoided or amended, but a potential risk that must be prevented. Thus, in the case of regulation of scientific research, there is a third party beyond the scientist and the regulator: the consumer.

In an analysis concerning application of the precautionary principle to nanotechnology, Chris Phoenix and Mike Treder posit that there are *two forms* of the principle, which they call the "strict form" and the "active form". The former "requires inaction when action might pose a risk", while the latter means "choosing less risky alternatives when they are available, and [...] taking responsibility for potential risks." Thomas Alured Faunce has argued for stronger application of the precautionary principle by chemical and health technology regulators particularly in relation to $Ti0_2$ and ZnO nanoparticles in sunscreens, biocidal nanosilver in waterways and products whose manufacture, handling or recycling exposes humans to the risk of inhaling multi-walled carbon nanotubes.

Resource Management

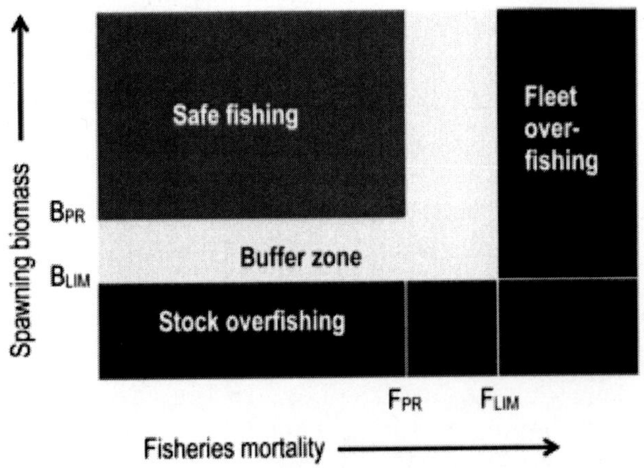

Figure: *The Traffic Light colour convention, showing the concept of Harvest Control Rule (HCR), specifying when a rebuilding plan is mandatory in terms of precautionary and limit reference points for spawning biomass and fishing mortality rate.*

Several natural resources like fish stocks are now managed by precautionary approach, through Harvest Control Rules (HCR) based upon the precautionary principle. The figure indicates how the principle is implemented in the cod fisheries management proposed by the International Council for the Exploration of the Sea.

In classifying endangered species, the precautionary principle means that if there is doubt about an animal's or plant's exact conservation status, the one that would cause the strongest protective measures to be realised should be chosen. Thus, a species like the Silvery Pigeon that might exist in considerable numbers and simply be under-recorded or might just as probably be long extinct is not classified as "data deficient" or "extinct" (which both do not require any protective action to be taken), but as "critically endangered" (the conservation status that confers the need for the strongest protection), whereas the increasingly rare, but probably not yet endangered Emerald Starling is classified as "data deficient", because there is urgent need for research to clarify its status rather than for conservation action to save it from extinction.

If, for example, a large ground-water body that many people use for drinking water is contaminated by bacteria (e-coli 0157 H7, campylobacter or leptospirosis) and the source of contamination is strongly suspected to be dairy cows but the exact science is not yet able to provide absolute proof, the cows should be removed from the environment until they are proved, by the dairy industry, not to be the source or until that industry ensures that such contamination will not recur.

Criticisms

Critics of the principle use arguments similar to those against other formulations of technological conservatism.

Internal Inconsistency - Applying Strong PP Risks Causing Harm

Strong formulations of the precautionary principle, without regard to its most basic provisions that it is to be applied only where risks are potentially high AND not easily calculable, applied to the principle itself as a policy decision, may rule out its own use. The reason suggested is that preventing innovation from coming to market means that only current technology may be used, and current technology itself may cause harm or leave needs unmet; there is a risk of causing harm by blocking innovation. As Michael Crichton wrote in his novel, *State of Fear*: "The 'precautionary principle', properly applied, forbids the precautionary principle." For example, forbidding nuclear power plants based on concerns about risk means continuing to rely on power plants that burn fossil fuels, which continue to release greenhouse gases. In another example, the Hazardous Air Pollutant provisions in the 1990 amendments to the U.S. Clean Air Act are an example of the Precautionary Principle where the onus is now on showing a listed compound is harmless. Under this rule no distinction is made between those air Pollutants that provide a higher or lower risk, so operators tend to choose less-examined agents that are not on the existing list.

Blocking Innovation and Progress Generally

Because applications of strong formulations of the PP can be used to block innovation, a technology which brings advantages may be banned by PP because of its potential for negative impacts, leaving the positive benefits unrealised.

The precautionary principle has been ethically questioned on the basis that its application could block progress in developing countries.

Waste Hierarchy

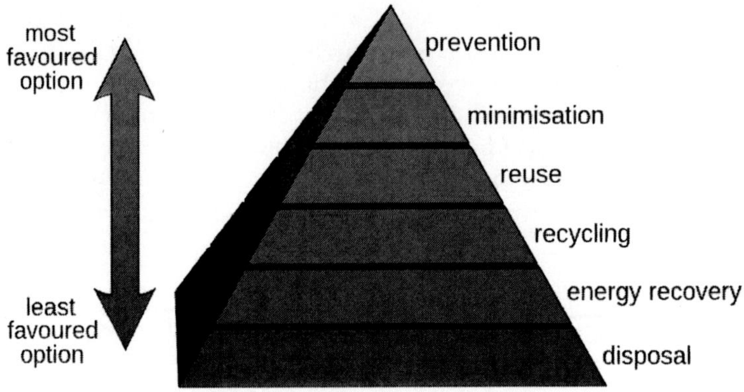

Figure: *The waste hierarchy*

The evaluation of processes that protect the environment alongside resource and energy consumption to most favourable to least favourable actions. The hierarchy establishes preferred program priorities based on sustainability. To be sustainable, waste management cannot be solved only with technical end-of-pipe solutions and an integrated approach is necessary.

The waste management hierarchy indicates an order of preference for action to reduce and manage waste, and is usually presented diagrammatically in the form of a pyramid. The hierarchy captures the progression of a material or product through successive stages of waste management, and represents the latter part of the life-cycle for each product.

The aim of the waste hierarchy is to extract the maximum practical benefits from products and to generate the minimum amount of waste. The proper application of the waste hierarchy can have several benefits. It can help prevent emissions of greenhouse gases, reduces pollutants, save energy, conserves resources, create jobs and stimulate the development of green technologies.

Stages

The waste hierarchy ranks waste management options according to what is best for the environment. It gives top priority to preventing waste in the first place. If waste is not produced then it has not to be disposed of. When waste is produced, it gives precedence to preparing it for reuse, then recycling, then recovery, and last of all disposal.

Stages

Prevention: The prevention of waste is the most vital point in the waste hierarchy. Prevention or reduction minimizes the generation of waste products in the first place. Prevention usually results in the least environmental and economic life cycle costs because it requires no collecting or processing of materials. Prevention also typically produces significant benefits in terms of production efficiencies and the use of resources. It involves using less material in design and manufacture, trying to keep products for longer, and using less hazardous materials.

Reuse: The reuse of waste is the next most desirable option. It is any operation where products or materials that are not waste are used again for the same purpose for which they were intended. Reusing waste often requires collection but relatively little or no processing. It involves checking, cleaning, repairing, and/or refurbishing, entire items or spare parts.

Recycle: Recycling of waste is the next step in priority. It is any activity that includes the collection of used, reused, or unused items that would otherwise be considered waste. Recycling involves sorting and processing the recyclable products into raw material and then remanufacturing the recycled raw materials into new products.

Recovery: The recovery of waste is further separated into categories: the recovery of materials and the recovery of energy. Whichever of these two choices is better for the environment and human health is the preferred option. The recovery of materials is most often preferred and includes activities such as recycling and composting. These management activities generally require a collection system and a method of material processing and conversion into a new product. Recovery of energy, such as incineration, is usually the less preferred option. The conversion of non-recyclable waste materials into usable heat, electricity, or fuel is done through a variety of processes, including anaerobic digestion, gasification, and pyrolysis.

Disposal: The last resort is disposal and is only considered once all other possibilities have been explored. Disposal is any operation that involves the dumping and incineration of waste without energy recovery. Before final disposal, a considerable amount of pre-treatment may be necessary to change the characteristics of the waste in order to reduce the quantity or harmfulness of the waste and that may include physical, thermal, chemical, or biological processes. Landfills are the most common form of waste disposal and the final disposal option.

Life-Cycle Thinking

All products and services have environmental impacts, from the extraction of raw materials for production to manufacture, distribution, use and disposal. Following the waste hierarchy will generally lead to the most resource-efficient and environmentally sound choice but in some cases refining decisions within the hierarchy or departing from it can lead to better environmental outcomes.

Life cycle thinking and assessment can be used to support decision-making in the area of waste management and to identify the best environmental options. It can help policy makers understand the benefits and trade-offs they have to face when making decisions on waste management strategies. Life-cycle assessment provides a scientifically sound approach to ensure that the best outcome for the environment can be identified and put in place. It involves looking at all stages of a product's life to ûnd where improvements can be made to reduce environmental impacts and improve the use or reuse of resources. A key goal is to avoid actions that shift negative impacts from one stage to another. Life cycle thinking can be applied to the five stages of the waste management hierarchy.

For example, life-cycle analysis has shown, that it is often better for the environment to replace an old washing machine, despite the waste generated, than to continue to use an older machine which is less energy efficient. This is because a washing machine's greatest environmental impact is during its use phase. Buying an energy-efficient machine and using low-temperature detergent reduce environmental impacts.

The European Union Waste Framework Directive has introduced the concept of life-cycle thinking into waste policies. This duality approach gives a broader view of all environmental aspects and ensures any action has an overall benefit compared to other options. The actions to deal with waste along the hierarchy should be compatible with other environmental initiatives.

Bibliography

Alka Pareek: *Environment and Nutritional Disorders*, Aavishkar Pub, Delhi, 2003.

Anshen, M. : *Corporate Strategies for Social Performance*, New York, United States, 1980.

Aswathappa, K. : *Essential of Business Environment*, New Delhi , Himalaya Publishing House, 2001.

Beesley, Michael : *Corporate Social Responsibility: A Reassessment,* London, Crrom Helm, 1978.

Campbell, Robert : *The Ethical Organisation,* London, Macmillan, 1996.

Carroll, A. : *Business and Society: Managing Corporate Social Performance,* Boston: Little, Brown & Company, 1981.

Chakraborty, S.K. : *Ethics in Management Ethics and Ethical behaviour are the Essential Parts of Healthy Management,* New Delhi, Oxford University Press, 1995.

Cheruniam, F. : *Global Economy and Business Environment,* New Delhi, Himalaya Publishing House, 2001.

Clover, Darlene Elaine: *Global Perspectives in Environmental Adult Education,* New York, Peter Lang, 2003.

Dunfee, T. : *That Bind: A Social Contracts Approach to Business Ethics,* Boston, HBS HBS Harvard Business School, 1999.

Francis J. : *Managing Corporate Ethics,* London, Oxford University Press, 1994.

Goodall, Steve: *Developing Environmental Education in the Curriculum,* London, David Fulton Publishers, 1994.

Gowdy, J., *Coevolution Economics: The Economy, Society and the Environment,* Kluwer, Boston, 1994.

Jagbir Sharma: *Advanced Environment Chemistry,* RBSA Pub, Delhi, 2006.

Keith Davis : *Business and Society.-Corporate Strategy, Public Policy, and Ethics,* New York, McGraw-Hill, 1992.

Larry J.: *Business Valuations, Advanced Topics*, Westport, CT, Quorum Books, 1997.

Manuel, G. Velasquez : *Business Ethics Concepts and Cases,* Delhi, Pearson Education, 2002.

Meyer, M. W.: *Theory of Organizational Structure*, Indianapolis, 1977.

Mohanty, R. : *Civil Society and Governance: A Research Study in India,* New Delhi, 2000.

Neil H. : *Corporate Power and Social Responsibility: A Blueprint for the Future,* New York, Macmillan, 1973.

Porter, M.E. : *The Competitive Advantage of Nations,* London, Macmillan, 1998.

Post , J.E. : *Business and Society,* New York, McGrawhill, 1988.

Richard, DeGeorge : *Business Ethics,* New York, MacMillan Publishing, 1990.

Robbins, P. : *Greening the Corporations: Management Strategy and the Environmental Challenge* , London: Earthscan, 2001.

Salancik, G. R.: *The External Control of Organizations, A Resource Dependence Perspective*, New York, 1978.

Shrivastava V.K. *: Environments and Social Concerns*, Concept, Delhi, 2011.

Sims, Ronald R. : *Ethics and Corporate Social Responsibility: Why Giants Fall,* New York, Praeger Publishers, 2003.

Som Nath Tiwari *: Global Warming and Its Effects on Environment*, Adhyayan, Delhi, 2007.

Venkateshwaran, Shanker : *The Business of Social Responsibility,* Bangalore, India, 2000.

Wartick, S. and Wood, D. : *International Business and Society*. Blackwell: Malden, 1998.

Watts, P. : *Corporate Social Responsibility: Making Good Business Sense.* World Business Council for Sustainable Development: Geneva, 2000.

Wood, A.: *The Corporate Economy*, London: Macmillan, 1971.

Index

A

Accidents Involving Radioactive Waste, 149.
Alternative Fuels, 23, 269.
Annexed Projects, 188.

B

Biodiversity, 12, 63, 71, 74, 75, 78, 79, 80, 81, 82, 83, 84, 88, 90, 92, 95, 203, 219, 292.
Blue Economy, 258.
Brine Management, 161.
Brine Treatment, 160, 161.
Building Design, 13, 217, 271, 272, 273.

C

Canadian Environmental Assessment Act, 183, 184.
Chemical Waste, 127, 141.
Clean Energy Trends, 18, 19.
Cleaner Production, 17, 18, 242.
Complex Organic Chemicals Industry, 159.
Construction Waste, 128.
Corporate Sustainability, 11, 15, 17, 161, 235, 248.
Current Laws, 215.

D

Diversity, 53, 54, 72, 75, 77, 79, 104, 231, 254, 284.

E

Eco-Industrial Development, 228, 229, 231.
Eco-Industrial Park, 173, 225, 226, 227.
Eco-Innovation, 252, 253.
Economy Wide Effects, 272, 274.
Electronics Industry, 215.
Environmental Assessment, 178, 181, 183, 184, 186, 193, 194, 195, 223.
Environmental Corporate Responsibility, 2.
Environmental Governance, 63, 64, 65, 67, 68, 69, 70, 71, 72, 75, 76, 77, 79, 80, 83, 84, 85, 86, 87, 88, 89, 90, 91, 92, 95, 261.
Environmental Impact Design, 197.
Environmental Policy, 9, 57, 58, 59, 60, 61, 62, 63, 90, 114, 122, 210, 236, 278, 285.
Environmental Tariff, 111.

F

Facing Environmental Governance, 68.
Forestry, 4, 24, 107.
Fuel Composition, 134.

G

Global Climate Coalition, 30, 31, 32.

Global Environment Facility, 68, 79, 83, 91.
Global Governance, 72, 81, 90.

H

High-Level Waste, 131, 134, 140, 141, 142, 145, 148.
Humane Tourism, 104, 105.

I

Illegal Dumping, 149.
Income Level Variation, 277.
Increased Energy Efficiency, 35.
Industrial Ecology, 166, 171, 175, 176, 177, 226, 231, 254, 260.
Industrial Wastewater Treatment, 157.
Insurance Industry, 34.
International Monetary Fund, 86.

K

Koch Industries, 33.

L

Legacy Waste, 136.
Life-Cycle Assessment, 176, 198, 216, 292.
Local Governance, 69.

M

Mapping Systems, 125.
Marine Stewardship Council, 117.
Mountain Tourism, 100.
Multilateral Environmental Agreements, 80.

N

National Management Plans, 148.
Non-Governmental Organisations, 89, 97.
Nuclear Industry, 159.
Nuclear Power, 20, 130, 138, 140, 192, 289.
Nuclear Weapons, 133, 135.

O

Ozone Layer, 1, 78, 83, 85, 90, 215.

P

Portland Cement, 126.
Pulp and Paper Industry, 159.

R

Radioactive Waste, 131, 132, 134, 136, 140, 141, 142, 143, 144, 145, 147, 148, 149, 150.
Registration Taxes, 110.
Responsible Tourism, 103, 104, 105, 106.

S

Social Sphere, 11.
Source Reduction, 17, 251, 252.
Sustainable Timber, 118.
Sustainable Tourism, 95, 96, 97, 98, 100, 101, 102, 103.

T

Tertiary Sector, 25.
Toxic Waste, 119, 120, 121, 122, 209.
Transuranic Waste, 141, 146.
Trickling Filter Process, 163.

U

Universal Wastes, 125, 126.
Uranium Tailings, 139.

W

Waste Hierarchy, 290, 291, 292.
Wastewater Constituents, 152.
Water Treatment, 159.
World Environment Organisation, 84.
World Trade Organisation, 68, 86, 91, 112.

❑❑❑